FIFTY YEARS OF MESOPOTAMIAN DISCOVERY

THE WORK OF THE BRITISH SCHOOL OF ARCHAEOLOGY IN IRAQ
1932–1982

With an Introduction by Seton Lloyd

Edited by John Curtis

Published by
THE BRITISH SCHOOL OF ARCHAEOLOGY IN
IRAQ (LONDON)
(GERTRUDE BELL MEMORIAL)

© British School of Archaeology in Iraq 1982

ISBN 0 903472 05 8

Printed in England by
Stephen Austin and Sons Ltd, Hertford

Contents

	Page
List of illustrations	4
Editor's Preface	6
Introduction by Seton Lloyd	7
Umm Dabaghiyah by Diana Kirkbride	11
Choga Mami by Joan Oates	22
Arpachiyah by John Curtis	30
Ras al 'Amiya by David Stronach	37
Hamrin Sites by Michael Roaf	40
Abu Salabikh by Nicholas Postgate	48
Tell Brak by David Oates	62
Tell Taya by Julian Reade	72
Chagar Bazar by John Curtis	79
Tell al Rimah by David Oates	86
Nimrud by Julian Reade	99
Balawat by John Curtis	113
Ain Sinu by David Oates	120
Acknowledgements	123

List of Illustrations

Cover   Ziggurat of Nimrud from the north-east.
Fig. 1. Map of Mesopotamia, p. 10
Fig. 2. Plan of levels 3–4, Umm Dabaghiyah, p. 12
Fig. 3. Domestic houses, Umm Dabaghiyah, p. 14
Fig. 4. Reconstruction of houses, Umm Dabaghiyah, p. 15
Fig. 5. Room with drain, Umm Dabaghiyah, p. 16
Fig. 6. Drying rack, Umm Dabaghiyah, p. 17
Fig. 7. Interior hearth, Umm Dabaghiyah, p. 18
Fig. 8. Frescoes of onager hunt, Umm Dabaghiyah, p. 20
Fig. 9. Arsenal, Umm Dabaghiyah, p. 21
Fig. 10. View of Choga Mami, p. 23
Fig. 11. Samarran house, Choga Mami, p. 23
Fig. 12. Guard tower, Choga Mami, p. 24
Fig. 13. Path by guard tower, Choga Mami, p. 25
Fig. 14. Figurine from Choga Mami, p. 26
Fig. 15. Samarran potsherd from Choga Mami, p. 26
Fig. 16. Section through Choga Mami, p. 27
Fig. 17. Map of irrigation canals in Choga Mami area, p. 28
Fig. 18. Aerial view of Arpachiyah, p. 31
Fig. 19. Aerial view of Arpachiyah, p. 32
Fig. 20. Work-force at Arpachiyah, p. 32
Fig. 21. 'Ubaid houses, Arpachiyah, p. 33
Fig. 22. Copper celt from Arpachiyah, p. 34
Fig. 23. "Tholoi" foundations, Arpachiyah, p. 34
Fig. 24. Halaf pottery from Arpachiyah, p. 35
Fig. 25. Section at Ras al 'Amiya, p. 37
Fig. 26. Plan of Ras al 'Amiya, p. 38
Fig. 27. Excavating 'Ubaid house, Tell Madhhur, p. 40
Fig. 28. 'Ubaid house, Tell Madhhur, p. 41
Fig. 29. 'Ubaid house, Tell Madhhur, p. 42
Fig. 30. Reconstruction of 'Ubaid house, Tell Madhhur, p. 43
Fig. 31. Curving building, Tell Madhhur, p. 44
Fig. 32. Reconstruction of curving building, Tell Madhhur, p. 44
Fig. 33. Grave at Tell Madhhur, p. 45
Fig. 34. Drawing of grave at Tell Madhhur, p. 46
Fig. 35. View of Abu Salabikh, p. 48
Fig. 36. Map of south Iraq, p. 49
Fig. 37. Tablet from Abu Salabikh, p. 51
Fig. 38. Pots from Grave 182, Abu Salabikh, p. 51
Fig. 39. Visitors at Abu Salabikh, p. 52
Fig. 40. Plan of Area E, Abu Salabikh, p. 53
Fig. 41. Clay sealings from Abu Salabikh, p. 54
Fig. 42. Grave 162, Abu Salabikh, p. 55
Fig. 43. Stemmed dish from Abu Salabikh, p. 56
Fig. 44. Seals from Abu Salabikh, p. 57
Fig. 45. Plan of Abu Salabikh, p. 58
Fig. 46. Grave 185, Abu Salabikh, p. 59
Fig. 47. Plan of square 51, Abu Salabikh, p. 60
Fig. 48. Contour plan of Tell Brak, p. 63
Fig. 49. Plan of Eye Temple, Tell Brak, p. 64
Fig. 50. Late Uruk pottery from Tell Brak, p. 65
Fig. 51. Tablet from Tell Brak, p. 65

List of illustrations

Fig. 52. Clay bullae from Tell Brak, p. 66
Fig. 53. Ninevite pottery from Tell Brak, p. 67
Fig. 54. Plan of Agade Palace, Tell Brak, p. 68
Fig. 55. Pottery basin from Tell Brak, p. 69
Fig. 56. View of central mound, Tell Taya, p. 73
Fig. 57. Stone wall footings, Tell Taya, p. 75
Fig. 58. Plan of stone wall footings, Tell Taya, p. 76
Fig. 59. View of Chagar Bazar, p. 79
Fig. 60. Contour plan of Chagar Bazar, p. 80
Fig. 61. Clay bullae from Chagar Bazar, p. 81
Fig. 62. Grave 186 at Chagar Bazar, p. 83
Fig. 63. Grave 151 at Chagar Bazar, p. 84
Fig. 64. Painted pottery from Chagar Bazar, p. 85
Fig. 65. View of Tell al Rimah, p. 86
Fig. 66. Contour plan of Tell al Rimah, p. 87
Fig. 67. Reconstruction of Palace reception suite, Tell al Rimah, p. 88
Fig. 68. Plan of Palace, Tell al Rimah, p. 90
Fig. 69. Plan of Temple, Tell al Rimah, p. 92
Fig. 70. Vault and arch construction, Tell al Rimah, p. 94
Fig. 71. Temple façade, Tell al Rimah, p. 95
Fig. 72. Late Assyrian shrine, Tell al Rimah, p. 96
Fig. 73. Stele of Adad-Nirari III, Tell al Rimah, p. 97
Fig. 74. Felix Jones' plan of Nimrud and surrounding area, p. 100-101
Fig. 75. Felix Jones' plan of Nimrud, p. 103
Fig. 76. Citadel wall, Nimrud, p. 104
Fig. 77. Postern gate, Nimrud, p. 104
Fig. 78. Inscription of Esarhaddon, Nimrud, p. 105
Fig. 79. Ivory from Nimrud, p. 107
Fig. 80. Ivory from Nimrud, p. 108
Fig. 81. Ivory from Nimrud, p. 110
Fig. 82. Ivory from Nimrud, p. 110
Fig. 83. Contour plan of Balawat, p. 114
Fig. 84. Excavations in Temple of Mamu, Balawat, p. 115
Fig. 85. Ashurnasirpal gates *in situ*, Balawat, p. 116
Fig. 86. Drawings of Ashurnasirpal gates, Balawat, p. 117
Fig. 87. Map of northern Iraq, p. 120
Fig. 88. Plan of Ain Sinu, p. 121

Colour plates (between pp. 36 and 37)
Plate 1a View of Umm Dabaghiyah
Plate 1b View south of Mandali
Plate 2a Pottery from Choga Mami
Plate 2b-c Pottery from Ras al 'Amiya
Plate 2d 'Ubaid levels at Tell Madhhur
Plate 3a Jar from Tell Madhhur
Plate 3b Jewellery from Abu Salabikh
Plate 3c Scraping surface, Abu Salabikh
Plate 4a View of Tell Brak
Plate 4b Shell pendant from Tell Brak
Plate 4c Ivory statuette from Tell Brak
Plate 5 Pottery from Tell Taya
Plate 6a View from Chagar Bazar
Plate 6b Glass beaker from Tell al Rimah
Plate 6c Frit mask from Tell al Rimah
Plate 7a View of Nimrud
Plate 7b-c Wall paintings at Nimrud
Plate 8a Furniture *in situ* at Nimrud
Plate 8b Shrine of Temple of Mamu, Balawat

Editor's Preface

For the sake of consistency I have modified the spelling of proper names in a few chapters. For this I apologise to the authors concerned, and hope they will be mollified by the admission that no set pattern of transliteration has been followed and that there is no pretence to have produced a "correct" form. My only concern has been that names should be easily recognizable. Similarly, I have sometimes used abbreviations (such as 1st, 2nd, etc.) that may not meet with universal approval, but have the advantage of brevity. For various reasons it was decided that in this book there should be no footnotes or references in the text. Instead, readers will find there is a short bibliography at the end of each chapter. These bibliographies are not intended to be comprehensive, but rather to serve as a starting-point for those wishing to delve deeper into a particular subject. The vexed question of how to represent dates for the earlier prehistoric periods affects this as it must any general book on Mesopotamian archaeology. Put simply, the problem is that radiocarbon dates earlier than *c.* 6500 before present cannot yet be calibrated by dated dendrochronological samples. Therefore, the currently accepted convention of using b.c. to indicate uncalibrated radiocarbon dates has been used in the appropriate chapters. Where they are available, calibrated dates have been used. There is unfortunately some overlapping, but it is felt that this is preferable to a more arbitrary usage of dates. In the preparation of this book I have received help from a number of quarters, but I should particularly like to acknowledge the assistance of David and Joan Oates. They have been most generous, both with their advice and in more practical matters such as supplying photographs.

Introduction
By Seton Lloyd

In the year 1956, the British School of Archaeology in Iraq celebrated its 'Silver Jubilee'. The occasion was marked by a meeting under the Presidency of Lord Salter, at which Sir Max Mallowan, already for many years Director of the School, reminded us of its foundation in 1932 as a memorial to Gertrude Bell and recounted its accomplishments in the years which followed. On that occasion also it had proved possible for the British Museum to organize an exhibition of the School's discoveries—characteristically described by Sir Max as a display "by which only a moron could fail to be roused"—and indeed, after its opening by Sir Leonard Woolley, it was seen by more than 12,000 visitors. Simultaneously, for more professional purposes, a useful handbook under the title *Twenty-Five Years of Mesopotamian Discovery* was also written and published by the Director, from whose own excavations the majority of the exhibits were derived.

Since that time, the progress of archaeological research would seem to have advanced a great deal faster than the history which it has helped to reveal; and today in 1982, it is the first half-century of the School's existence that we are able to celebrate. The collection of essays which follows might accordingly be regarded as a sequel to Sir Max's handbook, (of which a second impression was published in 1959), combining a re-assessment of its contents with a fuller account of subsequent enterprises undertaken by the School. In one important respect however, the present publication differs from its predecessor, in the pages of which the several archaeological operations described had been the sole responsibility of the author and could be most reliably reported by him. Since that time, the directorship of individual excavations has most frequently been deputed to a new generation of qualified specialists, and it is from their own writings that the new volume is composed. In the outline of our most recent work which follows, the successive mention of their names may serve as a preliminary introduction to their own written contributions.

The progress then, of the School's activities during its second quarter-century can most easily be traced in the bi-annual issues of its own journal *Iraq,* whose publication had been inaugurated by Sidney Smith as early as 1934 and subsequently edited in turn by R. Campbell-Thompson and C. J. Gadd. When this second instalment of the story begins, the immensely successful excavations at Nimrud are already in their seventh year. Mallowan himself is still in charge, supported by his remarkable wife and profiting as usual from the assistance of Barbara Parker. Most recently discovered and first excavated in 1957 are the ruins of the famous royal arsenal, "Fort Shalmaneser". The clearance of this vast complex was to prove the most productive single enterprise in the whole history of the expedition. In that year, David Oates and his future wife, Joan are also to be found exploring the Hellenistic settlement which overlay the Assyrian remains. By the following year, David has taken over the directorship of the Nimrud excavations from Sir Max, whose energies are temporarily diverted to preparations for the foundation of a new British Institute of Persian Studies at Teheran. In 1959 however, a pause in the School's fieldwork is necessitated by political events following the fall of the Hashemite Dynasty and the consequent re-organization of the Iraqi Government. During that time, changes have taken place in the department responsible for archaeological research, in which the most prominent figure had till then been that of Dr. Naji al-Asil, a long-standing friend and supporter of the School. The gap created by his transfer to the presidency of the Iraq Academy has now to be filled and guest excavators working in the country are soon to be greatly reassured by the appointment in his place of two younger but equally popular colleagues, Taha Baqir and Fuad Safar, to act respectively as Director- and Inspector-General of Antiquities.

When therefore, normal work is resumed by the School in 1959, one finds the prospect satisfactory. Where conservation is concerned, the antiquities from Nimrud and elsewhere are being ably cared for by Akram Shukri and his assistants in the much improved laboratory of the Iraq Museum. Meanwhile, our journal testifies to advances which are being made in the study and publication of textual material by scholars such as Saggs and Laessøe. Nor are contemporary developments in neighbouring countries ignored. Richard Barnett's interpretation of recent Russian discoveries at Karmir Blur and other Urartian sites adds a new dimension to Assyrian history. In a different context, Charles

Burney reports on prehistoric society at Yanik Tepe in north-west Iran, while back in south Iraq, David Stronach is planning his stratigraphic sounding at Ras al 'Amiyah.

In 1961, with the excavation of Fort Shalmaneser already in its fifth season, Donald Wiseman, now Editor of *Iraq*, is appointed to the chair of Assyriology in London University and, jointly with David Oates becomes co-Director of the School. Two years later, excavations at Nimrud are brought to a temporary conclusion, work on their publication having become imperative in view of the multiplicity of finds. But new names appear among the British specialists enlisted to help in the final operation. Jeffery Orchard, latterly acting as field-director, is joined by Julian Reade, Nicholas Kindersley, Ann Searight and Nan Shaw, while in the philological field, Saggs is supported by Lambert and others. Meanwhile, a new project is under consideration and 1964 sees the commencement of excavations at Tell al Rimah, south of the Sinjar hills in north-west Iraq, where preliminary explorations had been made by David Oates. This venture was, and continued for six years to be in the hands of Oates himself, assisted in part financially by the University Museum of Pennsylvania and in the field by the support of the new Director-General of Antiquities, Dr. Faisal el-Wailly. The walled city, temple and palace which Oates encountered at this site (ancient Karana), helped to identify it as capital of a fledgling principality in the time of Hammurabi, and the ruins which he was able to expose provided an illuminating vignette of political and domestic life in a province of Assyria. Its contribution, particularly to the history of Mesopotamian architecture, was considerable and could be supplemented by a collection of Old Babylonian tablets, subsequently published by Stephanie Dalley (née Page).

Annual reports of the work at Tell al Rimah fill the journal during the late 1960's, accompanied by much other material including *Festschrift* offerings to C. J. Gadd and other senior scholars. There are accounts also of independent operations by members in different parts of the country: Julian Reade's planning of a 3rd millennium township at Tell Taya; or Joan Oates' survey of the Mandali/Badra area on the Iranian frontier, which led to the discovery and excavation of Choga Mami. With the beginning of a new decade in 1970, a new Director is chosen in the person of Diana Helbaek and interest is again directed to prehistory by her discoveries at Umm Dabaghiyah in the Jazira desert. This four-year operation was highlighted by the unique vindication of a precocious conviction, when, in the face of much scepticism, the inhabitants of a pre-Hassuna settlement were proved to have hunted wild asses, trading in their hides and other products. In her report which follows, Mrs. Helbaek also provides us with a tentative but stimulating conception of the Neolithic world at large, envisaging in the 6th millennium an advance in technology and social administration far beyond that commonly imagined. In the same context 1973 saw the publication of a meticulous study, made by the Russian excavators Merpert and Munchaev of a Hassuna settlement at Yarim Tepe in the vicinity of Rimah.

In 1975, a new chapter opens with the appointment of Nicholas Postgate as Director. With a change of nomenclature, he soon finds himself in charge of a "British Archaeological Expedition to Iraq", working on cordial terms with the "Iraqi State Organization for Antiquities and Heritage" and its director, Dr. Muayad Sa'id Damerji. We see that in the following years he is able to resume excavations at the Sumerian site called Abu Salabikh, in collaboration with Americans from Chicago by whom it had already been tested. Despite the profitable results of this dig, the ingenious economy with which it has had to be conducted serves to emphasize a notable change in the contemporary approach to the revival of excavations in southern Iraq. "In a changing world", as I have written elsewhere, "new factors have to be considered in such an operation and diggers are faced with unfamiliar problems. They may find that, since the days of the 'great excavations', the cost of labour has increased by as much as one thousand percent, making the purely mechanical task of removing unstratified debris prohibitive. They will find that modern systems of excavation are still 'labour-intensive' and accordingly feel compelled to choose sites where the occupation-level of major relevance occurs near the surface". This has proved very much the case at Abu Salabikh.

Another result has been a great increase of interest in "rescue" operations in the prospective flood-area of hydro-electric barrage construction, especially when, as is the case in Iraq, the Government is prepared to take a share in the cost of labour, and this raises a subject of outstanding importance in relation to the work of foreign institutions operating in that country. In recent years, the grateful acceptance by ourselves and others of practical assistance in this most welcome form, has led indirectly to an improved system of collaboration, which may well set a new pattern for the future. Where recently, teams of excavators—both Iraqi and foreign—have taken part in a single project, aimed at the recovery of archaeological information from sites "at risk" in an exactly predictable area, some overall strategy has clearly been required, combining major excavations at regional centres with subsidiary soundings in related outposts, ('satellites' in today's 'nuclear' phraseology). In this way evidence can best be obtained of criteria indicating cultural fluctuations and their distribution. In marked contrast to an earlier régime, when such groups worked independently with no coherence of purpose or agreed objective, this has been made possible by a closer system of liaison and general consultation, even leading in some cases to a pooling of resources.

Such a situation is well illustrated by the Hamrin Dam Salvage Project, in which from 1979 onwards one finds Postgate and Michael Roaf participating with Cuyler Young and Anglo-Canadian financial support. The project itself is an international enterprise, organized by the Iraqi S.O.A.H. whose own excavating teams play a major role. The primary target allotted to Postgate was the mound called Tell Madhhur, but by agreement with his Iraqi colleagues his work was not rigidly restricted to this single site, and minor settlements in the vicinity could also be tested. In his essay here, Roaf, (who has more recently succeeded Postgate as Director of the "Expedition"), gives an account of his fascinating discoveries at Madhhur, but he refers at the same time to the unique success of the whole Hamrin Project. Clearly implied here is a well-deserved compliment to its organizers, and in particular to Dr. Damerji whose far-sighted wisdom and initiative may have created a new and favourable climate for Mesopotamian archaeology. The same system of collaboration now seems likely to be extended to other areas of rescue work in north Iraq: for instance at Eski Mosul and on the Middle Euphrates.

So, in the 1980's the work of the School proceeds from year to year with its enquiry into the secrets of Near Eastern antiquity, for which it was founded fifty years ago. And today, few would fail to be impressed by the fulfilment of that purpose, or to see it in the collection of writings that follow. A glance at their titles will show that the investigations which they record cover the whole saga of Mesopotamian history—from the precocious farmers and trappers of the Neolithic Age to the (perhaps less fortunate) victims of Roman imperialism. Indeed, the coverage of this book is so comprehensive that it might well serve others as an introduction to the subject with which we ourselves are so deeply concerned.

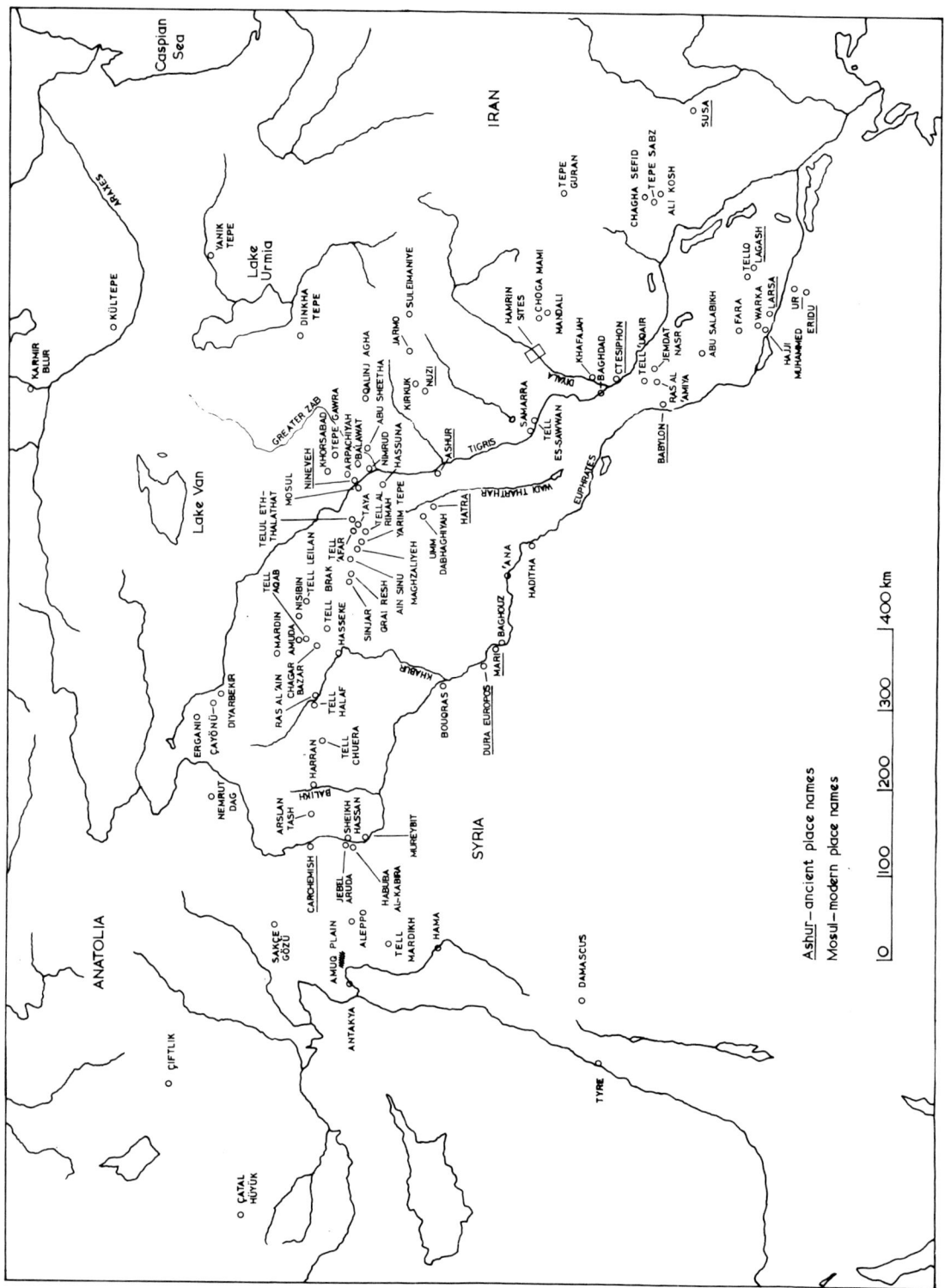

Fig. 1. Mesopotamia and surrounding areas. See also figs. 17, 36, 87.

Umm Dabaghiyah

By Diana Kirkbride

The occupation of Umm Dabaghiyah spans the period from about 6200 to 5750 b.c.,* a time when the origins of agriculture were already ancient, pottery had recently come into general use, and experiments in fashioning copper were already producing small vessels and objects of adornment. This stage of development is often referred to as the Late, or Pottery Neolithic. The village of Umm Dabaghiyah is sited in an environment that appears to be almost totally unfavourable for a Stone Age economy, a fact that poses many questions. In this context it might be useful to set the general background by tracing briefly the steps by which man had progressed to the stage of development in the Near East represented by Umm Dabaghiyah.

Everyone is aware that environment is the determining factor for settled life. Experiments in the cultivation of wild food plants began in those well watered parts where potentially domesticable plants were available in quantity, and the same applies to animal domestication. This immensely long process of experimentation, of mutation and human selection, lasted from the Upper Palaeolithic to the Late Neolithic before full domestication was accomplished.

The Mesolithic peoples were the pioneering settlers, and it seems reasonable to suggest that this initial step was more or less forced on them. Age-old previous experimentation with moving wild food plants out of their natural habitats and planting them in different, though still ecologically favourable areas elsewhere, had already shown that to be successful, man would have to stay put to protect the plants all the time. He could not simply put them in the ground and hope for the best. A form of ground clearance was necessary, and after sowing, the plants would have to be protected from birds and animal trampling, and later on from intense competition from other, indigenous, plants, not to mention holding off raids from other tribes and animals. Finally there would be the harvest. After that the cycle repeated itself endlessly. From that moment onwards the irrevocable mutual dependence between man and his food plants came into being, whereby although the plants were to become the slaves of men, men were equally to become the serfs of the plants, and the same applies to animal domestication.

Unfortunately this immensely slow process cannot be detected by botanical investigation because the plants under cultivation were physiologically wild. Only by man's selection and environmental manipulation did the physiological properties of the plants alter by continuous mutations into full domestication, after which they were helpless without the support of man. At the same time, man himself also changed genetically becoming, as the population densified, totally dependent on his plants and animals. In short, Mesolithic man was cultivating wild plants—not strictly speaking agriculture, but he was beginning to be tied to the soil in a primitive way. On the other hand his main subsistence continued to be based on hunting and gathering, only now the territory was based on the permanently manned settlement. The only difference between then and former times was that some part of the tribe was static, looking after the plants.

The early settlers continued to come down from the highlands to springs and river valleys where the necessary alluvial soil and moisture were present, a movement that led to the manipulation of water in a crude way and eventually to the larger, more permanent and relatively closely packed settlements of the Aceramic, pre-Pottery or Early Neolithic peoples. It was an evolution that took place along the bases of the hills that line the northern, western, and eastern arcs of the Near East.

These centres of emergence yielded different cultural traditions. Although within each one every local community would be stamped by its own environment, there would be discernible links originating in a common tradition—for example, flint types, certain architectural features and burial customs, pottery forms and decoration, still linked by tradition and a positive web of trade. By means of the latter new ideas and techniques reached the furthermost outposts, to be accepted, or accepted and modified locally. As we progressed from tentative beginnings through to the efficient self-supporting communities of the Aceramic Neolithic and on to what may have been a primitive form of founding colonies during the Late Neolithic, so our main food plants and animals became fully domesticated, thus enabling settlers to move out from the immediate vicinity of springs and rivers, and more technological processes were mastered. Until this

*See p. 6

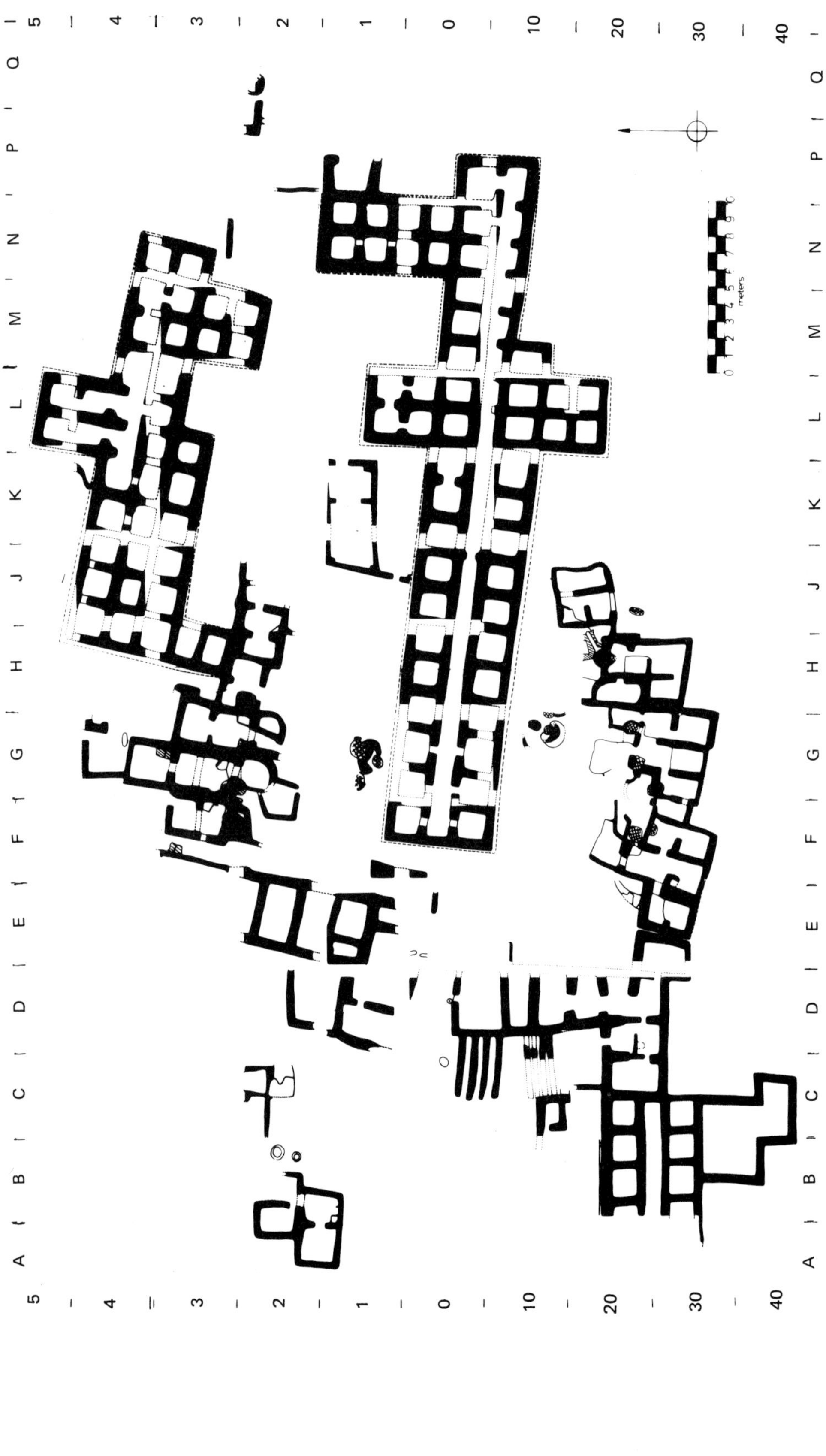

Fig. 2. Composite plan of lower levels 3–4.

time, the Late Neolithic, man's effect on his environment had been relatively light. True he had broken the soil for the first time and thereby opened the way for future erosional processes. Goats, those conspicuous devastators that prevent the rejuvenation of wood and shrublands by devouring saplings, had been herded since the Aceramic. Also man was manipulating water in a crude fashion which could, and did, lead to salinization of vast areas. The most important adverse effect on his environment was brought about by his need for fuel. Although initially by making inroads on arboreal stands near his settlements and by removing shrubby bushes in open country, he added areas for future erosion, this incessant need had not reached the dangerous proportions it assumed during the Pottery Neolithic and thereafter on an increasing scale. During the earlier periods, with very few if any exceptions, only small hearths for domestic purposes are found. But in the Pottery Neolithic ovens of all kinds proliferate alongside the domestic hearths, indicating that man had already become dependent on articles that could only be manufactured through the agency of heat—predominantly pottery at this time. By the Pottery Neolithic man was already enslaved by his plants, his animals and his need for fuel. Only the itinerant tribes revolving on the periphery of the settled areas were as free as humanly possible.

This was the general setting in which Umm Dabaghiyah was founded. The site was found as the result of a specific search undertaken when the writer was director of the British School of Archaeology in Iraq as the result of her strong conviction that the northern plains and foothills of Iraq, west of the Tigris, must contain settlements earlier than the period represented by the site of Hassuna, for over thirty years taken to typify the earliest stage of settlement in that region. The best area for such a search would have been in the more favourable environment along the foothills of Jebel Sinjar. This region would have had more rainfall, better springs with consequently more fertile soil in surroundings made up of open parkland shading into open forest, and owing to its proximity to the highlands there would have been a very good chance of finding Aceramic Neolithic or even Mesolithic settlements. However, for various reasons it was not possible to search this key area and instead a marginal area between desert and steppe some 90 km. south was selected. In the event, Umm Dabaghiyah was found and the fact that it is earlier than Hassuna upset the *status quo* a little. The culture, or phase, represented here is usually referred to as an "early facet of Hassuna", and so it is in a way. But the term is both vague and inaccurate: it ties Umm Dabaghiyah exclusively to Hassuna and denies the culture, or phase, existence in its own right. This may already be proving embarrassing as related sites are now being found round the Sinjar and even west of the Euphrates in Syria, and no doubt many more will be identified in the future. Part of the importance of what, for want of a better term, may be called the Dabaghiyah culture lies in its independent ancestral position, not to Hassuna alone but also, in certain aspects, to both Samarra and Halaf. An ancestor is rather different from a "facet": we all have ancestors and inherit different characteristics from them, and the same applies to the early village communities. By 'culture' it is not meant that every site large or small was exactly the same. Obviously each would have been created locally, but, as already mentioned, there would have been discernible those links introduced from a common tradition, or, as applied to ourselves, dominant genes. The other important aspect of Umm Dabaghiyah lies in the amount of information gained by the results of the excavation over a very large area of a site situated in such an unpromising environment.

Umm Dabaghiyah, then, covers a stage during which pottery had only recently come into general use thus, except in the initial stages, spanning the hiatus between the aceramic and Hassuna cultures in the northern plain of Iraq. Finally it is beginning to look as if it were a general period when small villages were being established for other than agricultural purposes in remote and ecologically unfavourable areas.

The environment appears to be singularly uninviting from the point of view of Stone Age settlement (col. pl. 1a). It forms the marginal land between true desert to the immediate south and more fertile steppe and former open parkland reaching up to the forested hills in the north. It lies at about 200 m. above sea level, and has an average rainfall of some 200 mm. a year. It is a vast expanse of open saline *Peganum* steppe, slightly rolling, stone- and treeless. The site lies close to an open clay pan depression which is the drainage centre for

Fig. 3. Domestic houses of the south-west residential quarter.

surrounding low ridges and a seasonal watercourse. After heavy rain this depression temporarily turns into a huge salty lake. One might visualize this as once having been a wide-stretched swamp area fringed by salt-resistant grasses and sedges with such shrubs as *tamarix*. The steppe is often broken by gypsum outcrops, a mineral that seems to form the substratum in most of the region, lying less than 30 cm. below the surface.

The climate is highly variable, very hot and dry for most of the year, with rain usually falling in violent and torrential thunderstorms. Periodically, total drought occurs and the area has to be evacuated; modern settlers, beduin and all their flocks are removed to the hills. Perhaps the rain was of a different pattern, more reliable, even and well distributed instead of the erratic downpours of today. Even so these particular areas were probably already somewhat salty and the water mainly brackish, though less so than today. In all this expanse of openness, Jebel Sinjar is clearly visible from the site some 90 km. away. Beyond the Sinjar lies the Khabur river, and at its confluence with the Euphrates, on the west bank of the latter, lies the contemporary site Bouqras. It is Umm Dabaghiyah's nearest neighbour as well as relative so far found to the west.

The archaeological records for both plants and animals throw further light on the ecology. The plant list does not differ in kind but only in degree from the species locally available today, while the almost total lack of arboreal charcoal suggests timber was not available. The fauna was infinitely more varied. Now, only occasional small foxes, hares, desert rats and jerboas are the sole inhabitants of an area that was once full of onager, gazelle and wild boar, with wild cattle available a little further north. The name of a neighbouring salt lake, Umm al-Dhiabba, Mother of Wolves, vouches for the former presence of those animals which, like jackals and hyenas, are not found in the region now.

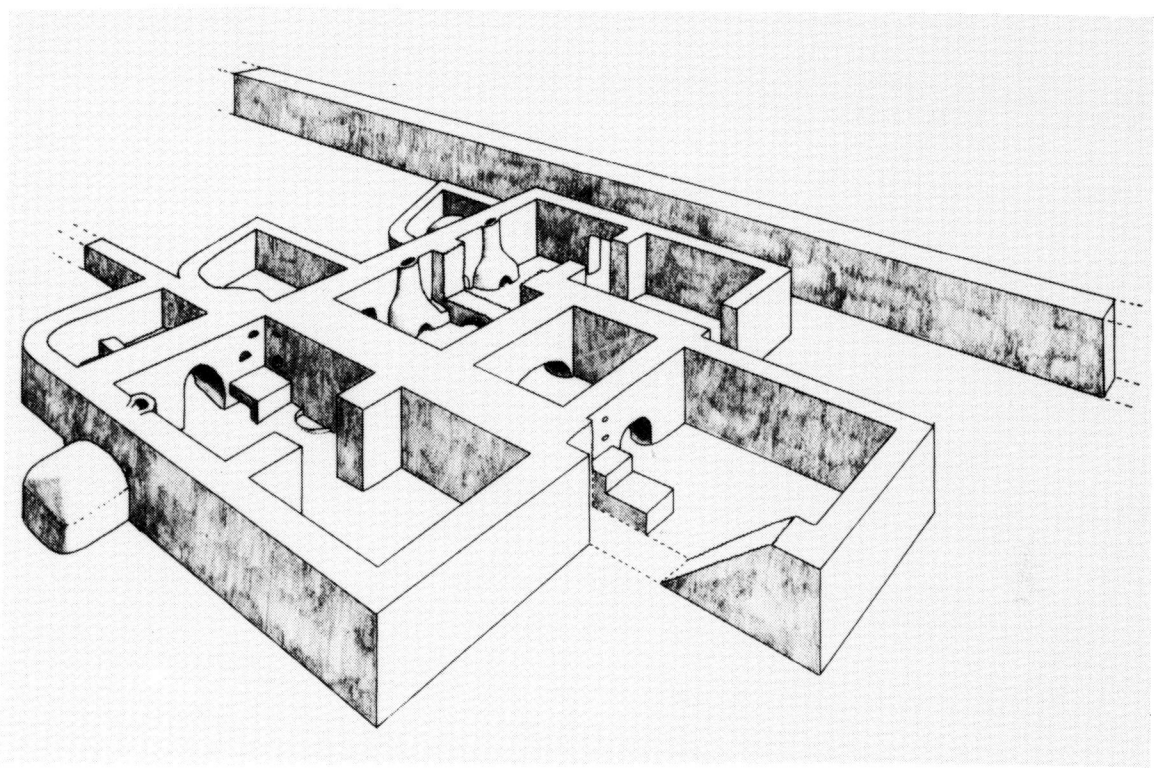

Fig. 4. Tentative reconstruction of a group of early houses.

The moment the first settlers arrived they inevitably altered things for the worse. They not only broke the soil for the first time, but the domesticated flocks and herds would have added their quota. To repeat, though, the worst agent for destruction, then as now, must have been man's insatiable demand for fuel. Umm Dabaghiyah contained a very large number of ovens of different kinds and one suspects that fuelling these would have reduced not only the immediate surroundings, but an ever-increasing area, to something approaching its modern aspect, or worse. All burnable shrubs and plants must have been used, and in dry years, as today, even the roots dug out and burnt. In short, a salty steppe without wood or appreciable stone, and a lack of sweet water — at least we failed to locate any — does not seem very conducive to Stone Age settlement. In days when the total settled population could not have been very large one would think that a fair amount of choice was available when it came to settling, and far more favourable surroundings could have been found. But that is a point to take up later.

The background of the site has been dealt with in some detail to show what possibilities were open to Stone Age settlers in that area. It remains to sketch in briefly a small selection of cultural elements and show their possible relationship to other sites, contemporary, earlier and later.

The plan of the settlement, at least in its main features, remained more or less constant during four complete rebuildings and some 18 phases, a total that adds up to about 500 years of occupation with periodic desertions (fig. 2). Apart from the ecology of the place, Umm Dabaghiyah exhibits many features, both architectural and cultural, unusual or even unique among the general run of contemporary farming communities. These taken together and allied to the local ecology point towards the settlement having been founded for some specialized purpose in which both agriculture and herding played a very insignificant part indeed.

One peculiarity is that the village appears to have been planned and built as a whole, and did not grow up in the haphazard way of ordinary settlements. Another peculiarity is the two long ranges of storage rooms containing over a hundred small chambers, mostly without communicating doors and without any external doors that we have found. Obviously these buildings were of supreme importance, the focal point and reason for the village's existence. Extremely strongly built of special clay heavily tempered with grasses, with interior buttresses, and with their external walls founded on widened, plaster-coated footings to protect their bases, they contrast strongly with the domestic buildings (figs. 3-4). The walls of the latter were of a sandy mixture with rare temper, and without protective footings. The houses themselves showed

Fig. 5. Two-level room showing central drain in lower part.

much evidence of alteration and rebuilding.

The plan of an individual storage block resembles smaller earlier examples from the Aceramic period. To west and north we have the sites of Mureybit, Sheikh Hassan and Çayönü. From their general situations, the first two on the Euphrates west of Bouqras, and the latter up in the mountains to the north not far from Diyarbekir they might well be ancestral to Umm Dabaghiyah. Slightly later examples of like plan but inferior workmanship have been found at Yarim Tepe, a Hassuna site about 70 km. north of Umm Dabaghiyah, but not, so far, at other Hassuna sites.

At Umm Dabaghiyah a few rooms were perhaps used as large, shallow basins. In the earliest levels these are characterized by very thick plaster floors, slightly canted, with drainage runnels in one corner leading out through the wall bases. These edifices were not necessarily roofed as one example had no entrance and only stubs of the walls remained. Another, in a house and therefore roofed, forms the lower part of a two-level room. In this case the drain was in the centre (fig. 5). In the later levels these rooms had their doorways built up with thick, rounded plaster kerbs, about 10 cm. high. An external step facilitated entry. In contrast to these rooms there also exist features that could have been used for drying some commodity. Basically they are individual groups of four or five low, non-load bearing walls built parallel to each other and about 30 cm. apart. One early example, built in a courtyard, consists of two separate units about a metre apart. Here the individual walls are three metres long (in centre on left side of plan, fig. 2). Indoor examples are smaller, in accordance with the proportions of the houses. There the walls are only 1.50 m. long. One complete example shows this unit situated across a corridor exactly facing the mouth of an interior oven (fig. 6). Obviously such a design is intended to allow warm, dry air to circulate freely. So one may conclude that these units were probably racks for drying some commodity that had, perhaps, been soaked first in the rooms with the drains. The only other examples of these drying racks known to the writer are later, again at Yarim Tepe, the Hassuna site to the north. At the earlier site of Çayönü, up in the hills, the same principle seems to have been applied in the form of long parallel lines of low walls forming raised foundations for floors. Again the idea of the free circulation of air seems to have been the same but adapted for different usage. So, a traditional connection could be suggested between the north and north-west and Umm Dabaghiyah.

The extremely small size of all rooms, both domestic and storage, roughly 1.50 x 1.75 m., must have been governed by the local ecology. Lacking roof timber, the only material on hand consisted of clay fortified by reeds and small branches from *tamarix* and other shrubs. Two other architectural features in the houses, on the other hand, could point towards ancestral links with the uplands of

Fig. 6. A drying rack facing the mouth of an interior oven across a narrow corridor.

Anatolia. One is the presence of exterior ovens built against outside house walls but with their mouths coming through the wall bases into rooms to form interior hearths with raised kerbs. More important, above these hearths are proper chimneys of plaster. These are of two kinds, either semi-circular (fig. 7) or with a full circle hood. One would have thought such an efficient heating system would not have been necessary on the plains except in freak winters. On the other hand, up in the mountains and on the Anatolian plateau there would have been urgent necessity to evolve a heating system that gave as little discomfort as possible. The other, perhaps diagnostic feature is associated with the use of the roofs for some purpose, either as in the case of the storerooms for access, or for other purposes. Access to the roof was by way of plastered steps set in corners of rooms, above which were toeholds in the walls leading up to some roof opening. The storage rooms did not have these features. Looking around the highlands for parallel traditions one comes to Çatal Hüyük on the Anatolian plateau about 1000 m. above sea level, which has a very rigorous winter climate while the summers are very hot. Çatal is the only contemporaneous site where access to the roofs by way of ladders set in the wall plaster of rooms is attested, but here the hearths were usually set immediately below the openings in the roofs which presumably acted as chimneys. However at Hacilar, also on the Anatolian plain, ovens set in recesses that formed rudimentary chimneys are reported, as is one example of a probable hooded chimney. In short, a tradition existed up on the plateau to the north-west of Umm Dabaghiyah, but the highlands immediately north of the site are still almost entirely *terra incognita* archaeologically speaking.

The inhabitants of Umm Dabaghiyah kept another ancient tradition alive. Using the white plastered walls and floors of their houses as a background they painted frescoes on the walls and sometimes a red band round the floor or over a sill.

Fig. 7. Interior hearth with semi-circular plastered chimney, the latter not fully excavated. Unexcavated doorway on left.

Painting bands round floors is a well-known feature from the aceramic period of the north-west and the Levant, while the wall-paintings of Çatal Hüyük are justly world famous. This tradition of painting murals is now attested at both Umm Dabaghiyah and Bouqras. These should be recognizable architectural characteristics which, singly or together might turn up at other sites of cultural affinity.

To repeat, the site is in an essentially stoneless environment though pebbles, brought in and used as grinders, pounders and burnishers are available in the larger wadis, for example in Wadi Tharthar about 30 km. away. A single deposit of very bad quality flint was located about 12 km. from the site. This material was much used for rough implements, scrapers and knives. The better class of implement was fashioned from high quality flint imported from outside the area, perhaps from the mountains. Another import used for tools was obsidian. Preliminary investigation shows this material to have come both from the Anatolian plateau near Çiftlik, and from either Nemrut Dag or the Lake Van area, roughly 800 km. away to the north-west and 500 km. to the north-east respectively. The tradition of flint-knapping shown by the implements is strongly based on that of the north, north-west and west where the antecedents can be traced back to the Aceramic Neolithic in many cases.

Fine polished stone bowls, jars, so-called mace-heads and beads of veined limestone and alabaster were also imported apparently ready-made, for nothing to indicate their fashioning has been found at the site. Here again the source for these stones and place of manufacture is unknown, but the makers were expert at their job and used the veining to its fullest advantage to enhance the excellence of their products. This is a tradition that continues strongly in Samarra.

Small basalt axe-heads were present in great numbers, usually found in the butchering yards. Again, all these axes were imported ready-made. A known source of greenstone and olivene lies in the Amanus mountains close to the Mediterranean, but other basaltic fields lies along the northern arc. The source of these axes is unknown at present, but that they were imported from some distance is certain.

Shells, for use as personal adornment, form a minor import. Those found have all been identified as eastern species. In other words, rather surprisingly in view of all the proven links with the western arc, they came from the Gulf rather than the Mediterranean.

Although pottery provides a good pointer towards cultural affiliations the subject is too broad to be covered here beyond pointing out that it is rather primitive, coarse and drab and its claim to posterity lies chiefly in the variety of its decoration. This includes high burnishing, painting, incising and applied work. It was a time when anything was tried in order to relieve the monotony of plain pottery by people who only recently had both fashioned and used exclusively vessels of stone, wood or basketry, all of them far more attractive materials.

The plant remains recovered not only bear out our deductions about climate and ecology but also cast doubt on whether agriculture played any part in the activities of the population at all. A few grains of *Emmer* wheat, hulled barley and *Einkorn* could suggest the cultivation of a few small plots at most. But, more important, the presence of a hexaploid wheat grain, peas and lentils, all plants that need humid soil conditions and could not possibly have been grown near the site, are proof that, to an important extent, the vegetable necessities of life also had to be brought in. The other identified plants are, rather naturally, salt resistant. *Chenopodiacae* (the goosefoot family), *Sueda maritima* (sea-blite) and *Salsola* (the salt worts) form the main part. The evidence shows that in their local collection of green foods the inhabitants gathered quantities of sea blite. They seem to have used the leaves raw, as is done today as a salad, throwing the stripped stems and immature fruits on the fires. This feature of hearth debris also indicates the plant fuel the inhabitants were forced to use, corroborated by the fine white ash left by plants that flare up quickly and burn right out. As today in the general area, they also used sheep or goat dung, evidence of which was found in the oven courtyards.

Needless to say the inhabitants also made good use of their underlying gypsum. They used it not only for plastering the floors and walls of their houses and occasionally a courtyard surface, but also to fashion a variety of scrapers, and loomweights, possible roof hatches, a few crude bowls and, with very many applied layers, they even tried to make a rare quern. The gypsum-burning ovens were located outside the walls, on the edge of the site furthest removed from the domestic quarters.

Thus we have a people deliberately settling in an area where they had to import their vital necessities from flint and stone to essential vegetable foods. Other plant sources such as pistachio and acorns were available not far north. Man does not live by meat alone, and one doubts whether he could except after millennia of conditioning as is probably the case with the eskimos.

For a probable explanation of the existence of the village we must now turn to the animal remains. The inhabitants seem to have kept a few cattle, sheep, goats and pigs, and they also had dogs. But all these domesticates, according to the faunal statistics, were of only minor importance accounting for a mere 11% of the whole. The overwhelming majority were of onager, about 70%, with gazelle trailing badly at some 16% and others such as boar, wild cattle and so on accounting for only 4%. The entire village seems to have been specialized for hunting onager. However, there must have been more to it than simply killing and eating onagers.

It is therefore suggested that this specialist settlement was founded as an industrial community to obtain various onager products, principally the hides, but no doubt also such things as sinews, even tail hairs, while the surplus meat above the needs of the villagers could have been dried, or salted and dried, and forwarded elsewhere. Although no remains of such a trade could ever be found, these people must have had something to give in return for their necessities, quite apart from their evident small luxuries.

Here two of the wall paintings help a little in showing fragmentary scenes of the hunt (fig.8). One depicts the initial stages of an onager stampede with men behind and others stationed along the way to keep the animals on the required line to the nets. For in a land without natural traps or precipices nets must have been used. Secondly, there is the arrival at what, although it is not shown, must be the net. The latter is outlined by

Fig. 8. Frescoes showing the start (above) and finish (below) of an onager hunt. Note the strong wooden hooks.

distinctive heavy duty wooden hooks which must have been used to keep the net in position under impact. The hooks are quite specific. Each consists of a slender tree trunk split vertically to include the spring of a stout branch, which when turned down makes a strong natural hook. Incidentally these hooks must also have been imports.

It is also suggested that the inhabitants came, or were sent out from a larger, one might call it more nuclear society, situated further north, probably quite high up, on purpose to obtain these products and forward them home. In return for these their home town saw to it that they were furnished regularly with their necessities. The habitation of Umm Dabaghiyah may well have been seasonal. There is no proof, but at least we know the site was deserted twice, each time for a considerable period necessitating complete rebuilding. On each of these occasions the houses were swept clean, doors bricked up and windows blocked, just as if their owners had simply intended to return the following year.

This explanation seems to cover the peculiarities of the site. The large storage blocks would have been for keeping perishable materials as well as such things as the wooden hooks and the nets themselves. One pair of rooms, presumably the paint store, contained numerous nodules of red ochre. This was probably another import. One other pair seems to have contained the arsenal where well over a thousand clay sling missiles and many large clay balls were found (fig.9). The rooms with drains could have been used for soaking the hides in brine before drying on the racks, one of the methods of curing hides to ensure their preservation before tanning. The actual tanning process probably took place up in the hills where the necessary vegetable substances would have been available. However, the preliminary curing, could this hypothesis only be proved, suggests that another major technology, ranking alongside agriculture and metallurgy according to some authorities, namely the use of salt for the preservation of food and curing of hides, was both known and in use by 6000 b.c.*. Some

Fig. 9. The arsenal containing over 1,000 clay sling missiles and many large clay balls.

such explanation for the site also accounts for the huge percentage of onager bones and it bears out the scenes on the murals. Finally it explains how the inhabitants could live there confidently dependent on the regular supply of their necessities.

Thus Umm Dabaghiyah spans a time when, as we know from Çatal Hüyük, members of large nuclear societies were well past living at subsistence level on what they could supply themselves. Further, they demanded their luxuries and may well have founded small satellite communities to produce them. They probably also forwarded surpluses for barter to other large or small communities, nuclear or not. It seems also to have been a time of increasing specialization in small settlements such as Umm Dabaghiyah, founded on the verge of the possible living areas, yet flourishing and even obtaining their own small luxuries. Probably, similar specialized communities producing fine stone bowls, axe-heads or other commodities were founded near the sources of their raw material. In such a hypothesis it is possible to see the embryonic beginnings of a process that would ultimately evolve into the full city state. But as in, for example, linguistics and the natural sciences, things seldom proceed along straight lines. The city states were not to appear for another three millennia. Instead, during the following stage the now fully domesticated plants were brought out and sown by great numbers of aspiring settlers all over the plains with a resultant plethora of small farming communities springing up all over the Near East. In the area around Umm Dabaghiyah these rather naturally were both tiny and short-lived, but further north in a more favourable environment they were large and of long duration. Probably it is true to say that the period encompassing such sites as Çatal Hüyük and Umm Dabaghiyah represents the zenith of the Late Neolithic in the northern region, that is on the Anatolian plateau and the adjacent plains, for there seems little doubt that in this area it was a period of great wealth, good organization and high technological achievement.

Bibliography

D. Kirkbride, Preliminary reports on Umm Dabaghiyah in *Iraq* XXXIV (1972), 3–15; XXXV (1973), 1–7; XXXV (1973), 205–9; XXXVI (1974), 85–92; XXXVII (1975), 3–10.

H. Helbaek, 'Traces of plants in the early ceramic site of Umm Dabaghiyah', *Iraq* XXXIV (1972), 17–19.

P. Dorrell, 'A note on the geomorphology of the country near Umm Dabaghiyah', *Iraq* XXXIV (1972), 69–72.

S. Bökönyi, 'The fauna of Umm Dabaghiyah: a preliminary report', *Iraq* XXXV (1973), 9–11.

C. L. Redman, *The Rise of Civilization* (San Francisco 1978).

J. Mellaart, *The Neolithic of the Near East* (London 1975).

J. Cauvin, *Les Premiers Villages de Syrie-Palestine du IXème au VIIème Millénaire avant J.C.* (Lyon 1978).

*See p. 6

Choga Mami

By Joan Oates

The prehistory of Babylonia remains little known, despite its importance for the understanding of early urban origins. The reasons for this lie to some extent in lack of exploration but largely in the heavy alluviation to which this region has been subjected during recent geological time and in the persistence of site location which has rendered inaccessible the early prehistoric levels of major centres such as Ur, Uruk and Nippur, at least for purposes of informative lateral excavation. It was with these problems in mind that we chose in 1966 to carry out a survey along the eastern margins of the alluvial plain, selecting the regions around Mandali and Badra as the most promising. Several geographical factors led us to this choice: firstly, the Mesopotamian flood plain slopes gently downwards from the Zagros foothills, beneath which Mandali and Badra lie (col. pl. 1*b*). The elevation of Mandali, for example, is 137 m. in contrast with 34 m. at Baghdad, 120 km. to the southwest. It was hoped, therefore, that in this area prehistoric mounds might be visible above the level of the plain. In the second place, Mandali lies roughly equidistant between Tell es-Sawwan, then the southernmost site at which material had been identified characteristic of northern Mesopotamia in the 6th millennium b.c.* (Samarra/Hassuna) and Ras al 'Amiya, then the northernmost known representative of an early phase of the 6th/5th millennium 'Ubaid occupation of southern Mesopotamia ("Hajji Muhammad", a ceramic style then thought to be equated solely with 'Ubaid 2). 'Ubaid 1 materials — "Eridu" — at that time appeared to be associated with a very limited area of southern Mesopotamia around Ur, Eridu and Uruk. Thus it seemed possible that in the Mandali area in particular information concerning the relationships, cultural, chronological and typological, among the very distinct and geographically differentiated prehistoric assemblages of northern and southern Mesopotamia might be found.

The third factor in our choice was climatic. Both Mandali and Badra lie on perennial mountain streams along the present border of viable rainfed agriculture, which skirts the Zagros chain. This led us to believe that at least the marginally better-watered area around Mandali would have been habitable in prehistoric times without recourse to irrigation and might therefore contain traces of early agricultural villages. A sweet water spring-line also connects the towns of Mandali and Badra, along the later route of the Achaemenid Royal Road.

The Mandali Survey

The survey was begun in the spring of 1966 with the co-operation of the Directorate-General of Antiquities and financial support from the American Philosophical Society. It was continued in 1967 with a Fellowship grant from the John Simon Guggenheim Memorial Foundation. A large number of sites was identified, of which the most interesting prehistoric mounds proved to be a group lying just to the north of Mandali. These included Tamerkhan (fig. 17), which yielded a small number of painted sherds bearing "tadpole" designs identical with a type known from early Zagros sites like Jarmo and Tepe Guran. This was the first, and remains the only, occurrence of such Zagros material in the Mesopotamian lowlands. Together with these and a large number of coarse undecorated sherds were an extensive chipped stone industry, including a large quantity of obsidian, and fragments of finely polished stone bowls, also in the tradition of Jarmo and Guran.

Among the other prehistoric sites identified were Choga Mami and Serik kabir; both appeared to have been extensively occupied throughout the Samarra, 'Ubaid and Uruk periods. A small site (survey no. 6) situated between Serik and Tamerkhan yielded a number of sherds in the "Hajji Muhammad" style, but of particular interest at Choga Mami was the presence among the surface materials of pottery closely resembling earlier 'Ubaid types from Eridu (levels XVIII–XVI) together with a large number of Samarran and a few Halaf sherds. Also found were a number of fine micro-blade "pencil cores" of a type common at Jarmo and Ali Kosh in Khuzistan; similar cores were recovered also from Tamerkhan.

Of these prehistoric sites Choga Mami was by far the largest on which there was no overlay of later occupation debris. We chose to begin excavation here partly for this reason, but largely because its surface materials were chronologically and culturally the most extensive. It was envisaged that ultimately a number of sites would be tested, in

*See p. 6

Fig. 10. View of tell.

Fig. 11. Samarran house in square H9.

particular Serik and Tamerkhan, which on the basis of their surface materials appeared to complement the sequence represented at Choga Mami. Unfortunately this has not proved possible.

Choga Mami: the excavations

Choga Mami is a low mound, standing some 6 m. high at its highest point, and extending some 350 by 100 m. (fig. 10). Samarran sherds have been recovered from all parts of the surface, suggesting it may have been an unusually large settlement for its time. The first season of excavations, which began

Fig. 12. Guard tower showing inner guard chamber, solid mud-brick platform and section of cobbled path.

on 2 December 1967 and continued to 26 February 1968, was sponsored by the British School of Archaeology in Iraq and generously supported by the Oriental Institute, Chicago. The excavations revealed that over most of the site the 'Ubaid and Uruk occupation, well-attested among the surface pottery, had been totally eroded, and that the latest preserved levels contained pottery and other artefacts similar to those found at Samarran sites such as Baghouz and Tell es-Sawwan. Two main areas of excavation were opened in which four phases of Samarran occupation were identified. In both areas a number of dwelling houses were excavated, all of a very uniform plan, consisting of two or three rows of three or four small chambers. The walls were constructed of long cigar-shaped *libn* (mud-bricks), laid in alternate courses of stretchers and headers; the external walls were buttressed, the lower courses often protected by an outer waterproof coating of *juss* or lime plaster. The debris associated with these structures appeared entirely domestic in character, with the exception of the contents of a single room (square H9, fig. 11), in which small plastered stone orthostats were set in the corners. In front of each was an area of heavy burning. A number of infant burials were found in pots concealed beneath the floors, in one instance at least apparently deliberately buried in the foundation level.

A slightly different picture emerged from the north-east corner of the mound, where the presence of a massive mud-brick guard-tower (fig. 12), which had once protected access to the village at this point, served to preserve levels of slightly later date. Here a cobbled path approached the settlement, turning at right angles around the tower and entering by way of a series of *libn* and polished limestone steps leading to an occupation level now lost (fig. 13). This substantial structure was responsible for the preservation here of several levels post-dating the classic Samarran levels excavated elsewhere and attributable to a phase characterized by pottery resembling both Samarran painted and incised wares and that associated with early 'Ubaid levels in southern Mesopotamia, in particular 'Ubaid 1 (Eridu levels XVIII–XVI). For this reason this pottery was designated "Transitional" (col. pl. 2a). Unfortunately the building remains associated with these poorly preserved "Transitional" levels were very fragmentary. A number of very characteristic "Hajji Muhammad" sherds was also recovered from the excavations in this area, unfortunately in unsealed deposits. Thus the exact chronological relationship between the Choga Mami Transitional, with its close parallels with both Samarra and 'Ubaid 1, and early 'Ubaid materials in Sumer was impossible to establish with certainty, although the approximate contemporan-

Fig. 13. Path on south side of guard tower, showing steps of alternate risers of stone and mud-bricks; the *libn* is marked with deep grooves or finger-marks.

eity of the Transitional and 'Ubaid 1/2 seemed indicated. This area of the site revealed also a well, dug through the preserved Transitional levels and containing an apparently homogeneous collection of pottery, much of which was clearly attributable to Late Halaf. Neutron activation analysis showed most of the Halaf sherds tested to have been manufactured locally, a result which was unexpected in view of the geographical position of Choga Mami, far to the south of the then known distribution of Halaf materials. A well excavated elsewhere on the site contained pottery in the 'Ubaid 2/3 tradition, closely comparable with that found at Ras al 'Amiya.

Among the small finds are the usual range of bone, clay and chipped and ground stone objects, characteristic of 6th millennium b.c.* settlements in Mesopotamia. Of some interest are a variety of studs and labrets, many closely paralleled at the Deh Luran sites in Khuzistan. A large group of female figurines was of particular importance.

Most were standing figures, either lizard-headed like the well-known, and much later, 'Ubaid figurines from Ur, or with remarkably realistic features (fig. 14). The Choga Mami ladies wore ear studs, labrets and bead necklaces, and bore three vertical tattoo(?) marks on each cheek, in the style of the well-known "face-pot" from Hassuna. Sherds of jars like that from Hassuna and of fenestrated pedestal bowls similarly ornamented were found at both Tell es-Sawwan and the Mandali sites. One of the most interesting features of the Choga Mami figurines is that the elegant hair style of the more realistic examples, such as fig. 14, persists in Mesopotamia until Late Uruk and even Early Dynastic times, a period of some 3000 years.

Irrigation

Among the most interesting, and unexpected, discoveries at Choga Mami was the recovery along the north side of the mound of a series of deliberately constructed water channels on the same

*See p. 6

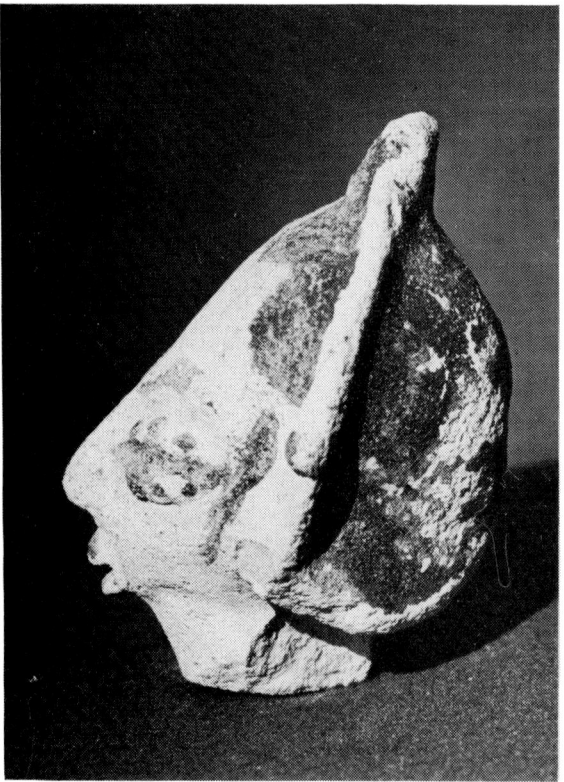

Fig. 14. Head of female figurine.

continued in use, with local realignments to compensate for silting and a rising land level, through 'Ubaid and Uruk times. Such developments imply a degree of planning and labour that must, however temporarily, have transcended the limits of individual settlements. We do not claim that irrigation technology was invented here, only that this is a so far unique example of the type of evidence that may be found elsewhere in comparable environmental situations.

We have as yet no knowledge of the background development of irrigation in Sumer, but the evidence from both Choga Mami and the newly excavated site of Abbadeh in the Hamrin (see below) suggests some contact between these areas and Sumer as early as 'Ubaid 1, while more detailed evidence from Chagha Sefid in Khuzistan strongly supports the view that a knowledge of irrigation technology was carried to Deh Luran from the Mandali region or some intermediate point. It is also evident that this technology was sufficiently developed by the 6th millenium b.c.* that its em-

alignment as one of the modern irrigation channels serving the area. The later channels at least were sited above ancient plain level, and this ancient sequence is associated stratigraphically with occupation levels of the Samarran phase (fig. 15). On modern analogy they may have formed part of a simple fan pattern of irrigation. On the south slope of the site was a larger and marginally later Samarran canal, which may have approached 6-8 m. in width, while some 100 m. further to the south we discovered another canal on the same alignment but of 'Ubaid 3 date (fig. 16). These later channels seem to represent an improvement in the irrigation system and an overall increase in the land available for cultivation, i.e. the replacement of a "fan" of small channels by one or more larger canals running parallel with the contours along the line of the *jebel* (fig. 17). Thus at Choga Mami there is evidence for small channel, possible fan, irrigation during the Samarran occupation of the site and for the existence, before the end of the period, of a much larger lateral canal, which

Fig. 15. Fragment of Samarran pot decorated with ibexes or goats, centipedes and swastikas.

*See p. 6

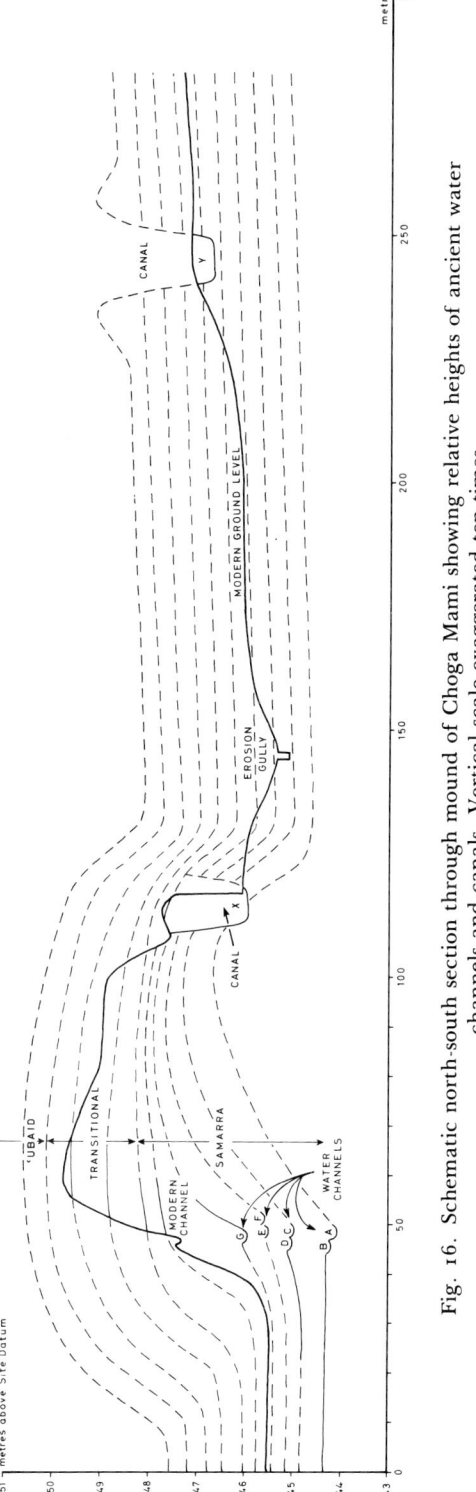

Fig. 16. Schematic north-south section through mound of Choga Mami showing relative heights of ancient water channels and canals. Vertical scale exaggerated ten times.

ployment in Sumer must have contributed to the increasing complexity of society attested from this time onwards.

Faunal and Botanical Data

Faunal specimens were studied at the site by Michael Jarman and later by Dr. Sandor Bökönyi. The full range of Near Eastern domesticates was present – sheep, goat, cattle, pig and dog, a feature we now know to be characteristic of even earlier 7th/6th millennium lowland sites such as Umm Dabaghiyah and Bouqras. Sheep/goat were predominant in all levels, including the 'Ubaid well and an Early Dynastic pit, and domesticated cattle apparently rare. This preoccupation with the herding of caprids is characteristic also of Samarran Tell es-Sawwan but appears in marked contrast with evidence from only marginally later lowland sites such as Ras al 'Amiya and Eridu where cattle predominate. At Choga Mami this may reflect the marginal position of the site, close to the Zagros foothills, but studies of settlement density in the Mandali region suggest that already in the 6th millennium there had been an intensification of agriculture that may have led to the development of some form of plough and a consequent need for traction animals.

5,329 seeds recovered by flotation have been identified. These include domesticated einkorn, emmer, "bread wheat", barley and linseed; lentil was also a major crop. Large-grain oat, ryegrasses, the linseed, naked barley and bread wheat, and probably also the clover, pea, lentil and blue vetchling suggest the availability of more water than modern conditions of rainfall would have supplied, a further indication of the practice of irrigation agriculture here in Samarran times. The plant inventory, both of cultivars and weeds, is too rich, however, for the site to be considered as representing early experimentation with irrigation, a purely botanical observation that is confirmed by the complexity of the irrigation schemes observed in the area. Certain species such as sea-blite, tuberous club-rush and swamp bedstraw indicate nearby marshes, a feature also of the modern environment.

Chronology

Since the excavation of Choga Mami, our knowledge of the new Transitional material, first identified here, has been much expanded by discoveries elsewhere, and it is now clear that our

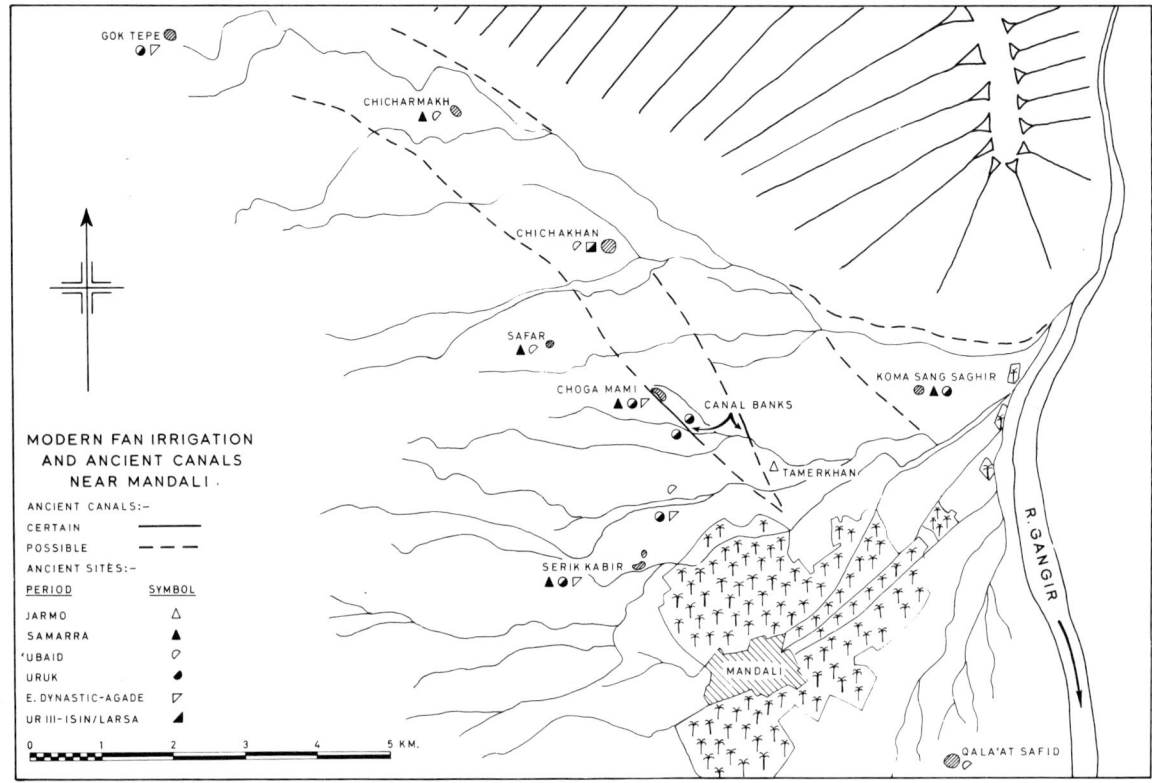

Fig. 17. Irrigation canals in the Choga Mami area.

original hope that the Mandali area would help to elucidate the complex relationships between north and south in the prehistoric periods has proved to be true. At Chagha Sefid in Khuzistan a large quantity of pottery identical with the Choga Mami Transitional has been recovered from level 5, preceding the Sabz phase (level 6), often (erroneously) equated with 'Ubaid 1 in Sumer. Moreover, at site WS-298 in the Warka survey sherds of 'Ubaid 1 type were found in association with a number which resemble some of the later Transitional forms. Occasional sherds of this type have been found at other southern sites, for example near Badra and Larsa, but the most informative new data come from recent excavations in the Hamrin just to the north of Choga Mami. Here, at the site of Abbadeh, the earliest level has produced a number of complete vessels and a variety of sherds which closely resemble examples from Eridu levels XVI–XIV (i.e. 'Ubaid 1/2), together with some specimens in the Choga Mami Transitional tradition (S.A. Jasim, personal communication). At Choga Mami it was observed that the closest affinities of this new ceramic type lay with the early 'Ubaid levels at Eridu, in particular levels XVIII–XVI ('Ubaid 1), and the Abbadeh evidence strongly reinforces this impression. In other words, it now seems certain that the Transitional ceramic tradition of central Mesopotamia is contemporary with 'Ubaid 1 and probably early 'Ubaid 2 in the south (*pace* Adams and Nissen); the presence of a very few Samarran sherds in the earliest level at Abbadeh and at Choga Mami, and of a few early 'Ubaid types in the latest Samarran levels, suggests also some contemporaneity between the end of the Samarran tradition and early 'Ubaid 1, a relationship which has always seemed likely. In sum, Choga Mami has provided evidence of a new prehistoric phase, apparently characteristic of central Mesopotamia and intrusive in Khuzistan, which is closely related both to Samarra, from which its pottery undoubtedly derives, and to the 'Ubaid 1 tradition characteristic of contemporary Sumer. Thin section analysis of the Choga Mami pottery has revealed an interesting continuity of potting tradition throughout the Samarran, Transitional and early 'Ubaid levels (as represented in the 'Ubaid well). These studies have revealed also that the Halaf potting tradition differed significantly from that of Samarra and 'Ubaid (D. Kamilli, personal communication), while recent work in the Hamrin has confirmed the contemporaneity of Late Halaf and 'Ubaid 2/3, suggested by the stratigraphic position of the Halaf well at Choga Mami.

A single radiocarbon determination from a Transitional level at Choga Mami, BM-483, 6846 ± 182 b.p. (4896/5101 b.c.*), accords well with recent determinations from other prehistoric sites in Mesopotamia, e.g. Arpachiyah, Yarim Tepe and Tell es-Sawwan, but these new dates are far too late in relation to existing determinations for comparable materials from Khuzistan. Such problems remain to be resolved, but the contemporaneity of the Choga Mami Transitional (and the earliest level at Abbadeh) with level 5 at Chagha Sefid is beyond question, a correlation which now clearly places 'Ubaid 1 before the Sabz phase with which it is often compared.

Although only one season of excavation was possible at Choga Mami, the results more than justified our expectation that the Mandali region would add much to our knowledge of Mesopotamian prehistory. New evidence for chronology, subsistence patterns and village life in general has been revealed. Recent excavations in the Hamrin have confirmed many of our tentative findings at Choga Mami, and it is to be hoped that one day it may be possible to continue work among what has proved one of the more promising concentrations of prehistoric sites in Mesopotamia.

Bibliography

J. Oates, 'Ur and Eridu, the prehistory', *Iraq* XXII (1960), 32–50.
—'First preliminary report on a survey in the region of Mandali and Badra', *Sumer* XXII (1966), 51–60.
—'Prehistoric investigations near Mandali, Iraq', *Iraq* XXX (1968), 1–20.
—'Choga Mami 1967–68: a preliminary report', *Iraq* XXXI (1969), 115–52.
—'Land use and population in prehistoric Mesopotamia', in *L'Archéologie de l'Iraq du début de l'époque néolithique à 333 avant notre ère* (CNRS colloque international no. 580, Paris 1980), 303–14.
—'Ubaid Mesopotamia reconsidered' (forthcoming article).
D. and J. Oates, *The Rise of Civilization* (Oxford 1976).
—'Early irrigation agriculture in Mesopotamia', in G. de G. Sieveking, I. H. Longworth and K. E. Wilson (eds.), *Problems in Economic and Social Archaeology* (London 1976), 109–35.
H. Helbaek, 'Samarran irrigation agriculture at Choga Mami in Iraq', *Iraq* XXXIV (1972), 35–48.
P. Mortensen, 'A sequence of Samarran flint and obsidian tools from Choga Mami', *Iraq* XXXV (1973), 37–55.
R. McC. Adams and H. J. Nissen, *The Uruk Countryside* (Chicago 1972).
F. Hole, *Studies in the Archaeological History of the Deh Luran Plain: the Excavation of Chagha Sefid* (Ann Arbor 1977).

*See p. 6

Arpachiyah

By John Curtis

In 1932, during the last season of Campbell Thompson's excavations at Nineveh, Sir Max Mallowan was entrusted with the task of making a deep sounding in the area of the Ishtar Temple. At a depth of about 22.5 m. beneath the modern surface of the mound, he encountered the distinctive painted pottery named after its discovery at Tell Halaf, nearly 300 km. away on the banks of the River Khabur. At that time Halaf pottery was also known from a few other sites, such as Sakçe Gözü and Carchemish, but apart from deducing that it was prehistoric little could be said about its date or about how it related to the pottery sequence for southern Mesopotamia. At Nineveh itself any further examination of the context in which the pottery occurred or of the settlement with which it was associated was clearly impossible on account of its great depth beneath the surface of the mound. Consequently, Sir Max cast about for a site in the vicinity where Halaf levels would be more easily accessible, and decided to excavate at the small mound of Tepe Rashwa next to the modern village of Arpachiyah, about 6 km. to the north-east of Nineveh (figs. 18–19). Here, Campbell Thompson had noticed Halaf-type sherds in 1928. The excavation, the first to be financed by the Gertrude Bell Memorial Fund, lasted for only six weeks in the spring of 1933, but was conducted with a workforce of up to 180 men (fig. 20). Nowadays the excavation of a prehistoric site with such a large number of men would never be contemplated, but it is an undeniable fact that the excavation was extraordinarily successful in achieving Mallowan's objectives.

In the centre of the mound Mallowan distinguished ten superimposed building levels (TT1–10) of which the top four had associated painted pottery of 'Ubaid type, so-called after its first identification at the site of that name near Ur in southern Iraq. Nowadays the 'Ubaid period is generally divided into four phases of which the first two, characterized by Eridu and Hajji Muhammed ware respectively, occur exclusively in southern Mesopotamia. It is, then, later 'Ubaid pottery that was found at Arpachiyah, and it is an extraordinary phenomenon that at about the same date 'Ubaid pottery appears at a large number of sites in northern Mesopotamia, and even as far afield as eastern Saudi Arabia. What this represents in political terms is unclear, especially as an 'Ubaid settlement large enough to give us this sort of information has never been excavated. Apart from similarity in pottery forms between north and south, however, parallels have been noted in architecture and in types of small object. There was clearly, then, an overwhelming cultural influence radiating from southern Iraq at this time.

To return to Arpachiyah, the 'Ubaid levels were characterized by poorly-built houses with flimsy walls, sometimes made of mud-brick and sometimes of *tauf* (packed mud) (fig. 21). Also attributed to the 'Ubaid period were some forty-five graves found in a cemetery on the west side of the mound. Most were simple inhumations and the bodies were generally accompanied by a humble selection of grave-goods such as pottery, both painted and plain, beads, and occasionally stone celts. One small find from the 'Ubaid levels, though, is of particular interest: this is a cast copper celt (fig. 22), testifying to a considerable proficiency in metalworking at this date. Although metal is rarely found on 'Ubaid sites the probability is that it was in quite common use. As copper was then a valuable commodity objects made from it would have been melted down if no longer required and never deliberately abandoned.

In the fifth level from the top (TT5), part of a building was excavated which, in marked contrast to the poor houses above, was solidly constructed with well-built walls and larger rooms. This contrast was even more marked in the level below (TT6), in which was found part of a spacious house, without central courtyard but with walls sometimes nearly 1.5 m. thick and with a thick mud-plaster covering. This house had been destroyed by a fierce fire which had the effect of largely preserving the contents of one room which Mallowan labelled "the potter's shop". Here were found clay figurines, mainly of "mother goddess" type, stone vases, amulets, flint and obsidian tools and pieces of Halaf pottery. Many of the latter were close to the walls of the room, lying on carbonized wood and thus indicating that originally they had probably stood on shelves. Also on the floor was a great number of flint and obsidian cores as well as a large lump of red ochre, palettes for mixing paint and bone tools for working pottery. Probably, then,

Fig. 18. Aerial view of excavations at Arpachiyah, looking north.

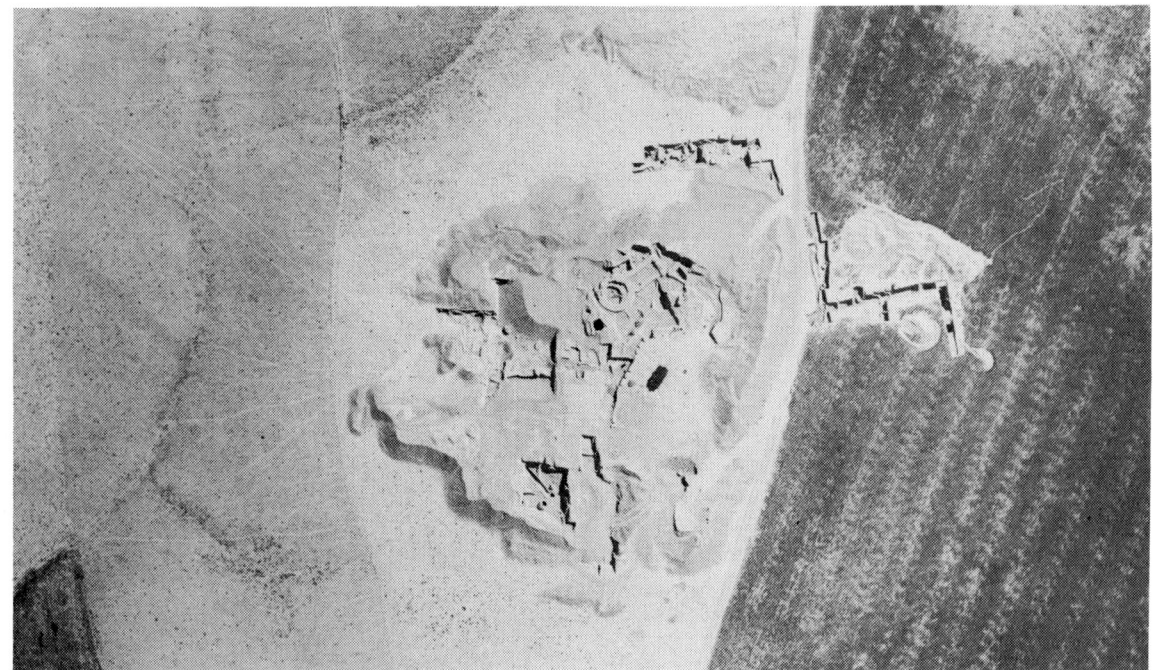

Fig. 19. Aerial view of excavations on completion of work showing "tholoi" in centre of mound.

Fig. 20. The work-force at Arpachiyah. The Mallowans are in the centre of the front row.

this room had been a workshop, perhaps occupied by both a stone-carver and a potter. Such was the profusion of pottery from TT6 that Mallowan suggested Arpachiyah must have been a centre specializing in the production of pottery, perhaps for export to nearby Nineveh. He also believed that the burning of TT6 represented a destruction of the Halaf settlement by people using 'Ubaid pottery, but this theory is contradicted by the evidence from nearby Tepe Gawra. It is clear here in levels XX to XVII that the transition from a Halaf to an 'Ubaid culture was a gradual process, implying that at Arpachiyah there was in fact a break in occupation. Further, it may be that the very latest phase of the Halaf civilization is not represented at Arpachiyah. Both these conclusions are borne out by the recent excavations at Tell Aqab in north-eastern Syria.

In the three lowest levels excavated by Mallowan (TT 7–10), a series of remarkable circular buildings was discovered, all firmly identified with the Halaf culture through their associated pottery. These buildings are often misleadingly referred to as "tholoi" because of their superficial resemblance to the well-known beehive tombs at Mycenae. The earliest of these circular structures at Arpachiyah consisted simply of a single room but later a long rectangular room, or antechamber, was abutted to the central part which now became bigger. The "tholoi" generally rested on stone foundations which supported *tauf* walls (fig. 23). It is possible that the "tholoi" were all domed, but some authorities dispute this.

It has become customary to divide the Halaf levels at Arpachiyah into three phases on the basis of the pottery (fig. 24). The pottery of the Early Phase, known only from pre-TT10 levels outside the central area of the mound, is hand-made, usually buff-coloured and commonly decorated

Fig. 21. 'Ubaid houses of level TT4.

Fig. 22. Cast copper celt from the 'Ubaid levels. BM 127757.

with red-brown paint. Naturalistic representations of birds, fishes and so on occur alongside stylized animal heads and geometric motifs. In this, as in subsequent phases, the "bukranium" or bull's head motif was particularly popular. The Middle Halaf Phase, corresponding to levels TT10-7, is characterized by pottery which is technically superior. Beautifully painted "cream bowls", shallow vessels with angular shoulders and flared rims, now become the distinctive form. In Late Halaf pottery, represented in the burnt house TT6, the use of brown, red and white paint on an apricot slip produced a brilliant polychrome effect. Shallow dishes now replace the "cream bowl" as the most popular form. The validity of these divisions has recently been confirmed by the carefully controlled excavations of Dr. Ismail Hijara at Arpachiyah, to which we shall refer later. They are further supported by the results from a programme of work undertaken at Edinburgh. Here we have an interesting example of how scientific techniques not

Fig. 23. Stone foundations of the "tholoi".

Fig. 24. Halaf pottery from Arpachiyah. From left, BM 127560 (top), BM 127530 (bottom), BM 127582.

available in Mallowan's day have in recent years been applied to archaeological problems with great effect. A number of sherds from Mallowan's excavations were selected for neutron activation analysis, care being taken to ensure that all the three phases outlined above were well represented. On the basis of their chemical composition it was possible to divide the samples into three distinct groups which corresponded to the divisions postulated on stratigraphical and stylistic grounds. The implication is that the Arpachiyah potters were using different clay sources at different periods, but why they should have done so remains obscure. There is no reason to suppose, however, that any of the clay sources were not in the immediate locality of the settlement. It is also clear from the same analysis programme that in the Late Halaf phase some pottery manufactured at Arpachiyah ended up at Tepe Gawra, thus confirming Mallowan's belief that Arpachiyah was producing painted pottery for use at other sites.

In 1976 a further season of excavation at Arpachiyah was undertaken by Dr. Ismail Hijara of the Iraqi State Organization for Antiquities and Heritage. The object was mainly to dig beneath the lowest level excavated by Mallowan in the central part of the site (TT 10), and in fact Halaf occupation was found to continue down to virgin soil. A further six building levels were identified, in the earliest of which the architecture was rectangular with the houses packed closely together. These houses were not, apparently, restricted to the central part of the mound. Later there was a transition to the circular architecture noted by Mallowan coinciding with a reduction in the overall size of the settlement. Evidence was found for a wall enclosing the "tholoi", suggesting to Hijara that they may have been in a special precinct and had some particular function, presumably religious. The settlement pattern at Arpachiyah during this period is in fact quite different to that observed in the contemporary levels at Yarim Tepe II, a site in the Sinjar Plain which has been excavated since 1969 by a Soviet expedition. Here, the "tholoi" appear to have been entirely domestic in character. There is some further evidence to suggest that the Arpachiyah "tholoi" were religious buildings. First, the stone foundations of most of them were left in position and not reused, which is curious given that the nearest source of stone was the River Khosr 3 km. away. Secondly, it appears that the fill around the "tholoi" was of clean reddish clay brought from beyond the mound rather than occupational debris and broken-down walls as is usually the case. In later periods this is certainly a feature of Mesopotamian religious buildings, as at Khafajah where the site of the Temple Oval was excavated down to virgin soil and filled with clean desert sand. Further, Hijara found three Halafian graves the character of which was in marked contrast to the Halafian burials found by Mallowan, which were in the form of ordinary inhumations. The new graves, on the other hand, consisted of skulls buried inside pots. If, as Hijara supposes, these are re-burials in a secondary context it would lend support to the view that during part of the Halaf period Arpachiyah had some special religious significance.

On the basis of the pottery types, Hijara has divided the Halaf occupation at Arpachiyah into four phases, of which the first three are earlier than Mallowan's TT 10. A charcoal sample from the second of these (BM 1531) has given a radiocarbon date of 4980 ± 60 b.c.* This determination, coupled with those for other Halaf sites, would suggest that the Halaf culture in Mesopotamia started at the end of the 6th millennium and continued for most of the 5th. At its widest extent, in the so-called "Middle Halaf phase", the Halaf culture covers northern Iraq, the foothills of southern Turkey and much of north Syria as far as the great bend in the Euphrates at Carchemish, all areas where dry farming is more or less practicable and which are suitable for the herding of cattle. Pottery typical of the "Late Halaf phase" has even been identified as far afield as Choga Mami (see the chapter by Joan Oates above) and Kültepe (Nakhichevan) in the Araxes Valley. Over the whole of this vast area there seems to have been a remarkable cultural homogeneity, with the widespread occurrence of "tholos"-type structures (usually having a domestic function) and extraordinary similarity in the shapes and decoration of pottery vessels. A form of statistical analysis has recently been applied to pottery from seven widely-separated Halaf sites, including Arpachiyah, which seems to underline this basic uniformity. That is not to say, though, that regional variations did not exist. Hijara, in his recently-completed thesis on the Halaf period, tends towards the view that they can be discerned.

Most of the settlements were clearly permanent, and had an agricultural basis. At Arpachiyah itself, the examination of soil samples has revealed the cultivation of emmer, barley, wheat, einkorn and lentils, while the bones recovered show that cattle, sheep, goats and pigs were all being domesticated. Also at this period we have further evidence for metallurgy in the form of fragments of copper pins from Arpachiyah as well as a copper stamp seal from Yarim Tepe II and a copper bead from Chagar Bazar. Earlier occurrences of metal in Mesopotamia are known at Yarim Tepe I and Tell es-Sawwan, dating from the so-called Hassuna and Samarran phases respectively.

For reasons that we have touched on above—its possible religious character during the middle period of its existence and its function as a specialist pottery-producing centre in the latest Halaf period—it may well be that Arpachiyah should not be regarded as a typical Halaf site. Nevertheless, it remains of crucial importance as one of only two Halaf sites—the other is Yarim Tepe II—to have been extensively investigated.

Bibliography

M. E. L. Mallowan and J. Cruikshank Rose, 'Excavations at Tall Arpachiyah, 1933', *Iraq* II (1935), 1-178.

I. Hijara, 'Three new graves at Arpachiyah', *World Archaeology* 10 (1978), 125-8.

I. Hijara et al., 'Arpachiyah 1976', *Iraq* XLII (1980), 131-54.

P. J. Watson and S. A. Leblanc, 'A comparative statistical analysis of painted pottery from seven Halafian sites', *Paléorient* 1 (1973), 117-33.

T. E. Davidson and H. Mckerrell, 'The neutron activation analysis of Halaf and 'Ubaid pottery from Tell Arpachiyah and Tepe Gawra', *Iraq* XLII (1980), 155-67.

P. S. de Jesus, *The Development of Prehistoric Mining and Metallurgy in Anatolia*, 2 parts (Oxford 1980): for analysis of Arpachiyah celt.

*See p. 6

Plate 1a View of Umm Dabaghiyah showing the typical environment of this part of the Jazira.

Plate 1b View south of Mandali, of the gap through which the R. Gangir debouches onto the Mesopotamian plain.

Plate 2a Transitional pottery from Choga Mami.

Plate 2b-c. Painted pottery of 'Ubaid 3 type from Ras al 'Amiya.

Plate 2d Work in progress on the later 'Ubaid levels at Tell Madhhur.

Plate 3a A scarlet ware jar found in the Early Dynastic I curving building at Tell Madhhur.

Plate 3b Jewellery from Grave 176, Abu Salabikh. The lapis lazuli seal is also illustrated fig. 44, top left.

Plate 3c Scraping the surface of the west mound, Abu Salabikh, after rain.

Plate 4a View of Tell Brak from the south-west.

Plate 4b Shell pendant from Tell Brak.

Plate 4c Ivory statuette of a nude female from Tell Brak.

Plate 5 Fine and incised wares of Taya 9–6. Top row, Taya 9; others mainly Taya 8–7.

Plate 6*a* View looking northwards from Chagar Bazar. Part of trench BD in foreground.

Plate 6*b* Inlaid glass beaker from Tell al Rimah.

Plate 6*c* Glazed frit mask from Tell al Rimah.

Plate 7*a* Nimrud citadel seen from Fort Shalmaneser.

Plate 7*b-c* Wall paintings of genies in fish cloaks. Nimrud, Fort Shalmaneser, T 27.

Plate 8a Elements of possible couch as found at Nimrud in NE 26, Fort Shalmaneser.

Plate 8b The shrine at the N.W. end of the Temple of Mamu, Balawat.

Ras al 'Amiya

By David Stronach

As has been stressed elsewhere in this volume, the problem of heavy alluviation has done much to limit out understanding of the earliest patterns of settlement in southern Mesopotamia. One or two observations may serve to underline this point. An extensive survey of the Uruk region undertaken in 1967 identified only one site that was possibly contemporary with the earliest 'Ubaid occupation ('Ubaid 1) and only three mounds that could be identified with the subsequent Hajji Muhammad or 'Ubaid 2 horizon. Moreover, it is worth recalling the unusual circumstances which allowed the excavators of Uruk, more than forty years ago, to locate the neighbouring site of Qal'at Hajji Muhammad where the distinctive pottery of the 'Ubaid 2 period was first found. This probably late 6th millennium site had come to be overlaid in the course of time by three metres of alluvium and it was only an inspection of the meandering bed of the Euphrates — made at a time when the river was low — that led to the discovery of the site.

It was in fact a still more random chance that led to the location of Ras al 'Amiya. In the late 1950's two drainage canals, cutting across a once occupied area, happened to bring to the surface a quantity of Hajji Muhammad sherds. This circumstance at once extended the known distribution of 'Ubaid 2 pottery and at the same time narrowed the physical gap between the northern and southern ceramic sequences of Mesopotamia.

By the time that I came to learn of the presence of the site, the canals were not too far away from being brought into operation. The relevance of an attempt to excavate was accepted without delay, however, by the Directorate-General of Antiquities, by the appropriate irrigation authorities and, not least, by the British School of Archaeology in Iraq.

Fig. 25. The CW Cut in the west wall of the side canal after the removal of the alluvial overburden and a partial exposure of the site's upper building levels. The oval outline of an oven can be seen in the foreground.

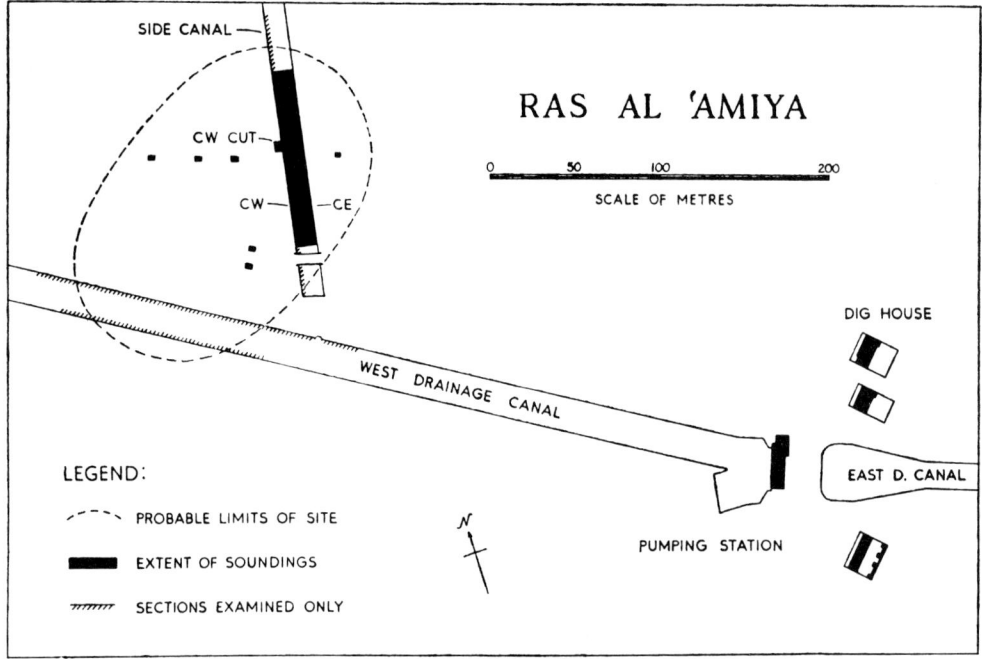

Fig. 26. Plan of Ras al 'Amiya.

Thus it came about that David French, Jeffery Orchard, Eva Strommenger and I set out for Ras al 'Amiya for a brief season of three weeks duration early in May 1960.

Ral al 'Amiya is situated 80 km. south of Baghdad in the flat alluvial plain between the Euphrates and Tigris rivers. As can be inferred from the presence of such adjacent sites as Kish, Jemdat Nasr and 'Uqair, this was for long one of the more favoured regions for early settlement in central Mesopotamia. But the very difficulty which has deprived us of so much information, notably before the 4th millennium, is emphasized by the fact that the highest point of the deposit at Ras al 'Amiya still lies 1.20 m. below the present surface of the alluvium (fig. 25).

The first days of the work also served to confirm a second unusual attribute of the site: namely the transitional character of the pottery. While a good part of the pottery accords with the closely painted Hajji Muhammad style (in which the patterns often appear in reserve) a still larger sample can be seen to illustrate the more open painted style of the 'Ubaid 3 period (col. pls. 2b-c).

From traces of occupational strata in the side walls of the two canals, and from small probes introduced elsewhere, it seems legitimate to suggest that the village covered a total area of about 2.5 hectares (fig. 26). In terms of the site's relatively short existence, further soundings in the narrow side canal revealed the presence of five probable building levels, the lower two of which already stood below the level of the water table at the time of the 1960 excavations. It should be added that no sign of destruction was encountered in level I—the latest level—and that, if salinization was not yet a problem, sudden movements in a local river regime are likely to offer the best explanation for the foundation and desertion of villages of this more or less standard size.

To the limited extent that the architecture of Ras al 'Amiya has been exposed to date, it offers no hint of distinction. *Tauf* walls were preferred to mud-brick walls and at only one point were we able to document the use of relatively crude 'mud-slab' bricks. Although no complete house plans were recovered, it is clear that small square rooms—and very often more nearly oval compartments—were ranged round open courtyards. Such courtyards usually contained an oven, either constructed as a free-standing unit or built into a side wall.

No concentrated deposits of plant material

chanced to be found during the work (which preceded the introduction of flotation techniques), but since the average rainfall in this part of Iraq stands today at only 150 mm. per annum it is safe to assume that the villagers at Ras al 'Amiya already engaged in irrigation agriculture. With reference to the faunal sample, the most striking feature is the high percentage of cattle bones. The foundation of the local economy appears, therefore, to have been cattle herding and irrigation agriculture. Sheep and goats were also herded; fresh-water mussels were collected; and such animals as gazelle, onager and wild pig appear to have been hunted on occasion.

Following the passage of more than twenty years many perspectives have changed. Down to the late 1950's the essential continuity of the 'Ubaid pottery sequence was not universally recognized and Louis le Breton felt able to suggest that Hajji Muhammad pottery could have reached Sumer from Khuzistan rather than *vice versa*. Today, in the wake of Joan Oates' important article written in 1960, and in the light of the work carried out at Ras al 'Amiya and other sites since that same year, Hajji Muhammad pottery is seen as an undoubted link in the evolution of the 'Ubaid sequence. Moreover, Ras al 'Amiya offered early and valuable confirmation of the link between 'Ubaid 2 and 'Ubaid 3, not to mention the persistence of Hajji Muhammad designs (already well documented at Eridu) and the sometimes notable quality of early 'Ubaid 3 pottery.

It is also possible (if the present water table is not too high to preclude such a course) that the recovery of a larger sample of pottery from Ras al 'Amiya, and a very careful study of such material, would help to determine the extent and nature of local ceramic production at the village level at a time when the mass production of 'Ubaid pottery seems to have begun in earnest. Certainly, if we wish to know more about the various factors which contributed to the new character of 'Ubaid pottery from the 'Ubaid 3 period onwards, studies of this kind will not be irrelevant.

After an interval of two decades we should perhaps find it a matter of concern that Ras al 'Amiya still provides one of the very few indications of early village size in southern Mesopotamia. It is also worth stressing, with reference to palaeobotanical studies, that flotation techniques have yet to be introduced at any Hajji Muhammad site situated in southern Iraq.

The fact that 45% of all the animal bones recovered from Ras al 'Amiya were cattle bones was originally taken to be an almost suspect finding. In retrospect, however, this signal interest in cattle can be understood as a vital element in a distinct type of economy which evolved in Mesopotamia and which eventually proved strong enough to support the beginnings of urban life. Comparable evidence for cattle breeding has since been found at several other early lowland sites and, at this moment at least, it could be surmised that a domestication of cattle took place in Mesopotamia.

Finally, the recent findings from Umm Dabaghiyah and the pre-pottery settlement of Maghzaliyeh show that the north Mesopotamian plain was far from being an agricultural vacuum in the 7th millennium. If we add to this intelligence the new evidence for pioneer irrigation skills in the region of Choga Mami to the north-east, it is not difficult to suppose that central Mesopotamia became one of the first parts of the Near East outside the zone of marginal dry farming to be transformed and enriched by irrigation agriculture. In this reconstruction, too, the aboriginal population of adjacent Sumer could have been introduced to the advantages of irrigation at an earlier date than is generally suspected. At all events it would seem bizarre indeed for Ras al 'Amiya—a modest link in a long chain of discovery—to remain for much longer the earliest known site in the long stretch of low lying alluvium between Nippur, 80 km. to the south, and Tell es-Sawwan, 180 km. to the north.

Bibliography
D. Stronach, 'The excavations at Ras al 'Amiya', *Iraq* XXIII (1961), 95-137.
K. V. Flannery and I. W. Cornwall, 'The fauna from Ras al 'Amiya, Iraq: a comparison with the Deh Luran sequence', in F. Hole, K. V. Flannery and J. A. Neely, *Prehistory and Human Ecology of the Deh Luran Plain* (Ann Arbor 1969), 435-8.
J. Oates, 'Ur and Eridu, the prehistory', *Iraq* XXII (1960), 32-50.
— 'Choga Mami, 1967-68: a preliminary report', *Iraq* XXXI (1969), 115-52.
R. McC. Adams and H. J. Nissen, *The Uruk Countryside* (Chicago 1972).
L. le Breton, 'The early periods at Susa, Mesopotamian relations', *Iraq* XIX (1957), 79-124.
C. Ziegler, *Die Keramik von der Qal'a des Haǧǧi Mohammed* (Berlin 1953).

The Hamrin Sites

By Michael Roaf

Perhaps the most exciting project undertaken in the last fifty years of Mesopotamian archaeology has been the Hamrin Dam Salvage Project: other sites have produced more impressive finds, such as the beautiful ivories from Nimrud or the spectacular architecture of the temple at Tell al Rimah, but nowhere else in Mesopotamia has there been such successful international co-operation on such a wide variety of sites in such a small area producing such important and interesting results. When the results of the numerous excavations have been published the Hamrin Basin will be the area best known archaeologically in Mesopotamia and we will be able to discuss regional settlement patterns not only superficially, from surface collections of potsherds, but also in depth from the more complete and reliable evidence of excavations. Most of the credit must go to the Iraqi State Organization for Antiquities and Heritage which initiated the project, provided the largest share of the finance, and indeed undertook the majority of the excavations. The contribution of the British Archaeological Expedition to Iraq was only a small part of the whole project, but the results of our work were extremely worthwhile, though they will only achieve their full significance when the results of the excavations at the other sites have been published in detail.

In 1977 the British Archaeological Expedition to Iraq was invited by the Iraqi State Organization for Antiquities and Heritage to excavate one of the many sites which were to be flooded by the dam built across the Diyala River where it passes through the Jebel Hamrin, and in December Nicholas Postgate started work at Tell Madhhur. In all the British Archaeological Expedition spent some fourteen months in the field and during that

Fig. 27. Excavating down to the 'Ubaid house at Tell Madhhur. The walls of the house are visible in the foreground.

Fig. 28. A view of the well preserved 'Ubaid house at Tell Madhhur from the north-east, showing the cruciform central hall.

time as well as excavating at Tell Madhhur was able to work for about two months at Tell Rubeidheh and to carry out a small sondage at Tell Haizalun. Our work in the Hamrin was sponsored by the British School of Archaeology in Iraq and the Royal Ontario Museum, with grants from the British Academy, Edinburgh University, the Johns' Fund of Cambridge University and an anonymous donation.

Tell Madhhur

Tell Madhhur lies in the north-eastern part of the area to be flooded. It is a small mound about 90 m. in diameter rising 2.50 m. above the surrounding plain, but extending a further 4 m. below the present level of the alluvium suggesting that at least 4 m. of silt have been deposited since the site was first occupied. The bulk of the mound was formed during the Late 'Ubaid period, with a small village settlement in the Early Dynastic I period being responsible for the top metre or so of deposit on the highest part of the site. When the site was not occupied it was subject to intense erosion and most of the later Early Dynastic I layers and much of the latest 'Ubaid levels have been lost. At various periods the site was re-used: in the mid-3rd millennium a number of rich tombs were dug into the surface of the mound, subsequently a well was dug at an uncertain date, there are traces of a medieval Islamic occupation of the 13th or 14th centuries A.D. of which only storage pits survive, and finally the mound was used until recently as a cemetery by local villagers. Excavations here were directed by Nicholas Postgate, T. Cuyler Young and Michael Roaf.

The earliest occupation level at Tell Madhhur was only investigated in three small sondages and no walls were found. The pottery was similar to that of the later 'Ubaid levels, and in fact there was very little change throughout the 'Ubaid occupation on the site.

During the first season walls standing to a height of about 2 m. were found in a deep trench (col. pl. 2d). The excavation of the whole of this building, subsequently to become known as the level 2 'Ubaid house, was the main aim of the next three seasons (fig. 27). Although the building was quite small, about 14 m. square, it lay at the heart of the mound and was covered by numerous levels of later 'Ubaid and Early Dynastic I buildings which took a considerable amount of time to excavate before reaching the house. When the house was completely excavated with its intact windows and doors, it could be seen to be one of the best-preserved prehistoric buildings ever to have been found in Mesopotamia (figs. 28–29). It had a tripartite plan, consisting of a central cruciform hall running the whole width of the house, with rows of rooms to the north and south. The walls were made out of rectangular mud-bricks (53 x 28–30 x 8–10 and 53 x 14.5–15 x 8–10 cm.) and the outside wall stepped out wherever it was met by an internal wall. The building was reinforced by a heavily plastered low mud-brick revetment built at the base of the outer wall; this feature was also found in the later 'Ubaid buildings at Tell Madhhur but as far as I know has not been identified on any other 'Ubaid sites.

The only entrance to the house was at the north-west corner, leading through an antechamber into the central hall. The north wall of this central hall had collapsed but the fallen bricks were visible in one of the sections dug across it. By counting the number of courses it could be calculated that the original height of the hall was at least 3.5 m. On the floor of this room were a few fragments of mud-plaster painted white with a red stripe or band, but the original scheme of decoration could not be reconstructed.

The building had been destroyed by fire: several of the rooms had been heavily burnt and the charred beams were lying on the floor where they had fallen. When the house was abandoned, all the domestic equipment was left *in situ:* more than 70 pots, many with painted or incised decoration, and typical everyday artefacts such as baked clay nail-shaped mullers, grindstones, stone hoes, flint and obsidian blades (but no baked clay sickles), baked clay spindle whorls, and a few animal figurines. Sun-dried, egg-shaped clay sling bullets were found in remarkable numbers, there being more than 3,800 in the house. In one of the heavily burnt rooms at the south-west of the house were found

Fig. 29. A view of the well preserved 'Ubaid house at Tell Madhhur from the south-east, showing the east end of the cruciform central hall.

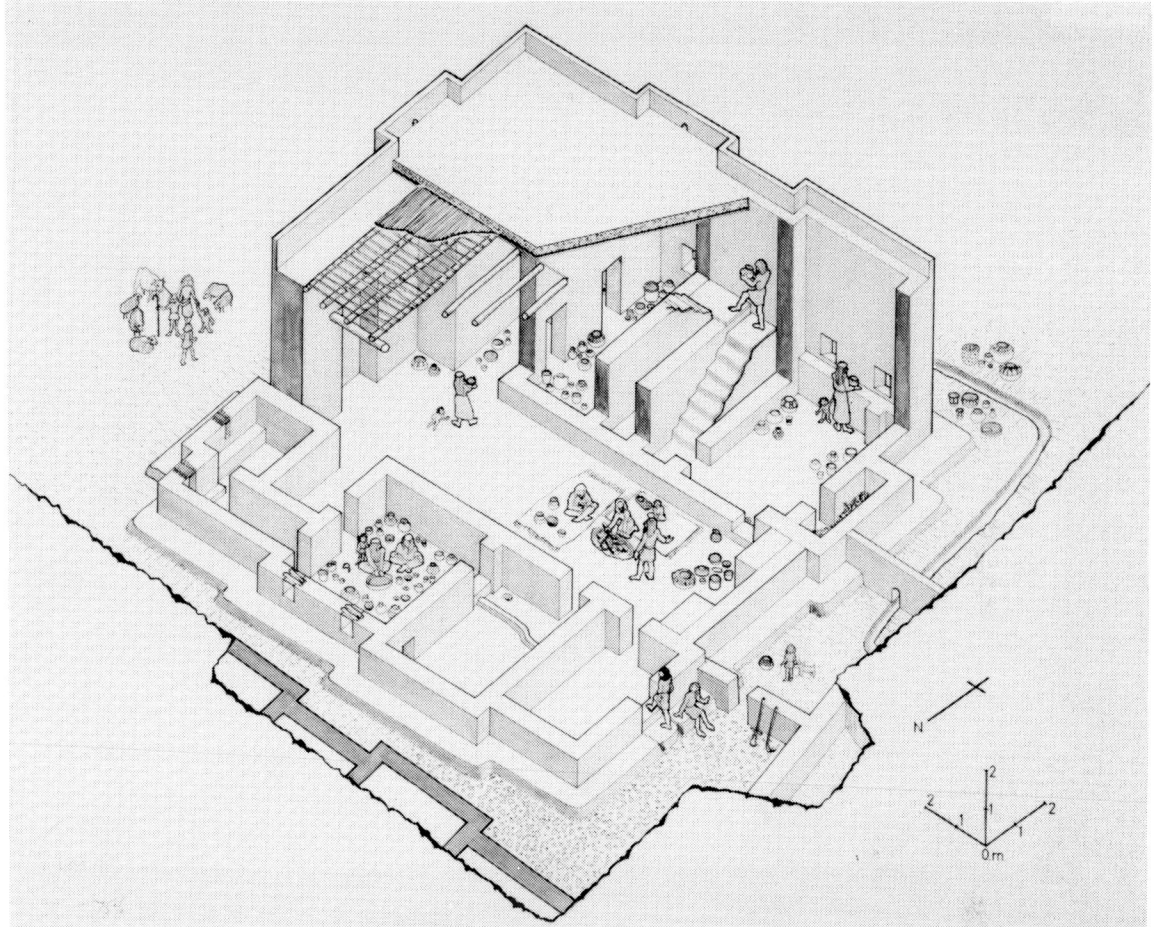

Fig. 30. An isometric partial reconstruction of the 'Ubaid house in level 2 by Susan Roaf. The pots are drawn reconstructed and replaced in approximately their original positions. Note the low revetment round the outside of the house. No evidence for the nature of the staircase was observed but it must have been in the position shown.

large quantities of carbonized grain, provisionally identified as 6-row hulled barley, which has yielded a Carbon-14 date of $5,570 \pm 55$ b.p. or a calibrated date of $4,470 \pm 80$ B.C. As this is one of the very few Carbon-14 determinations to be made for the 'Ubaid period it is particularly interesting.

The plan of the Tell Madhhur level 2 'Ubaid building has close parallels at other 'Ubaid period sites in the Hamrin Basin (Tell Abbadeh, Tell Rashid, and Kheit Qasim) and with 'Ubaid sites in the north of Iraq (Telul eth-Thalathat and Tepe Gawra). In pottery also the links are closer with the north (Nuzi and Tepe Gawra) than with the south.

The discovery of a complete building constructed as a unit and destroyed with all its pots and other furnishings left *in situ* is a rare and fortunate occurrence for the excavator (fig. 30). Normally domestic village houses grow and decay gradually and irregularly, and this was the case with the 'Ubaid occupation levels above the level 2 house. Here rooms were added to existing buildings, dilapidated walls were rebuilt, abandoned structures were levelled and used as courtyards, and pits and drains were dug into them. The resulting stratigraphy was very complex and difficult to unravel. Four main building levels with numerous phases were identified and it was clear that the character of the settlement was much the same as that un-

Fig. 31. A view of the Early Dynastic I curving building at Tell Madhhur from the east, much damaged by Islamic pits and graves.

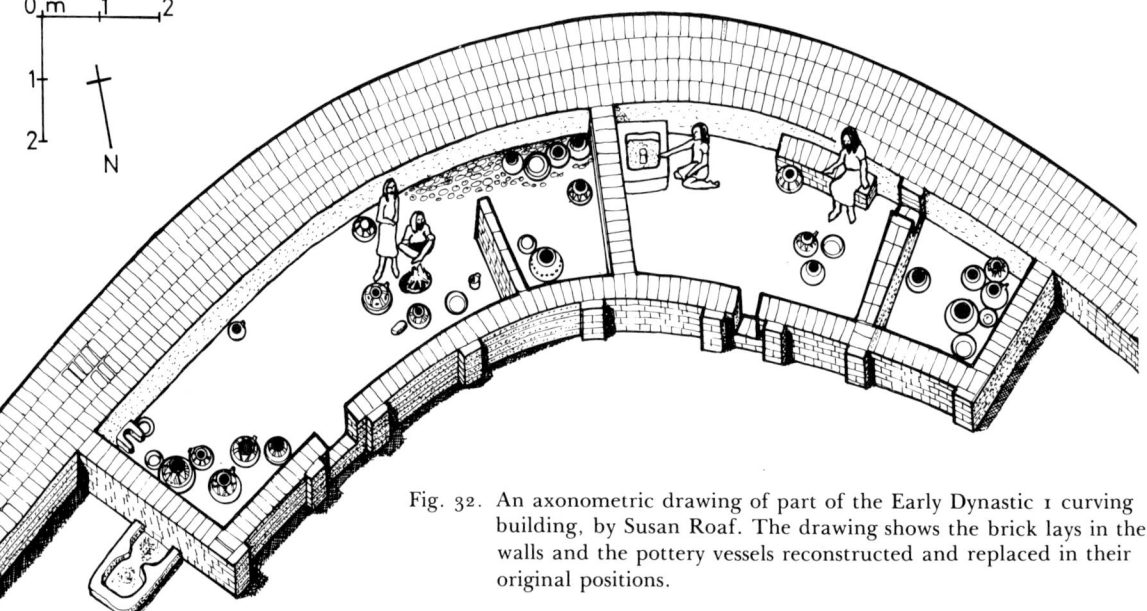

Fig. 32. An axonometric drawing of part of the Early Dynastic I curving building, by Susan Roaf. The drawing shows the brick lays in the walls and the pottery vessels reconstructed and replaced in their original positions.

covered in level 2, and the pottery and other small finds were very similar. As the latest level was very eroded there was no evidence to suggest why the site was abandoned at the end of the 'Ubaid period.

Apart from a few Uruk sherds found in Early Dynastic I contexts there was no evidence of any occupation in the Uruk period at Tell Madhhur and the Early Dynastic I occupation represents a new settlement. The Early Dynastic I buildings were for the most part fragmentary, damaged by later pits and graves and destroyed by erosion off the top of the mound, but one building was of particular interest. Only the southern half of this building was preserved (the rest being lost by erosion) and it consisted of a thick curving wall on the inside of which a number of rooms with thin walls had been built (figs. 31–32). If the building had originally formed a complete circle it would have been about 30 m. in diameter. On the floors of the four rooms of this curving building were several smashed pots including both scarlet ware jars (col. pl. 3a) and coarse grog-tempered bag-shaped pots with cylinder seal impressions on their rims and on the applied bands beneath the rim. Similar coarse pots with seal impressions have been found on the other Early Dynastic I sites excavated in the Hamrin Basin. In fact the Hamrin Basin seems to have formed a distinct cultural enclave in this period, with a definite tendency towards buildings with curving walls (seen spectacularly at Tell Gubba and Tell Razuk) and with its own corpus of pottery including pots with seal impressions and styles of scarlet ware painting similar to but distinguishable from the Diyala scarlet ware further south. It is striking that the solid-footed goblet which was taken as a hall-mark of the Early Dynastic I period in the Diyala region was totally absent from the Tell Madhhur assemblage.

During the excavations at Tell Madhhur four large rich graves dug into the surface of the mound were excavated. Three of them were badly damaged by later pits and graves, but enough could be recovered to show that all four shared a number of common characteristics. They all had a similar alignment with the long axis running from east to west, the body (when found) was laid along the east edge of the tomb with its head to the north, and on the west side of the tomb were the skeletons of two equids. Similar tombs have been found at Tell Gubba and at Tell Razuk of roughly the same date.

The earliest of the tombs at Tell Madhhur may have belonged to the end of the Early Dynastic I period (perhaps contemporary with Early Dynastic II in the Diyala), two more to the Early Dynastic III period and the fourth, the largest, the richest, and the best preserved to the Akkadian period (figs. 33–34).

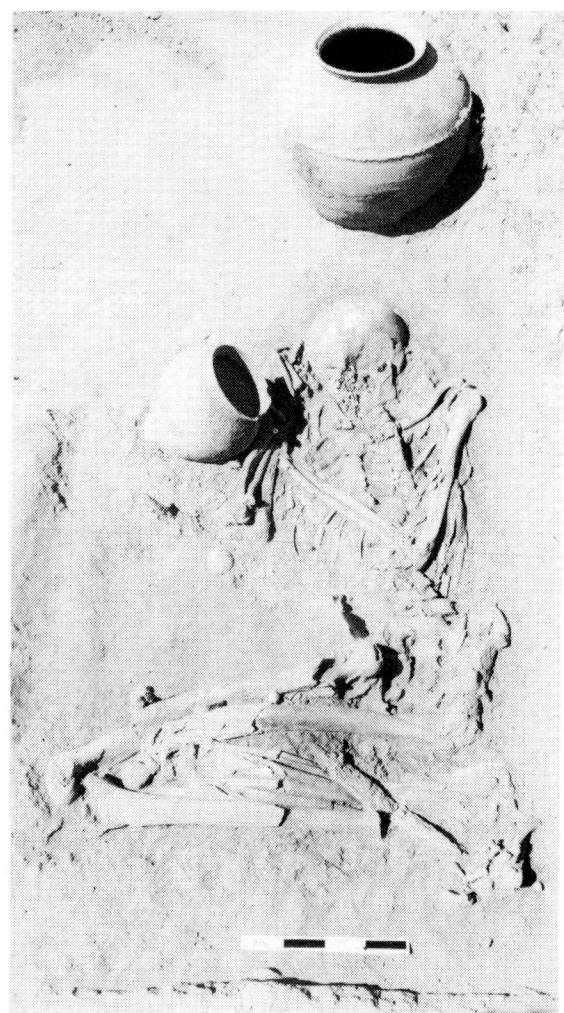

Fig. 33. The human skeleton in the 5G grave at Tell Madhhur.

This grave, called the 5G grave as it was located in trench 5G, was roughly square with each side measuring about 4 m. The skeleton lay in the north-east corner with lapis lazuli and carnelian jewellery, cockleshells containing pigments, a

Fig. 34. A perspective drawing of the mid-3rd millennium grave in trench 5G by Susan Roaf.

bronze cosmetic set, a bronze adze and dagger, and a number of bronze and pottery vessels. The skeleton was that of a young adult male aged between 17 and 20 years old. On the west side of the tomb were the skeletons of two equids, probably asses. They were an ill assorted pair, one only about 2½ years old and the other more than 20 years old. There was no evidence of a cart or chariot, like those found in the tombs at Ur and Kish. Elsewhere in the tomb were many bronze implements (small spearheads, chisels, saws, etc.) and pottery vessels. The forms and decoration of these pots were very similar to the pottery excavated at the nearby site of Tell Abqa and it is possible that Tell Madhhur was the burial place of the chiefs of that settlement.

Tell Rubeidheh

Tell Rubeidheh lies on undulating ground in the north-west part of the Hamrin Basin just below the slopes of the Jebel Hamrin. It was discovered by the team working at Tell Madhhur on one of their rest-days. Because the surface sherds could be recognized as belonging to the Uruk period and because no other site belonging to this period had at that time been identified in the Hamrin Basin, it was decided to make a preliminary investigation of the site in the late spring of 1978. A further short season of excavation was carried out in the following year. Operations at Tell Rubeidheh were directed by Nicholas Postgate and Robert Killick. As well as the scatter of Uruk sherds, which covered an area about 150 m. in diameter, there were two small areas with 'Ubaid and Halaf sherds. The site had suffered from considerable erosion and the remaining occupational deposits were confined to an area of about 40 by 50 m.

Three building levels were distinguished but only in the middle level could any coherent plan be identified. In this level parts of four rectangular rooms were excavated. On the floor of one of these was a stamp seal with the typical Uruk design of two pairs of drilled holes with oblique slashes at each corner. In a pit just below the surface was found a collection of fifteen pots associated with some animal bones: this may have been part of a grave but no human bones were found. A second grave contained a single bowl and the skeleton of an adult male who had suffered from a hunch back and a wry neck.

A good assemblage of Late Uruk pottery was

recovered from the site with bevelled rim bowls in profusion, as well as spouted jars, four-lugged jars, and a variety of wares, including Uruk grey and red burnished pottery. Other finds included a complete lead bowl, a second drilled stamp seal, a stone cube (perhaps a weight), stone pendants, and stone and clay beads. The pottery and finds belonged to the Late Uruk period and find their closest parallels with Uruk material from the south of Iraq.

After the work at Tell Rubeidheh had started a second Uruk site was discovered and excavated by a German expedition at Tell Ahmed al-Hattu in the north-west of the Hamrin Basin. These are the only two Uruk sites found in the area and it is clear that there was a discontinuity in the settlement pattern between the end of the 'Ubaid period and the beginning of the Early Dynastic I period. Perhaps the Uruk occupation represents the arrival of new settlers, who chose to live on new sites on the alluvium rather than on previously occupied mounds and perhaps these settlements have been buried by the considerable accumulation of silt that has occurred since that time.

Tell Haizalun

During the course of the excavations at Tell Rubeidheh in the spring of 1979 a small sounding was made by Robert Killick in the mound of Tell Haizalun lying to the south of Tell Rubeidheh near the west bank of the Narin River. In the limited area of the sounding no buildings were discovered but the pottery, including an infant pot burial, showed that the site had been occupied in the Late 'Ubaid period, slightly earlier than the 'Ubaid levels at Tell Madhhur.

Conclusion

The Hamrin Dam Salvage Project is the first large-scale international rescue project to have taken place in Iraq, and it has proved to be immensely rewarding. So often in the past excavators have tended to work in isolation, but in the Hamrin the archaeologists were part of a larger organization and able to share and discuss their discoveries with others working on similar problems in the same area. Furthermore the great variety of sites both large and small has given a view of the regional archaeology which would not have been possible if excavations had been confined to the massive tells favoured by earlier excavators, and indeed sometimes the smaller tells have proved much more informative than the larger.

The pattern of co-operation established in the Hamrin Dam Salvage Project has been continued in the Haditha Dam Salvage Project on the middle Euphrates where the British Archaeological Expedition to Iraq is already at work on the island of 'Ana. It is hoped that there will be British participation in any future rescue projects, for as the Hamrin Project has shown, such excavations are justified not only because the sites are threatened by flooding, but also because they are well worth digging in their own right.

Bibliography

R. G. Killick and M. D. Roaf, 'Excavations at Tell Madhhur', *Sumer* XXXV (1979), 534-42.

J. N. Postgate and P. J. Watson, 'Excavations in Iraq, 1977-78', *Iraq* XLI (1979), 141-81.

J. N. Postgate and M. D. Roaf, 'Excavations in Iraq, 1979-80', *Iraq* XLIII (1981), 167-98.

Further reports are in press and are to be published shortly by the Iraqi State Organization for Antiquities and Heritage:

M. D. Roaf, J. A. Moon, D. Downs and P. J. Watson, 'Tell Madhhur, a summary report on the excavations'.

R. G. Killick, E. MacAdam, D. Downs and P. J. Watson, 'Tell Rubeidheh'.

R. G. Killick and J. A. Moon, 'Tell Haizalun'.

Abu Salabikh

By Nicholas Postgate

The cluster of barren, sherd-strewn mounds today called Abu Salabikh rises only some 5 m. above the plain at the highest points, and even before 1977, when huge irrigation ditches were dug, fencing the site in with their banks, it did not break the horizon from any distance (fig. 35). The site and the village from which we draw most of our work-force lie on the eastern fringes of cultivation, which relies on the waters of the Daghghara branch of the Euphrates. Only a kilometre to the east begin the sand-dunes of the desert which still separates Euphrates from Tigris, and in which stands the major Islamic site of Zibliyyat, with its brick tower making an imposing landmark visible from Abu Salabikh in all but the thickest dust-storms. Despite its sand and sunshine, Abu Salabikh is hardly a place one would choose for a holiday, with its sand-flies in hot weather, and amazingly slippery mud when the surface salts are wet from the winter rains. Once, though, it must have been very different: a branch of the Euphrates, or at least a canal, must have flowed by the houses, and there was no doubt a belt of date-palms and pomegranates along the river banks, and outside these, fed by its waters, wheat and barley fields perhaps only beginning to suffer the effects of salinization which is the plague of all agriculture in southern Iraq.

We have been working here since 1975 — and hope to continue for a while yet — in an effort to fill out this picture, and illustrate a Sumerian city in all its aspects. Our hope is that this will help us to understand *the* Sumerian city (if such an abstraction has any significance!), and so to understand the conditions and processes which converted southern Mesopotamia into the world's first major urban society. Although there is settlement at the site during the Uruk period, when the urbanization process began, we have concentrated on the Early Dynastic levels (roughly 3000–2400 B.C.). This may seem perverse, when there are more major excavated sites of Early Dynastic date in Mesopotamia

Fig. 35. View looking towards Area A on the main mound from the east.

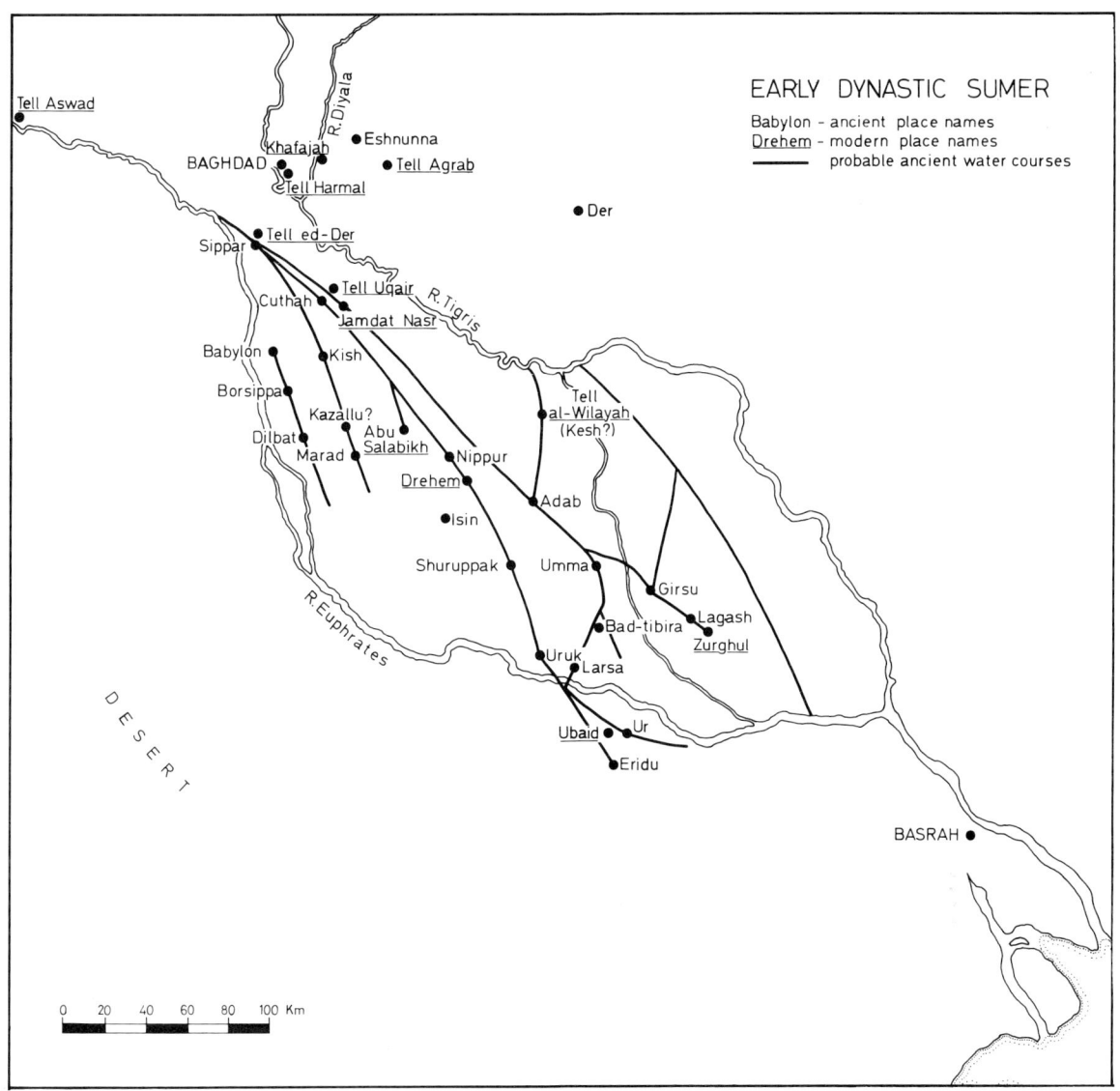

Fig. 36. South Iraq in the ED III period (c. 2400 B.C.) showing major cities and reconstructed water-courses.

than of any other time (fig. 36), whereas the Uruk period before and Akkadian and Ur III periods directly after Early Dynastic are badly neglected, but in fact the Early Dynastic scene itself is extremely patchy: only at Girsu (modern Tello), where accurate archaeological results were minimal, have we enough written sources to begin to reconstruct a historical outline, while ironically at Ur and the Diyala sites, which between them supply the archaeological backbone, there was found pitifully little in the way of inscribed material. Nor are we much better served if we try to reconstruct from the excavations a general view of the Sumerian city: at the Diyala sites we learn a great deal about the architecture and decoration of temples, and at Ur we have the brilliant grave-furniture of the Royal Cemetery, but there is no every-day context in which to set these things. Some ordinary houses have been dug, notably at Khafajah on the Diyala, but even there the excavated remains cannot tell us much about the layout and social composition of a Sumerian city: the size of the sample is too small in relation to the entire site, and too many integral questions remain unanswered for any generalizations to have validity. Yet this was the formative age of Mesopotamia, when the cuneiform writing system developed and a truly urban society emerged for the first time.

While this was the broad line of thought which led us to an Early Dynastic site, there were of course specific reasons for choosing Abu Salabikh. There were some cogent negative arguments: unlike so many of the major Sumerian cities, like Warka or Nippur, there were not metres of later deposits above the layers we were interested in: the 3rd millennium city was at the surface. Also, it was small: not perhaps by most standards, but by comparison with contemporary cities like Warka or Al-Hiba (= Lagash), Abu Salabikh comes a good way down the league, and if we were to have any chance of investigating a significant proportion of the city, it would be pointless to set our sights any higher. Nevertheless, we did know that we would at least be dealing with an urban centre, perhaps even the capital of a little city-state. Quite apart from its size, which is still daunting, more than 500 Old Sumerian tablets found at the site in 1963-65 were enough to guarantee that the city boasted a scribal school, and administrative texts show that it had an *ensi*, or city-ruler. And since it is these tablets which are still Abu Salabikh's principal claim to fame, we had better begin by describing them and their discovery.

The site first features in archaeological literature in the 1950's, when it was visited during their 1956-57 survey of Akkad by Drs. Vaughn Crawford and R. McC. Adams. Actual excavation began in 1963 under Vaughn Crawford and Donald Hansen on behalf of the American Schools of Oriental Research, and the results of that season were striking enough to ensure a second season in 1965. The attraction of the place in the first instance had been the accessibility of Uruk period levels, which were buried hopelessly deep at Nippur (only 20 km. to the south-east and in sight on a clear day), where the main Chicago expedition was digging. In the event, though, archaeology sprang one of its regular surprises, in the shape of cuneiform tablets which began to appear in a sounding on the main Early Dynastic mound. It emerged that they had an importance which can hardly be overstressed: they included lexical texts previously known in contemporary versions from Fara (Shuruppak) as well as from earlier and later copies, but also—and this was the great revelation—substantial literary compositions. Some of these are unknown and unintelligible, but there are at least two major texts found in the repertoire of the post-Sumerian scribal schools of Babylonia: the Instructions of Shuruppak and the Kesh Temple Hymn. Although the writing system is still in a rudimentary stage, there is no doubt that we have here the selfsame poems, and the history of Sumerian literature was pushed back half a millennium at one stroke by this discovery.

As the study of these texts has progressed, principally at the hands of Robert Biggs, various interesting general points have emerged. Many of the literary texts were written in a scribal tradition rather different from that known at Fara, which was the precursor of subsequent practice in the writing of Sumerian. The newly revealed tradition, known from a recurring phrase as UD.GAL.NUN, adds a new dimension to the development of writing at the hands of its Sumerian inventors. Or should we rather say "south Mesopotamian" inventors, because another surprise concerns the people who actually wrote the tablets: Prof. Biggs showed that more of the scribes have undeniably Semitic than have Sumerian names. Taken in conjunction with the occasional Semitic feature in the language of the few administrative documents from the site (cf. fig. 37), this argues a strong Semitic presence in the area, something that could hardly have been predicted for this period in the vicinity of Nippur, the cultural and religious "navel" of Sumer. Since Prof. Biggs first wrote about these names—which he carefully refrained from calling "Akkadian" and thereby identifying these people with the later population of Mesopotamia—a whole new angle on our texts has been given us by the recovery of the royal archives of the city-state of Ebla (Tell Mardikh, near Aleppo in Syria). The palace there had an active scribal school at about the same time, and it shared with Abu Salabikh a whole range of writing practices, such as the use of Semitic numerals, some month names, and even entire duplicate texts, such as a geographical list found at both sites. At this date Abu Salabikh surely fell within the cultural, if not actually the political, orbit of Kish, and shared with Kish close links with the west: up the Euphrates through Mari to Ebla, and doubtless other Syrian cities. This cultural

Fig. 37. Both faces of an administrative tablet from the Central Complex (AbS 1045 = IAS 519). The text lists 13,972 small domestic animals and uses the Semitic numerals *mi-at* '100' and *li-im* '1000'.

in the social and political life of the city, and indeed to wonder about the role of the city itself within the complex politics of Early Dynastic Sumer.

If we have failed to answer these questions so far, it is not for want of trying. Each season we have searched for the limits of the Area E building, but with only some success. The plan of the whole complex speaks for itself (fig. 40), and there is no need to describe it room by room. On two sides only have we reached any sort of limit: in the east, separating the Central Complex from another building, is a wide street. At its south end this street turns to the west and becomes a wide roofed corridor, which separates the Central Complex

affinity, reconstructed first by Gelb on the written evidence, is also reflected in our pottery repertoire, for example, at Abu Salabikh, which differs markedly from neighbouring sites to the south (like Fara), but has close parallels as far to the northwest as Mari and even Tell Chuera (cf. fig. 38).

While the tablets from Abu Salabikh have given Sumerologists plenty to scratch their heads about for some years to come, there are other problems about them which can only be solved by excavation. When we began our work in 1975, after a survey season in 1973 (fig. 39), our first obvious task was to find more about the provenance of the tablets. The plan of the building excavated in the 1960's was incomplete and parts of it hard to understand, and although some administrative tablets had been found scattered in with the literary and lexical texts, none of them offered any sure clue to the nature of the building. The size of the establishment, coupled with the very existence of the tablets, made it unlikely that we were dealing with a "private house", but there seemed no way to decide whether it was a "religious" or a "secular" administrative complex — in other words, a temple or a palace. Once we could determine that, the tablets themselves would gain in significance, and it would be time to consider what part the institution played

Fig. 38. "Set" of pots found in Grave 182. Several such "sets" have been found in graves at Abu Salabikh, and are attested to the north and west, at Kish and Mari.

Fig. 39. A welcome visitation during the survey season of 1973. From left: Sherqati Khalaf Taleb, Julian Reade, McGuire Gibson, S. Nan Shaw Reade, Hilary Stuart-Williams, Diana Kirkbride, Douglas Kennedy, Miguel Civil, site guards.

from another major building to its south, which we investigated in 1981 and have called the South-East Complex. Beyond this to the east the south wall of the corridor backed onto a steep drop of several metres, which was filled up in Early Dynastic III times by a continuous accumulation of stratified rubbish. Rubbish tips are the archaeologist's stock-in-trade, and this one has been gratifyingly productive. In 1975 we came upon the complete skeleton of an equid—a donkey or an onager—lying within the ashy layers, and in 1978 and 1981 it yielded a quantity of small clay items: there was a good number of clay figurines, both human and animal but uniformly rudimentary, there were miniature bowls and jars, all of doll's house size, and over a hundred "counters" usually made from shaved-down potsherds. Perhaps the most suggestive finds are the sealings: these were lumps of clay, used to seal up the mouths of jars or door-locks and such like, and then impressed with the seal of the person who owned or was responsible for the goods in question. Most of the lumps we find are quite small fragments, but the subject and style of the seals used can often be discerned and is often unexpected (fig. 41). One of the interesting features is the occurrence of stamp seals, which are otherwise very rare at this time. Some of the sealings must have been applied to the doors at Abu Salabikh, and the seals used must therefore have belonged to local inhabitants or institutions, but other sealings very likely came off imported goods, and should provide us with evidence for the city's trading links. In either case, the presence of these sealings, of which more than 200 have been registered, shows that this rubbish is being thrown out from rooms which had a more than merely domestic function.

Unfortunately, we are unlikely ever to identify these rooms, because both the stratigraphy and the dating of the potsherds in the rubbish tip indicate that the layers of ash were thrown out from a

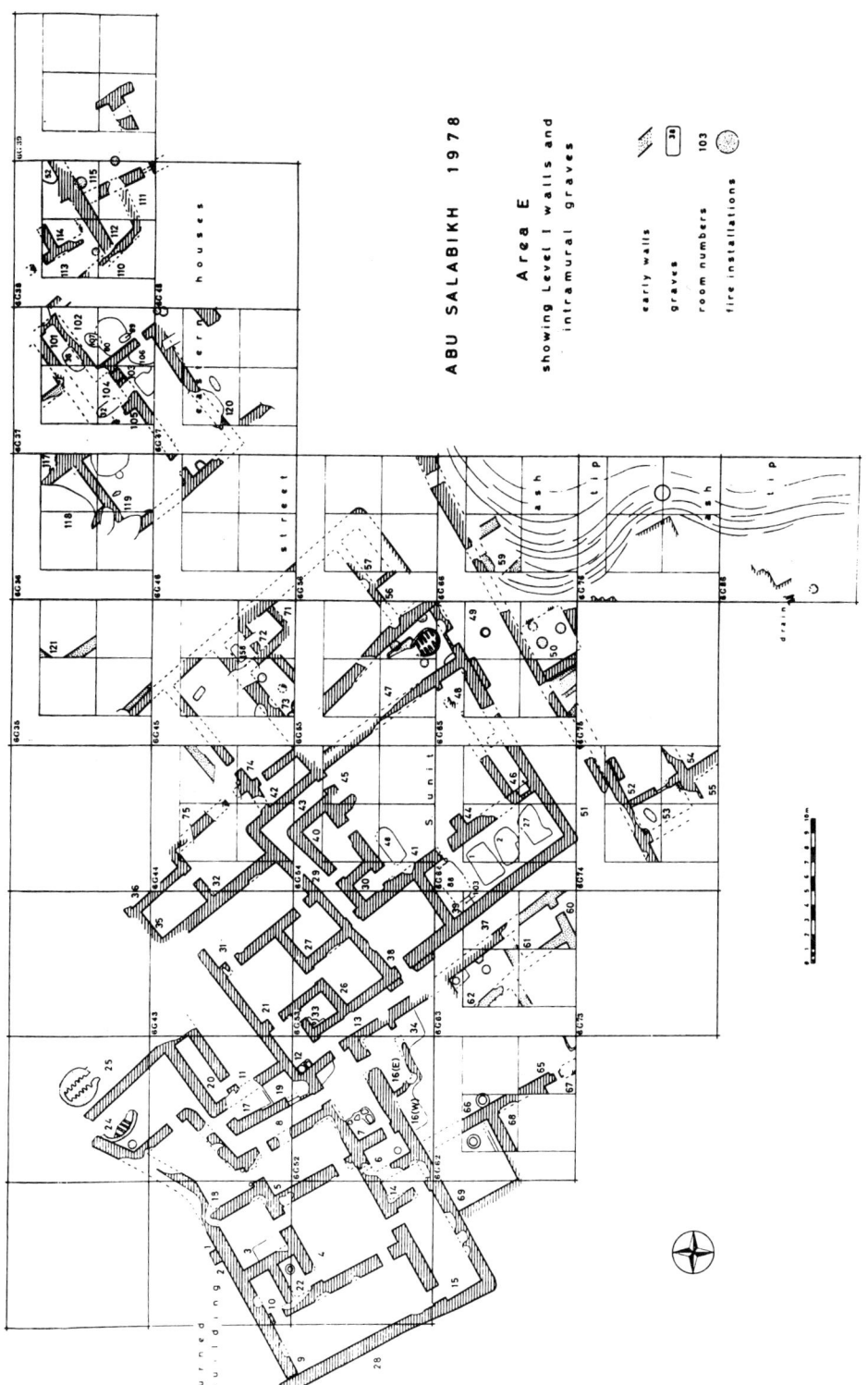

Fig. 40. The main administrative complex in Area E, before the 1981 season.

Fig. 41. A large sealing (AbS 437) with the impression of a cylinder seal, a stamp seal, and an unidentified L-shaped object. The smaller sealing (AbS 1902) has several impressions of an amulet(?) in the shape of a foot. Both from the Area E rubbish tip.

building level which has now been entirely eroded from the summit of the mound. All we can do is guess that at this later date, at the end of the Early Dynastic III period, the layout of the rooms had not changed much from the earlier levels we do have, and that the activities attested by the contents of the ash tip would have taken place earlier too. Obviously either a temple or a palace could have been engaged in business activities involving counters and sealings, and either would have produced large quantities of wood ash to throw out from its ovens; but in my opinion the presence of the figurines and miniature vessels is a hint that it was a temple, since they could have had a role in the cult, but are hard to place in the daily routine of a palace. Another hint favouring a temple is supplied by a land allocation text found by us in 1975, which begins suggestively with "the lady" (n i n), the "god Shara", and (only then) "the *ensí*" (or city-ruler). The lady must surely be a goddess, and if Prof. Biggs and I are right to guess that Abu Salabikh is the ancient city of Eresh, it could then mean that we are working in the temple of Nisaba, goddess of reeds and writing.

Until we have a certain identification of the building as temple or palace, we can only interpret the function of different parts of the complex hesitantly. On the west there is a complete courtyard unit with an obvious domestic character, with a bathroom and cooking places, and elsewhere throughout the building there are hearths, ovens, or bitumened features. The rooms in the north-east are particularly hard to interpret, but the tablets found there, although the great majority, were all out of their original context anyway. The Southern Unit is the only part of the building that has yielded tablets definitely *in situ:* some were found on the floors in Rooms 39, 44 and 48. Possibly, therefore, this courtyard with its rooms should be taken to be the "scriptorium", but not with any certainty because when we continued digging here in 1975 we discovered that Room 39, the main room on the west side, had been used as a burial place. Let into the floor of the room were four large graves and a subsidiary infant burial; a fifth grave was in the courtyard just outside the door. Although only one of the big graves was preserved intact, it was of exceptional interest; the goods with the body included over 100 conical bowls, other pottery, jewellery of silver, lapis lazuli and carnelian, joints of meat, etc. Half-way up the shaft there was a secondary deposit of four more pots, one still containing fish bones, and there were also stray little items of copper ornament mixed in with the fill. Right at the top of the shaft, just under the floor of the room, was a bowl lying with three ungainly clay "feet" which may have served to support it. Perhaps even more important were the finds above the floor, because graves are so rarely preserved intact right up to the surface from which they were dug. The floor had been replastered several times as the earth settled within the shaft, fires had clearly been lit above the grave, and there were many holes in the floor which must have been made by the pointed ends of something wooden, perhaps standards erected over the grave. On a slightly higher floor Donald Hansen had already found a large pottery bowl filled with ash directly above the grave, and the conclusion is inescapable that all these unusual features are connected with rites for the dead person.

Room 39 was not the only one to be used as a burial place. Several people were buried at different times in the Eastern Houses, and in the South-East Complex there were also graves which had been dug within the occupancy of the rooms. What these graves seem to show is that people lived their normal lives in those parts of the building, which agrees with the evidence of the fire and washing installations. The consequence seems to be that virtually all the complex in Area E so far excavated consists of a number of domestic units with little to distinguish them from private houses. Indeed, it is difficult to be certain, merely looking at the plan, that we are not dealing with a number of independent residences. It is only when we take into account the testimony of the tablets, note that the corridors are internal, not outside alleyways, and consider the quality of construction and regularity of plan, that we remain convinced that we are in fact dealing with a single establishment. And if we are right, it is significantly large: the rooms north of the corridor measure some 40 x 50 m., while the South-East Complex stretches southwards at least another 50 m. and an unknown distance to the west. This makes an area as big as the Temple Oval at Khafajah, for instance, and more intensively occupied, and as the size of the establishment grows, so it becomes more urgent to define its limits, its identity, and its

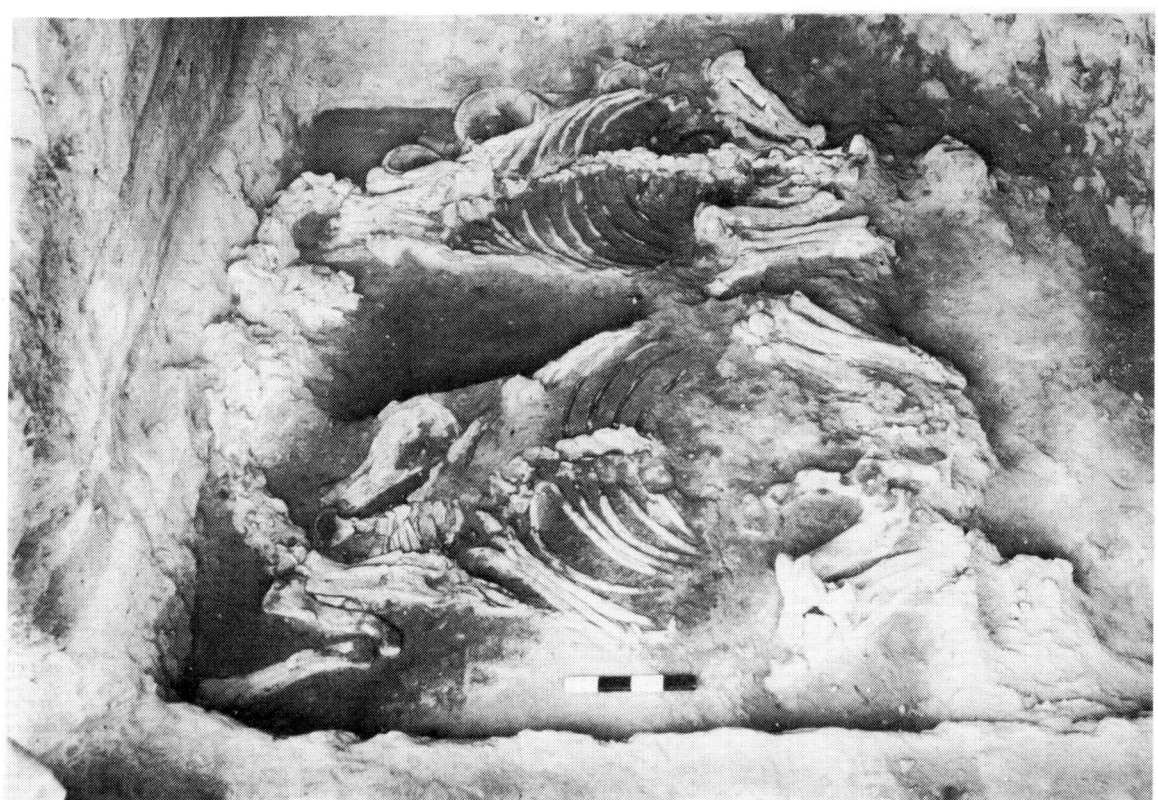

Fig. 42. Skeletons of two equids in northern chamber of Grave 162.

relationship to the rest of the city. In our next season we should like to seek some answers by moving further west, but of course this is precisely where our main dump is sitting, according to one of the ineluctable laws of archaeology.

Now that we have mentioned the existence of graves within the rooms of the building, we should say something about the graves in general, since they are inevitably our most prolific source of "finds". Wherever we dig on the main mound we find the surface of the site riddled with graves which cut both walls and floors. Many of the graves have themselves been accidentally disturbed or deliberately robbed, but mercifully they do all seem to be of Early Dynastic date, and provide us with evidence for a period of occupation the architecture of which had been washed away by the rains before our arrival. We suspect that these graves were dug from the floors of later houses, for this is a practice known at other Early Dynastic sites and certainly represented slightly earlier at Abu Salabikh itself as we have seen. One particularly interesting intramural grave is in Room 57, just south of the corridor, where Grave 162 was clearly stratified beneath the floor: unfortunately the main part had been badly robbed, but in a subsidiary chamber to the north there lay undisturbed the skeletons of two equids, side by side (figs. 42–43). At the time of writing we have not finished the excavation of the grave, but it seems likely that they had been harnessed to a wheeled vehicle, a cart or a chariot.

As yet this is our only instance of draught animals in a grave, although they are known from Ur, Kish and Susa, and equids were found in our graves at Tell Madhhur. Otherwise grave goods are mainly pottery, sometimes in very large quantities, personal ornaments, and the animal bones from joints of meat. By the head there is often a long copper pin—Grave 176 (col. pl. 3b) with no less than seven of them is exceptional—and one may

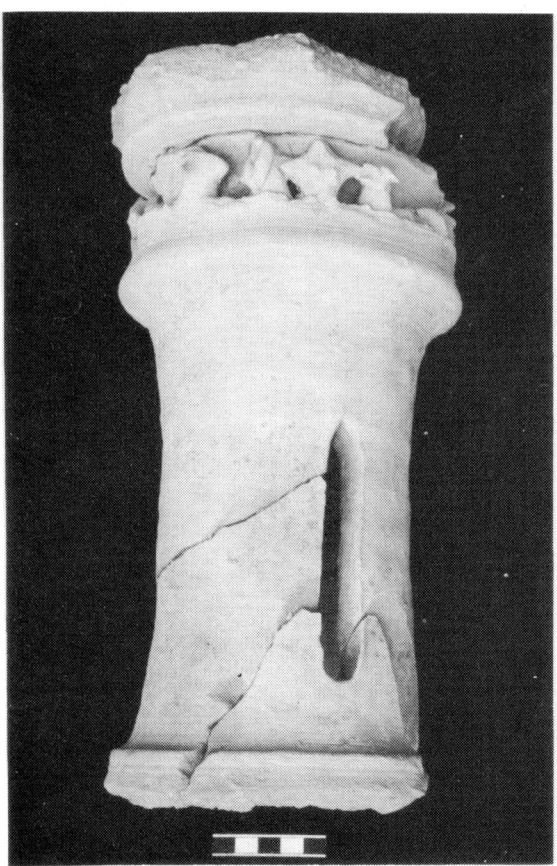
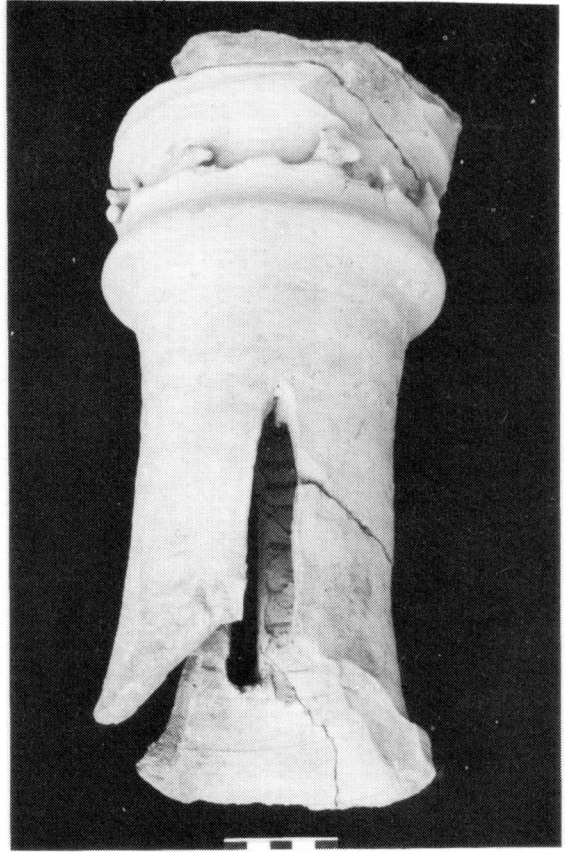

Fig. 43. Stemmed dish from Grave 162 with frieze of humans and animals around top of stem. AbS 2057.

Fig. 44. Seals found in 1981. Those in the top row (AbS 1950, AbS 1906) come from Grave 176, that bottom left (AbS 1850) from Grave 164, and the last (AbS 1872) was found in the ash tip.

also find copper or silver discs, copper vanity-sets, and the occasional cylinder seal (fig. 44). One grave of a young person included a silver eye-patch and silver sandals. Most undisturbed graves have necklaces of lapis lazuli and carnelian, also sometimes quite elaborate frit beads. It is difficult to guess from the jewellery whether the dead person was male or female, but when the grave goods include copper weapons or tools it seems fair to assume the occupant was a man. Unfortunately the human bones are frequently too spongey to preserve the evidence needed by the anthropologist to determine sex. Despite the attractiveness of the personal ornament in graves, it is probably the pottery that is for us the most valuable: for even from the disturbed graves we are often able to recover groups of different types of vessel which are contemporary, enabling us to build up a series of associations which are especially useful where the floor from which the grave was originally dug can be pinpointed, so tying the grave and its contents directly to the architectural phases of the building.

Welcome though the graves are in their way, they are a tribulation for those interested in the architecture, not simply because they actually destroy parts of the buildings, but also because they slow down the process of excavation agonizingly. This slowness, which is only aggravated by today's higher wages and more exacting standards of recording, has led us to experiment with a different approach. Digging must of course remain the archaeologist's most rewarding means of attack, but it did not take any fine calculation to convince ourselves that if we stuck to digging we should never probe more than a tiny portion of the city. The situation can be starkly expressed in figures: at the most optimistic estimate we would not dig more than ten 10 m. squares to a depth of 1 m. in the course of a season. The *visible* area of the site at Abu Salabikh is roughly 50 hectares (cf. fig. 45), or 500,000 m². So, if we dug ten squares per season for ten years — an ideal we are unlikely to achieve — we should have revealed the top layer of only some 2% of the site. Put another way, if a house measures 20 x 20 m., which is quite plausible when the reception rooms are roughly 9 m. in length, a season's work would dig hardly more than two houses to a depth of a metre, so that over ten years we could not aspire to recover more than 20 or 25 house plans, not a glittering prospect for those interested in the layout of the entire city.

Some other approach was obviously needed, and

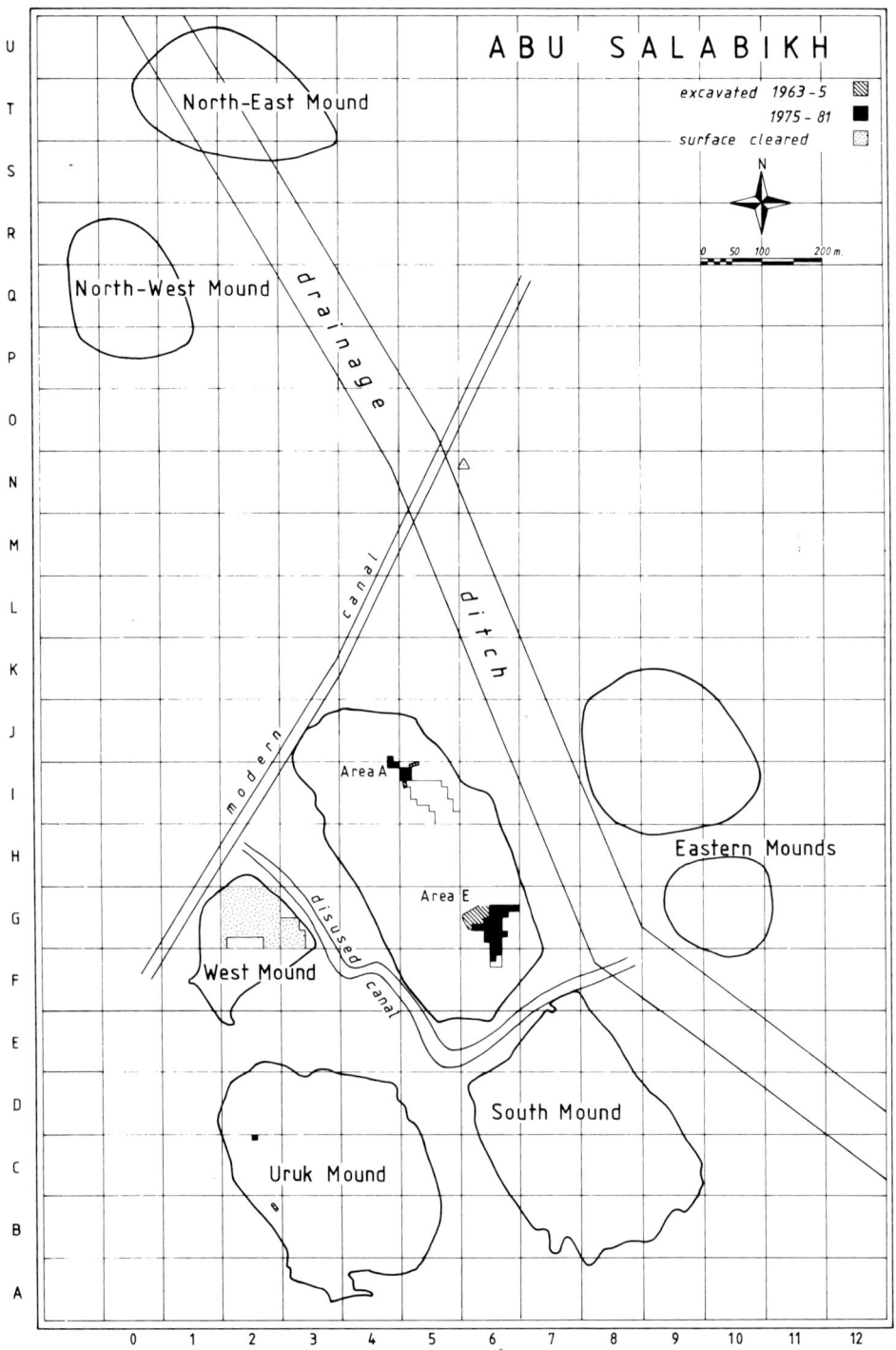

Fig. 45. Plan of Abu Salabikh showing the various mounds and excavated areas.

we have therefore adopted a policy of "scrape and plan" (col. pl. 3c). As a result of the constant erosion of the site, the walls and floors of the buildings which compose the mounds lie literally at the surface. By scraping away quite a shallow layer of loose soil, one can generally expose clear layers and wall-lines, which can be planned quite as accurately as after actual excavation, and very much faster. We applied this technique to a wide area on the West Mound first, and in 1981 transferred our attentions to the main mound, south of Area A. There are drawbacks: one is well advised to wait, if necessary, until the surface is damp from rain and the colours accordingly show up much better, and there are whole squares where we could see nothing at all of interest. By and large, though, the operation gave exactly the results we were hoping for in both areas, and they are worth describing.

We had initially branded the West Mound, which was previously unexcavated, as "early", meaning Early Dynastic I. Scraping and collection of the surface potsherds quite confirmed our suspicions, although it also revealed, what we had not suspected, that at least towards the south-east the occupation of the mound began in the Uruk period. As for buildings, the most informative area was further north, where we encountered thick walls — up to 4 m. wide — built of the characteristic plano-convex Early Dynastic bricks, and forming three or four enclosures or compounds within which stood independent ordinary rectangular houses with courtyards, storerooms, and drainage and fire installations. This suggests that at the beginning of the Early Dynastic I period we should envisage a city composed architecturally of large, self-contained compounds, and socially of corresponding groups of persons. Inevitably we are reminded that the Sumerologists, especially Diakonoff and Gelb, have recently laid great stress on the importance of the extended family in Sumerian city life, and agree that the word "house" (é) embraces not merely the building and its owners, but their servants, animals, sheep-pens, etc.

It is too early to say whether this layout is typical of the whole city. A different one has emerged on the main mound, where we selected an area between our two presumed public buildings of the Early Dynastic III period in the hope that it would consist of private houses. This is indeed what we found, although it emerges that here too we are in Early Dynastic I levels, since an unusual multiple grave with five bodies and a dozen pots of Early Dynastic I date was found virtually on the surface, implying that the buildings into which the grave was dug are still earlier (fig. 46). In contrast to the houses on the West Mound, though, these are packed tightly side by side, with the occasional narrow street between them (fig. 47). They have thin, often apparently un-plastered walls, with frequent alterations, and minor changes of alignment.

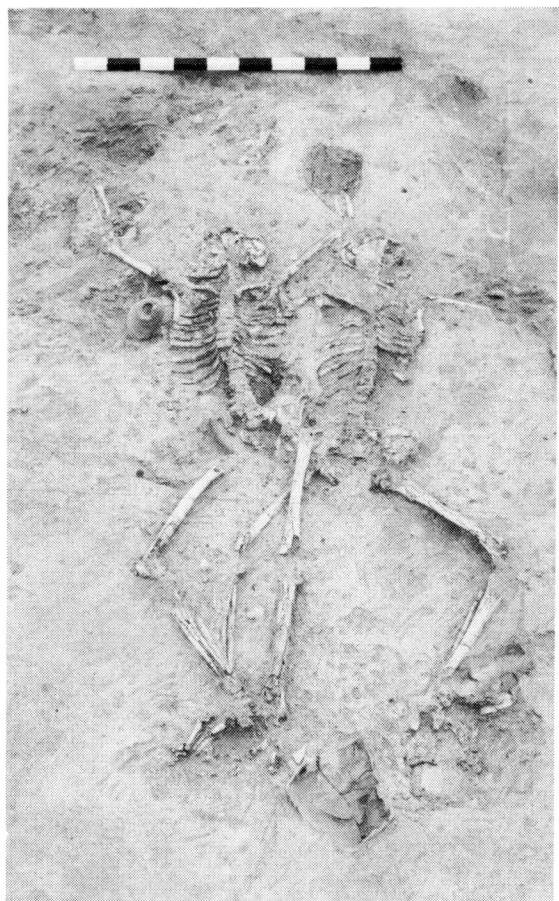

Fig. 46. Grave 185, which originally held at least five bodies.

Almost every house seems to have had its big oval oven in the courtyard, of a type well-known in later levels at Abu Salabikh and elsewhere in Sumer, but hitherto absent on the West Mound. This may be explained by the difference in date, because it does appear that the long span recently attributed to the Early Dynastic I period is entirely borne out at Abu Salabikh, with the undoubted ED I levels on the

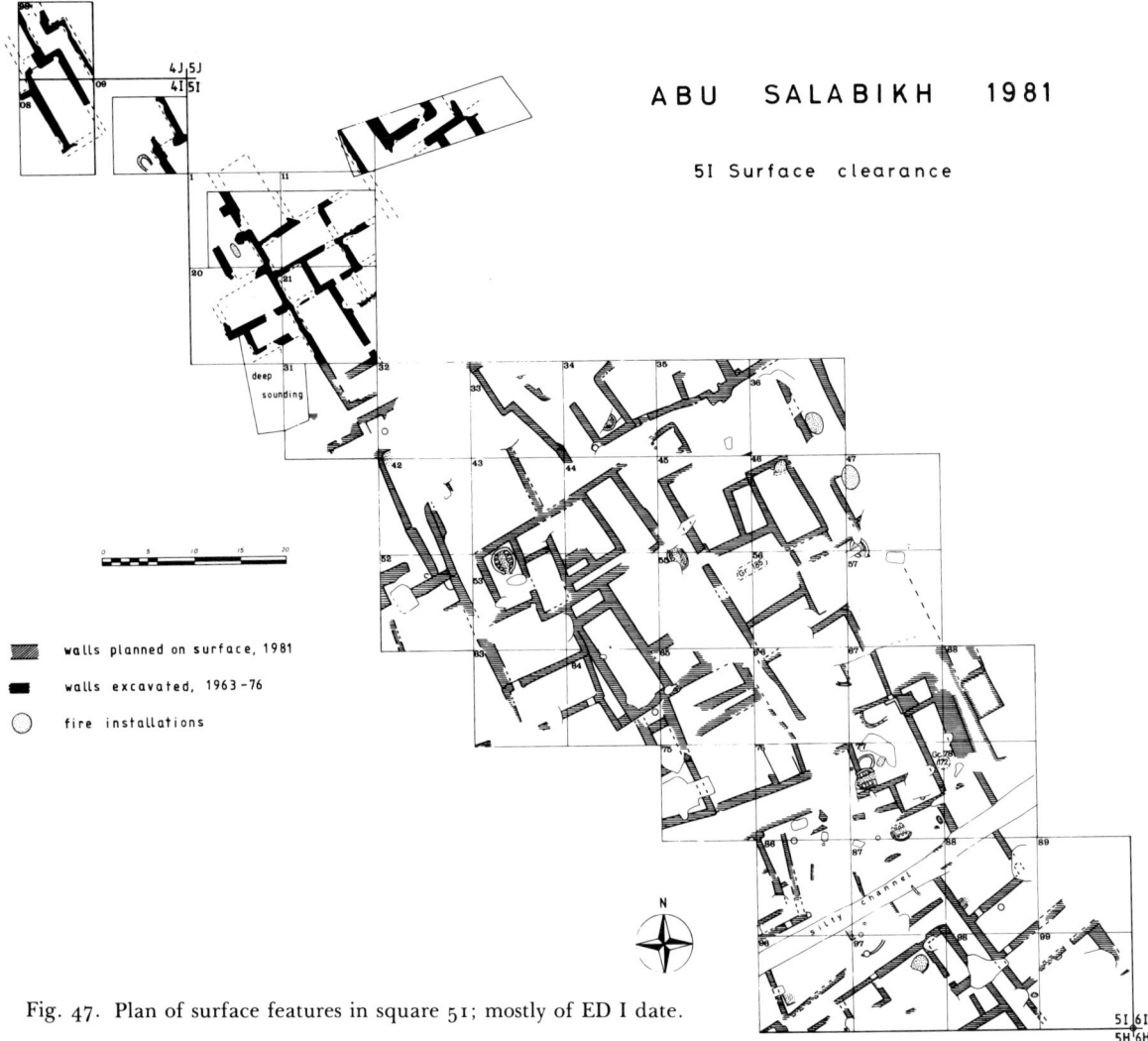

Fig. 47. Plan of surface features in square 5I; mostly of ED I date.

West Mound earlier than anything on the main mounds, either on the surface or in the deep soundings.

The success of the surface clearance has given us a real opportunity of learning a significant amount about the archaeology of a Sumerian city. We can look at the results and select for excavation areas of the date and character we prefer. There are specific questions the procedure will help to solve: was there a city wall? Or how far does the building in Area E extend, and does it jostle in with the rest of the city, or, as we rather suspect, stand in a substantial compound of its own? But almost more important are the ordinary houses and streets, and it may prove possible to say whether the layout of the settlement in Early Dynastic III times was radically different from the earlier city-quarters we already have on plan. Of course we shall still only be able to examine a fraction of the site, but that fraction will be more like 10% than 2%, and already we have planned the largest sector of housing from any 3rd millennium site in south Iraq (pride of place in the north being held of course by Tell Taya).

The existence of written documents in Sumer in general and at Abu Salabikh in particular gives us opportunities denied to most archaeologists. Sumerologists are advancing their comprehension of the difficult Old Sumerian texts yearly, and much progress is being, and will be, made in the exploitation of archives from sites like Fara and Lagash, as well as Abu Salabikh. In reconstructing the life of these earliest cities the written sources give the archaeologist a wider historical context, and precious detail about such mundane matters as food and drink, with the occasional glimpses of law and social organization. With luck we may yet find more administrative texts at Abu Salabikh which will contribute to the picture of our city, and perhaps even tell us the identity of the major building in Area E or of the city itself; but even if not, it is essential that the archaeological side of the research continues. All the evidence suggests that at this date the extensive use of documents was restricted to the large organizations, and our aim is to encompass the whole city, from temple and palace down to the poorest and most emphatically illiterate family dwelling.

*   *   *

For their continual support of our work our thanks are due in the first instance to Dr. Muayad Sa'id Damerji, President of the State Organization for Antiquities and Heritage, and to his predecessors as Director-General of Antiquities. We cannot name here all members of the Organization from whose help we have benefited, whether in the field or in Baghdad, but we cannot pass over the names of the late Fuad Safar, whose encouragement as Inspector-General is greatly missed, and of Dr. Abd-as-Sittar al-Azzawi, Director-General of the Southern Region. During 1975–1981 we have received financial support from the following institutions, to which we are most grateful: The British Academy, the National Geographic Society, Washington D.C., the British Museum, the Royal Ontario Museum, the C.H.W. Johns Fund, Trinity College, Cambridge, The City of Birmingham Museum, Manchester City Museum, and the University of Edinburgh.

Bibliography

J. N. Postgate, Preliminary reports on Abu Salabikh in *Iraq* XXXVIII (1976), 133–69 (with P. R. S. Moorey); XXXIX (1977), 269–99; XL (1978), 77–88; XLII (1980), 87–104.

— 'Early Dynastic burial practices at Abu Salabikh', *Sumer* XXXVI (1980), 65–82.

J. Clutton-Brock and R. Burleigh, 'The animal remains from Abu Salabikh: preliminary report', *Iraq* XL (1978), 89–100.

R. D. Biggs and J. N. Postgate, 'Inscriptions from Abu Salabikh, 1975', *Iraq* XL (1978), 101–17.

J. C. Payne, 'An Early Dynastic III flint industry from Abu Salabikh', *Iraq* XLII (1980), 105–19.

J. A. Moon, 'Some new Early Dynastic pottery from Abu Salabikh', *Iraq* XLIII (1981), 47–75.

R. D. Biggs, *Inscriptions from Tell Abū Ṣalābīkh* (OIP XCIX, Chicago 1974): for the earlier excavations of 1963 and 1965.

R. McC. Adams, *Heartland of Cities* (Chicago 1981), *passim*: for the position of Abu Salabikh within the cities of Sumer.

Tell Brak

By David Oates

Tell Brak is the largest ancient site in the Khabur basin of north-eastern Syria and one of the most important early urban centres in northern Mesopotamia. It is over 40 hectares in extent and 43 m. high, approximately the area of Kuyunjik, the Late Assyrian citadel of Nineveh (fig. 48 and col. pl. 4*a*). It was first excavated on behalf of the British School by M. E. L. Mallowan, who conducted three campaigns of excavation, the first in the spring of 1937, the second and third in the spring and autumn of 1938. Mallowan found there a series of temples of the late 4th millennium B.C. and an administrative building of the Agade and Ur III periods, *c.* 2300–2100 B.C., both demonstrating direct connections with southern Mesopotamia. There can be little doubt that these connections reflect the strategic position of Brak on an important metal trade route that linked the ancient copper mines of Ergani Maden in eastern Anatolia with Sumer by way of Ashur and the Tigris Valley. Mallowan's work in north-eastern Syria was interrupted by the war, and the decision to reopen the excavations at Tell Brak was taken as the result of a survey carried out by the writer and Sayid Kassem Tuweir of the Syrian Department of Antiquities in February and March 1975.

Excavation at Brak is a formidable undertaking at any time, and doubly so in a period of financial stringency and galloping inflation, yet it seemed that many important questions about the history of the region could best be answered at this important site, or in its immediate vicinity. One of the most obvious problems that emerged from the survey, and from previous work in comparable marginal areas of northern Iraq (for example, at Tell al Rimah), is the extension of settlement that took place in the 4th and continued, at least intermittently, in the 3rd millennium B.C., followed by an apparent recession after the Old Babylonian period. Brak's size alone suggests that it was the capital of the whole region for a considerable length of time during these periods, and it seemed obvious that evidence for major political and economic developments could only be recovered here. Brak clearly controlled an important crossing of the Wadi Jaghjagh, of which the present bed lies some 3 km. to the south. The significance of this crossing, near the confluence with the Wadi al Radd, is greatly enhanced when we observe that there are marshes to the east along the Radd and that a short distance to the west there is a field of volcanic rock around the extinct volcano of Kaukab, extending almost to the Khabur. Moreover, to the south-east from the mound one can see a notch in the line of hills marking the Bara pass between Jebel Sinjar and Jebel Jeribe, over which runs one of the few negotiable tracks linking the Khabur basin with the north Mesopotamian plain, Ashur and the Tigris valley route to the south.

We can only guess at the course of this road north of Brak, but to the south Lake Khatuniyah is a traditional staging post, and it is interesting to notice that a direct continuation of the line from Khatuniyah to Brak passes through Chagar Bazar, whence an existing road leads north to Mardin and eventually to Diyarbekir and the copper sources of Ergani Maden. Indeed, during the course of the 1981 season we identified on the ground the Roman staging post between Brak and the Lake, previously photographed by Poidebard, confirmation of the importance of this route as late as Severan times.

The fact that Brak lies in an area climatically marginal for cereal cultivation promised also the possibility of new evidence relevant to ancient climate and patterns of agriculture. Moreover, much of the mound has no surviving occupation levels after 2000 B.C., and this made Brak an attractive historical choice, in that our previous excavations at Rimah and Nimrud had concentrated on periods after this date. Indeed exploration of any major 4th or 3rd millennium site further to the east in Assyria would have been out of the question owing to the heavy overlay of later occupational debris. Such were the reasons that led us to resume work at Brak in 1976. Four seasons of excavation have taken place since that time, in the spring of 1976, 1978, 1980 and 1981.

Prehistoric and Late Uruk Brak

No levels earlier than the Late Uruk period have so far been excavated, but the Late Uruk levels now lie at least 12 m. above the plain, and it is clear that Brak was a prehistoric mound of some considerable importance. In the excavation of an Early Dynastic well or cistern near the Agade Palace site (CH), we encountered brick work of an Al 'Ubaid building situated still some 12 m. above modern plain level,

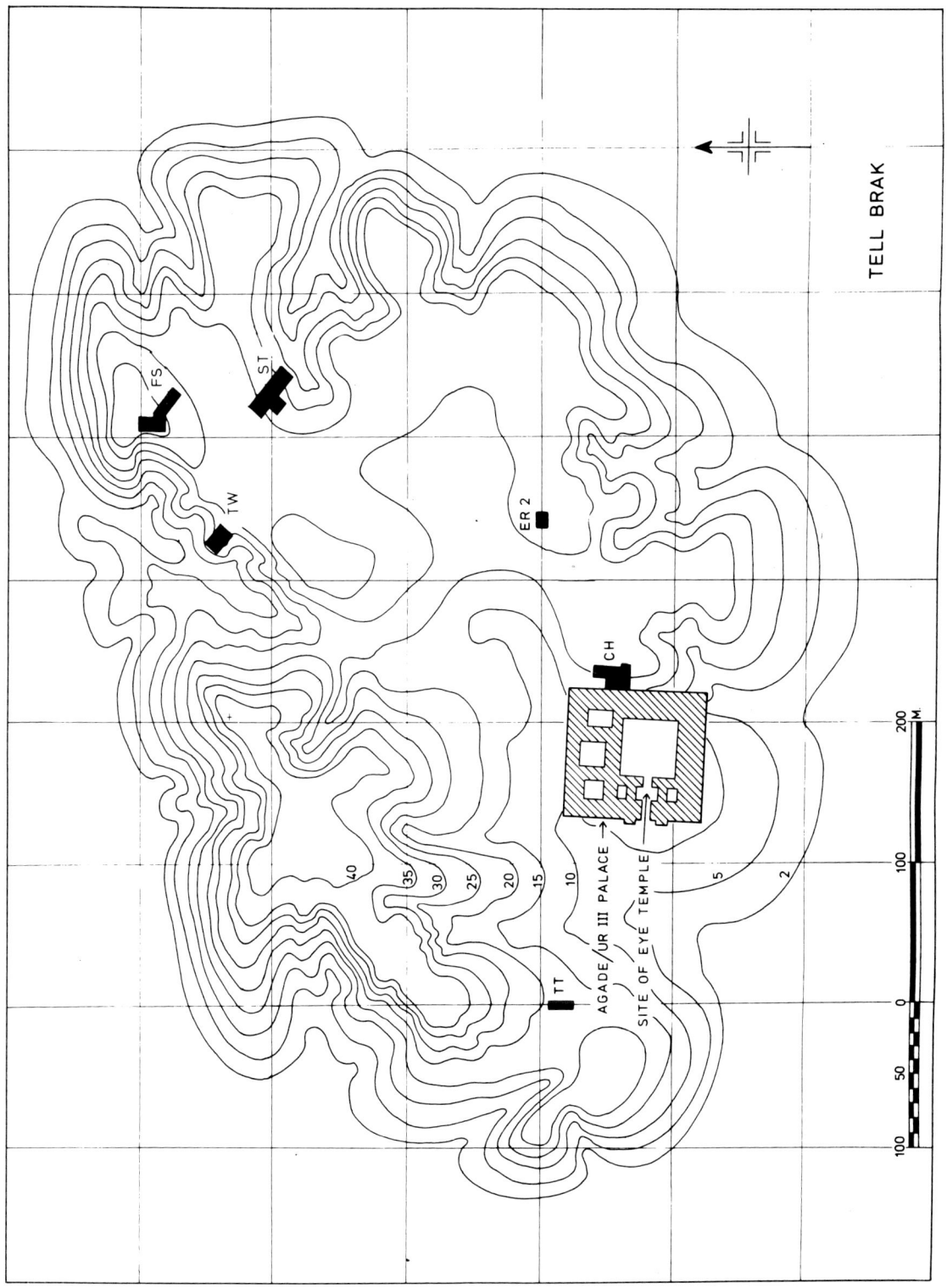

Fig. 48. Contour plan (after Mallowan) showing excavated areas.

and Mallowan recovered large numbers of Halaf, 'Ubaid and early Uruk ("sealing wax") sherds, especially in the excavation of the latter site. We ourselves have found many more, including several examples of 'Ubaid tortoise vases indistinguishable from those at southern sites such as Ras al 'Amiya. Although it is probable that not all the site was occupied in prehistoric times, there would appear to be a great depth of 6th–5th millennium and

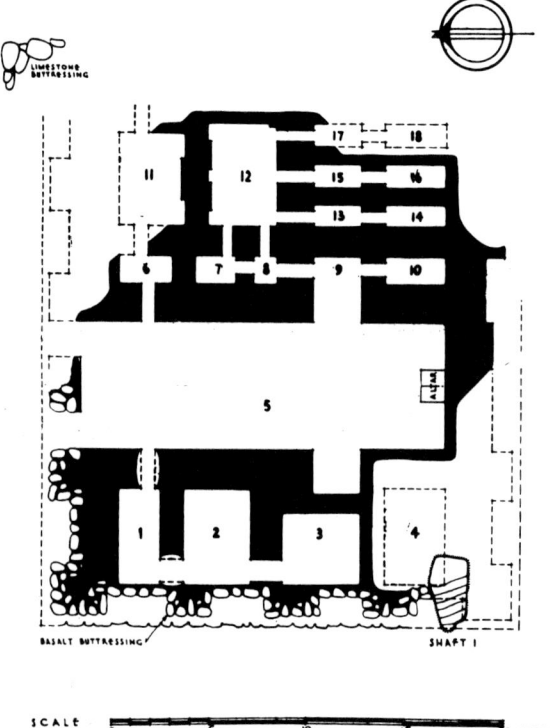

Fig. 49. Plan of the Eye Temple.

perhaps even earlier settlement. The earliest sherds so far identified closely resemble examples found in the Transitional levels excavated at Choga Mami, some 500 km. to the east, while one rim sherd, also found out of context in the massive foundation trench of the Palace, may date from the Samarran phase.

The Late Uruk occupation is better-known, though the depth of 3rd millennium occupation makes exploration of this phase both costly and difficult. The wealth of the Eye Temple, excavated by Mallowan (fig. 49), shows not only that Brak was an important centre at this time, but that links with Sumer were close. The temple plan, its contents, the cone mosaic decoration and indeed the method of construction, on a high platform enclosing the remains of earlier versions of the shrine, can be precisely paralleled in the south, for example at Uruk and Eridu. Moreover, the Eye Temple plan is one of the earliest so far recovered in which are preserved the heavily defended storage areas which were to be such an important part of later temple precincts.

Our own observations show that the whole of Brak was occupied in Late Uruk times, and not only is Uruk pottery widespread on the mound itself (fig. 50), but it has been found on eleven small sites within a radius of one mile. Bevelled rim bowls and the characteristic nose-lug jars are numerous at Brak itself, while the former have also been discovered at the small modern village of Majnunah, where the post-war expedition has made its base. Undoubtedly the single most interesting find of this date is a numerical tablet (fig. 51) recovered in 1978 in the area (CH) adjoining the administrative precinct, the first evidence in northern Mesopotamia of an accounting system that was at this time employed from Iran through Sumer to western Syria.

It is difficult to believe that Brak's importance in the late prehistoric period derived only from the agricultural resources of its immediate territory, and on the basis of the evidence so far recovered it is tempting to postulate some political connection with the south already in the 4th millennium. The idea of a "proto-Sumerian" presence in this area, many hundreds of miles from Sumer, has become much more plausible since the discovery of Habuba South and Jebel Aruda, on the bend of the Euphrates east of Aleppo, where not only the pottery and sealings, but the *riemchen* bricks would not have been out of place at Warka itself. There is, however, one significant difference between such Sumerian "colonies" to the west and Brak itself. Brak is essentially a Mesopotamian site with a long previous tradition of contact with Sumer and Assyria. It was thus not an artificial Uruk foundation, though without written documentation the precise nature of its relationship with Sumer, or indeed the "colonies" of the upper Euphrates, may be impossible to ascertain. In this respect, Brak's geographical position, controlling the ancient route from the Tigris to Ergani Maden, is of undoubted importance.

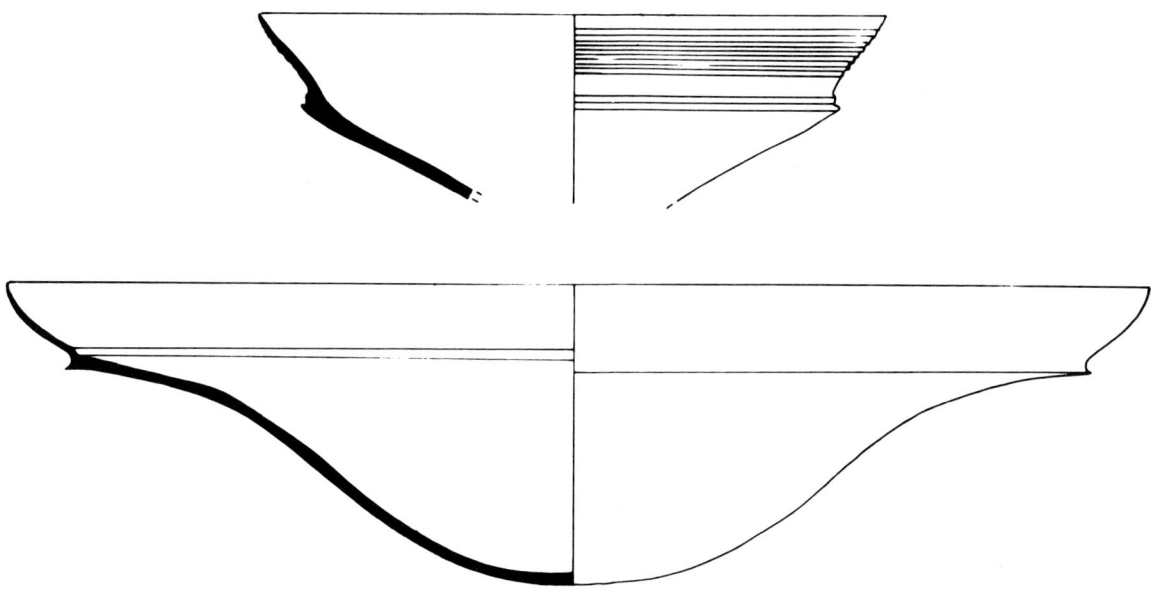

Fig. 50. Drawings of Late Uruk pottery.

Fig. 51. Late Uruk numerical tablet.

Early Dynastic Brak

The superimposition of the Naram-Sin palace on the sequence of Eye temples appears in this area of the site to have destroyed virtually all trace of occupation during the Early Dynastic period, although Mallowan found remnants of an intervening structure apparently built of typically Early Dynastic plano-convex bricks. In the same way the rasing of the Agade building to floor level before the construction of its Ur III successor left a similar, though much shorter, gap in our knowledge of the 3rd millennium sequence of occupation. What was clearly needed was a coherent series of levels covering as much as possible of the late prehistoric and early historic periods, not only as a guide to the history of Brak itself but as an index to the development of pottery types, without which no precise analysis of site distribution in the area is possible. This has been one of the major objectives of the recent excavations; although in many respects we have been successful, evidence for extensive Early Dynastic occupation remains rare.

Much of our detailed stratigraphic study has been carried out in an area of some 600 sq.m. to the east of the Agade Palace (CH, where Mallowan excavated private houses of the Agade and Ur III periods). Here in 1980 was revealed an important new ED III building, dated by seal impressions on a very interesting group of bullae recovered from its remains (fig. 52). A very similar but inscribed bulla was found by Mallowan in 1936 at Chagar Bazar (fig. 61, top). Another important find was a shell pendant in the form of a bull (col. pl. 4*b*). The new building at Brak had been heavily burnt, almost certainly in the Agade destruction of the city, though whether by Sargon or Naram-Sin remains uncertain. The destruction level was excavated more extensively in 1981, one room revealing large quantities of complete pots, stone bowls, grinding stones, burnt grain and a bulla of the same general type as those from the storage area excavated the previous season. This heavily burnt level immediately precedes a complicated series of Agade structural phases which can be stratigraphically correlated with the erection of the Palace in the reign of Naram-Sin. It must, therefore, be dated to the very end of the Early Dynastic period, and we are tempted to think of a possible destruction by Sargon. Although there is as yet no documentary evidence to support this suggestion, it would accord with the probable sequence of events at Ebla, and stylistically the material from this level — although late ED in aspect — could well be dated to Sargon's reign.

In 1980 large quantities of identical pottery, including a large storage vessel with a late ED III sealing impressed on its shoulder, were recovered from a substantial private house excavated in area ER, further up the main southern ridge of the site. The publication of pottery from both these areas is now in preparation, and will provide an invaluable guide to the identification of Late ED III/early Agade materials and settlements in northern Mesopotamia. Radiocarbon determinations from grain samples from this destruction level have proved surprisingly unsatisfactory, the calibrated dates running consistently, and unbelievably, too low (BM 1760–65).

One of the most interesting architectural discoveries in area CH was a boundary wall running parallel to the Agade Palace wall but demonstrably earlier since it is cut by the foundation trench associated with the Naram-Sin construction. This implies the existence in the late Early Dynastic period of some substantial building or complex occupying at least in part the Palace site, but completely destroyed when the Palace was built. We have already noted the series of Late Uruk Eye

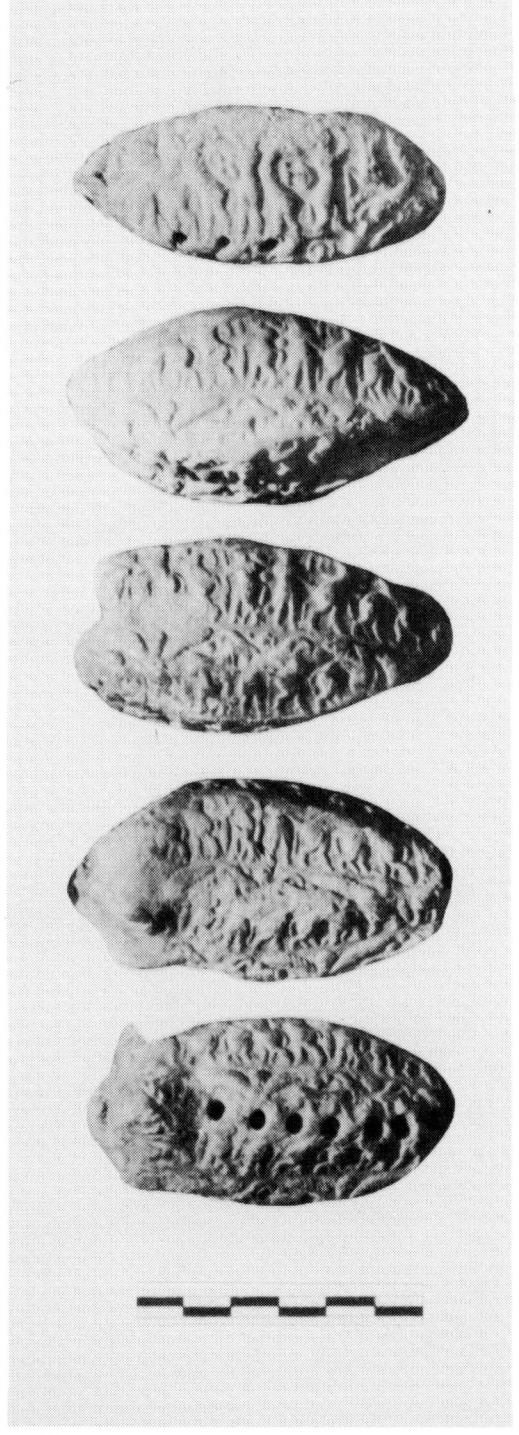

Fig. 52. Group of clay bullae found in 1980.

Temples that occupied the western part of the Palace site, but whether the intervening occupation was religious or secular in character we shall never know. It seems probable, however, that the boundary wall delineated some formal ED building or complex of buildings. Between the boundary wall and the Palace we found in 1978-80 a circular pit containing a large number of conical cups and bowls. Further clearance in 1981 to a depth of some 6 m. strongly indicates that this was a well associated with some phase or phases of the late ED complex. The presence of grey *libn* in the side of this well, apparently similar to that found in one of the Eye Temple platforms to the west, further supports the view that the earlier precinct extended under the whole of the Agade Palace, but we cannot prove this. Both in this well and in another pit excavated in 1981 further to the east in CH were found hundreds of enigmatic, triangular-section objects of sun-dried clay. Most were tapered at both ends and could possibly be interpreted as sling bullets, although the more conventional type of sling bullet is also found at the site; others, however, are of regular width throughout, with squared ends, and we are at a loss to explain their function.

With the exception of a very small number of sherds, which are clearly out of context, no Ninevite V pottery, painted or incised, has been found among the large quantity of ceramic materials recovered from these late ED III contexts at Brak, or indeed from later levels. A sounding in the south-east corner of CH in 1978 (in which the Late Uruk numerical tablet was found) showed that the late ED III building immediately overlay levels containing Ninevite V and Late Uruk material, which must be some 500 years earlier and more, and which we hope to explore in a future season. This strongly implies an earlier levelling of the site to make way for the Early Dynastic III building, presumably associated also with the vanished complex to the west of which only the boundary wall survives. This follows so closely the pattern of Agade building operations that we suggest, with due reservations, an Early Dynastic III settlement on this part of Tell Brak that had some official — political or military — character, and was not simply an indigenous phase in the continuous occupation of the city as a whole.

Although levelling operations in CH have destroyed most of the Early Dynastic occupation in this area, it is hoped that excavation in another area of the site to the north-east (ST) will provide a longer sequence of 3rd millennium materials. A step trench, excavated in 1978-81, revealed occupation levels of the Agade period, bounded on the lower east side by a massive mud-brick wall which may have been a retaining wall for the early Agade buildings. Below this wall we found vestiges of houses containing Late Uruk/ED I material, including Ninevite V incised sherds (fig. 53) and bevelled rim bowls. The intervening sequence of occupation was masked by the retaining wall, but excavation in 1981, continuing the line of the step

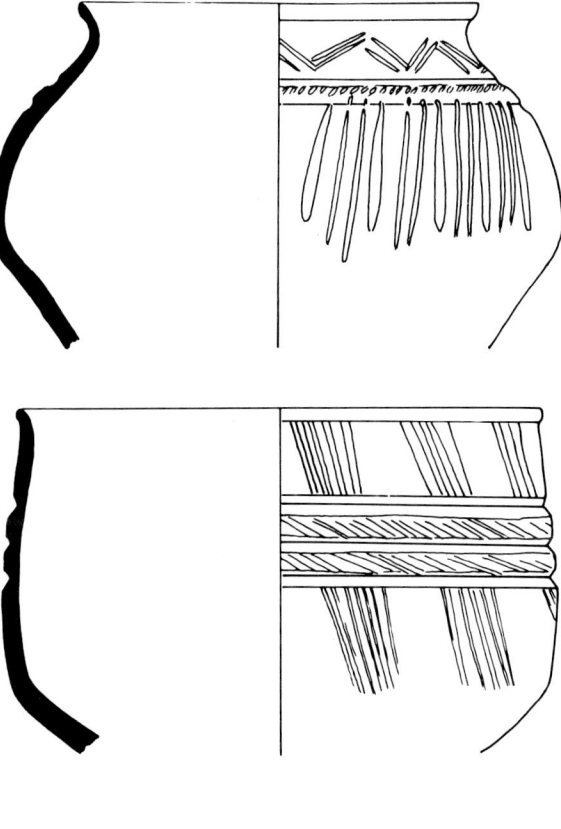

Fig. 53. Drawings of Ninevite V potsherds.

trench on the upper surface of the mound to the west, revealed two large Agade buildings below which it is hoped the Early Dynastic sequence may be preserved. In area TW, discussed below, pottery of ED I date, of types hitherto not found at Brak, has also been recovered. Future seasons will undoubtedly reveal more detailed evidence of the earlier 3rd millennium at Brak, and will undoubtedly place the very distinctive pottery known as Ninevite V in a proper context. All we can say at present is that it is to be dated earlier than the end of ED III, and that we have unequivocal evidence for the association of bevelled rim bowls and incised Ninevite V.

Agade and Ur III

Mallowan's excavations at Brak produced substantial evidence of the occupation of the site during the Agade, Ur III and intervening periods. Most important was the excavation of a heavily fortified administrative building, referred to as the Agade "Palace" (fig. 54), in which were found unbaked bricks inscribed with the name of Naram-Sin. One of these is now in the British Museum. The objects discovered in the Palace and in a group of private houses adjacent to it (CH, ER) reflect the widespread distribution of certain standard types of metal work, pottery and seals throughout the Tigris Valley and north-eastern Syria. Similar materials have also been found at Tell Taya, south of Jebel Sinjar. Recent discoveries at Ebla have highlighted the Akkadian presence in Syria and Anatolia, while, as we have seen, at Brak and at western sites such as Habuba, close commercial if not political connections with Sumer are attested at least a thousand years before. Brak was extensively occupied during the Agade period, and it is one purpose of the current excavations further to elucidate this

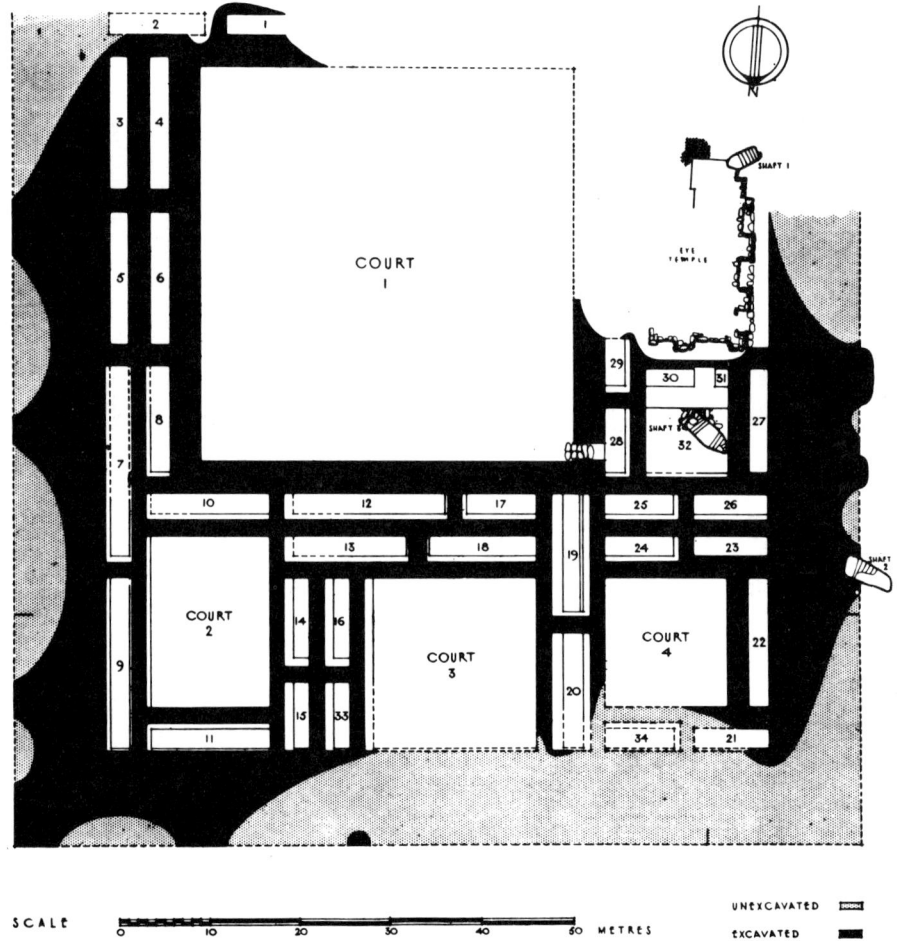

Fig. 54. Plan of the Agade Palace, also showing outlines of post-Akkadian walls.

Fig. 55. Rectangular pottery basin with decoration of applied snakes.

important phase. The 1976-78 excavations revealed in CH a regular and well-built structure of Agade date, which was tentatively identified as a temple but which we now believe to be a substantial private house or official building. Between this building and the boundary wall lay a street which sloped downwards towards the centre of the site and on which wheel or sledge marks were still visible. At the bottom of the sequence of Agade building levels was a more open area, partly surfaced with gypsum cement, in which were a number of ovens or kilns, and which may represent a working level associated with the construction of the Palace.

Area ST, where two large Agade buildings were identified in 1981, seems especially promising. In one of these buildings two rectangular snake-pots (fig. 55), similar to examples found by Mallowan in the 1930's, and a unique ivory statuette of a nude female (col. pl. 4c) were of particular interst. Two points of historical importance have also arisen from work in this area. Firstly, there was no trace of definitely identifiable Ur III material, suggesting perhaps that this eastern part of the mound was not reoccupied in the Ur III period. Secondly, the original Agade buildings were aligned on either side of a previously existing gully, demonstrating a considerable phase of erosion at some earlier time. Indeed the modern contours of the mound seem already to have been in existence.

The most important building associated with the Ur III occupation of the mound is the later Palace, excavated by Mallowan, conventionally linked with the name of Ur-Nammu, although there is no unequivocal identification of this Ur III king at Brak. Certainly a major reconstruction of the Palace took place approximately at this time, while seals and pottery show a continuing close relationship with southern Mesopotamia. The Agade Palace seems to have been destroyed, although whether by Gutians, Amorites or some other unidentified group remains uncertain. The length of time between the end of the Agade Dynasty and the re-assertion of authority under the kings of Ur remains one of the unsolved problems in Mesopotamian chronology, and the continuous occupation of Brak during this "interregnum" may well contribute to a more precise assessment of its duration. Certainly it would appear on present evidence that the gap is unlikely to exceed 100 years.

Brak in the Early 2nd Millennium

"After the abandonment of the (Ur III) palace more than half the town became a ruin and was never again rebuilt. The western flanks of the mound were, however, continuously occupied and the later houses tower over the plain, for they were built over the ruins of settlements which had been piled up one over the other for many millennia. The standard Khabur ware and metal work of this period was more lavishly distributed at Chagar Bazar and followed a similar development at Brak . . . In the top three levels of the mound Khabur ware began to disappear and to be replaced by new types (Nuzi ware) which reflected a widespread phase in the development of ceramic throughout the whole of North Syria and Mesopotamia". So wrote Mallowan in 1956. This view must now be altered as a result of the most recent excavations at Tell Brak, when the exploration of a strikingly regular building on the slope north-west of ST (TW), the outlines of which had been visible as vegetation marks in the early days of the season, revealed part of a substantial fortification system to be dated to the Old Assyrian period, possibly to the time of Shamshi-Adad I. The very regular walls observed at the beginning of the season proved on excavation to be a complex of approximately square chambers of a distinctive red mud-brick. They had been built down the slope of a ridge between two gullies and appear to be substructures, originally covered by a mud-brick platform itself stepped down the slope of the ridge. The fill within the structure contained a mass of Late Uruk and some Ninevite V sherds, but the surface actually associated with it yielded two sherds of painted Khabur ware, c. 1800 B.C. We believe that this structure formed part of a massive building of Old Assyrian date on the northern side of the mound, and the occurrence of the same heavily eroded but distinctive red brick over long stretches of the northern perimeter suggests that it formed part of a city wall. Moreover, there is a very substantial platform of the same material extending over the highest ridge of the mound on which the modern survey point stands. It is worth observing that the presence of red mud-brick implies the use of fresh earth from outside the mound and in itself implies a major building operation. If this indeed represents the erection of a city wall when Khabur ware was in use — roughly the time of Shamshi-Adad I of Assyria — then Tell Brak must then have been a much more important site than hitherto suspected. We badly need epigraphic evidence to give us its ancient name, but it must be one of the major cities mentioned in the Mari archives, and an identification with Shubat-Enlil is not out of the question.

Although the Old Assyrian construction had obliterated much of the occupation in the area of TW, the untouched levels beneath produced pottery of approximately ED I date, of types hitherto not found at Brak. This encourages us to believe that we shall in due course find a complete sequence of occupation throughout the 3rd millennium. The early ED levels beneath the 2nd millennium building and the mass of Late Uruk material used as fill within it and obviously taken from occupation levels nearby emphasize once again the extraordinary extent of settlement at Brak in the 4th and 3rd millennia B.C. Everywhere we have dug to any considerable depth on both the north and south sides of the mound Uruk occupation levels have been found, and the distribution of eroded floors and surface pottery elsewhere confirms that the whole area of the tell was occupied at this date. Brak, with an area of 40 hectares or something over 80 acres, and surrounded by a number of Late Uruk satellite villages, must be one of the largest 4th millennium sites in Mesopotamia. The very meticulous excavation of TW provides also a useful cautionary tale in the days of computerized pottery studies. Virtually 100% of the pottery recovered from this building was Late Uruk, including complete examples of bevelled rim bowls, yet careful observation of two Khabur ware sherds lying on the foundation level confirmed its 2nd rather than 4th millennium date, indeed the only interpretation which makes sense in view of the massive platforms of similar red-brick clearly associated with 2nd millennium occupation not only elsewhere at Brak but at a number of neighbouring mounds.

Brak after the Old Assyrian Period

By the middle of the 2nd millennium the occupation at Brak appears to have been restricted to the very highest (northern) portion of the tell, where a series of occupation levels was excavated by

Mallowan abutting against the red brick platform referred to above. The latest pottery recovered here is conventionally identified as Middle Assyrian, but need be no later than c. 1400 B.C. This retrenchment at Brak appears to correspond with a considerable retraction of settlement in the 2nd millennium in this part of the Khabur basin. We are uncertain as yet of the precise reasons for the retrenchment, but such phenomena are often related to climatic, economic or—in a general sense—political developments, which in such marginal climatic zones are often mutually dependent.

With the exception of a single Hellenistic floor, excavated on the high southern ridge of the mound in 1981, no later occupation levels have as yet been found. There is no evidence of extensive Hellenistic occupation, however, although we have identified Hellenistic pottery at a number of nearby sites. We may recall that at Nimrud a Hellenistic village, closely dated by coins between 250 and 150 B.C., was found in a very similar situation on a high point of the tell. Occupation had by then normally retreated in times of peace to low-lying land with closer access to fields and water, and we suggest here, as at Nimrud, that the position on high ground was chosen for defensive purposes, probably during the long struggle between the Parthian and Seleucid kingdoms for the control of Mesopotamia.

In Roman times Brak was clearly an important staging post. Although there is no evidence of Roman occupation on the tell itself, a number of Roman settlements and camps are known in the neighbourhood. Several of these were identified by Poidebard, and one excavated by him in 1930. This season we found yet another Roman site just north of the main tell, at one of the mounds now known as Majnunah.

Thus the occupation of Tell Brak seems to have been more or less continuous from prehistoric times to about 1400 B.C., or slightly later, a period of at least 4500 years. During most, if not all, of this time Brak was the largest site in the Upper Khabur basin. The city, for such it was, appears to have been of the greatest importance during the 4th and 3rd millennia, with settlement apparently contracting after both the Agade and Old Babylonian periods, perhaps reflecting not only the marginal climatic shifts and the breakdown in political control attested elsewhere in the 2nd millennium, but also the Babylonians' access to new sources of copper. We have yet to learn the ancient name of Brak, and many of its secrets; of its historical importance there can be no doubt.

Bibliography

M. E. L. Mallowan 'Excavations at Brak and Chagar Bazar', *Iraq* IX (1947), 1-259.
— *Twenty-Five Years of Mesopotamian Discovery* (London 1956), 24-38.
D. Oates, 'The excavations at Tell Brak, 1976', *Iraq* XXXIX (1977), 233-44.
— *Studies in the Ancient History of Northern Iraq* (London 1968).
C. J. Gadd, 'Tablets from Chagar Bazar and Tall Brak, 1937-38', *Iraq* VII (1940), 22-66.
D. and J. Oates, 'Nimrud 1957: the Hellenistic settlement', *Iraq* XX (1958), 114-57.
A. Poidebard, *La Trace de Rome dans le Désert de Syrie* (Paris 1934).

Tell Taya

By Julian Reade

Tell Taya lies on the lower slopes of a range of hills overlooking the wide Tell 'Afar plain in northwestern Iraq. The hills are an outlying fold of the Zagros mountains, that run north-west to southeast along the Iraq-Iran frontier. The plain itself is dominated on the north-west by the hulk of Jebel Sinjar, but to the south it extends to the horizon, finally merging into the Syrian Desert. The Wadi Tharthar, which ends in a salt lake between the Tigris and Euphrates rivers, rises in this region; it is fed, most years but not all, by winter and spring rains the first of which turn the landscape from brown to green within a very few days.

This is excellent farming land, and the hundreds of mounds of many periods which dot the plain show how heavily it was exploited in antiquity. Today it is used primarily for grain, small mountains of which appear on the outskirts of modern settlements in a good year. Pastoralists use the land too, mainly with flocks of sheep; in the nineteenth century, under weak Ottoman government, they controlled the plain, but today their activities are restricted for fear of damage to the crops. The proximity of desert, and the unreliable rainfall, mean that here the traditional conflict of interest between nomadic and settled people, with their distinctive forms of land-use, is conspicuously reflected in the archaeological remains: Ottoman settlements, for instance, were confined to a few sources of permanent water by the hills.

The School's excavations at Taya developed naturally from its earlier work in northern Iraq and Syria. Originally there had been Mallowan's explorations in the Khabur and Balikh regions which, combined with the previous deep sounding at Nineveh and later work at Nimrud, provided a rough stratigraphical framework for northern Mesopotamia from the Hellenistic age back far into prehistory. More detailed excavations, by the School and other institutions, enlarged our understanding of several periods but still left notable gaps. It was partly to fill one of these that the School, under David Oates, moved in 1964 from Nimrud to Tell al Rimah, a few miles south of 'Afar. The principal occupation of Rimah, as described elsewhere in this volume, covered much of the 2nd millennium B.C.; it had been occupied earlier, but there did not seem much likelihood of easy access to earlier levels.

It was apparent, however, from surface pottery, that many sites in the 'Afar plain had been occupied and attained considerable size in the 3rd millennium B.C. The first person to draw attention to them had been Seton Lloyd, in a pioneering survey supplemented by soundings in 1938–39. The 3rd millennium pottery found by Lloyd, and by ourselves at sites visited from Rimah, was evidently related to some of that excavated at Ashur, Gawra, Brak, and elsewhere, but there seemed to be anomalies and complications, in the published evidence, which obstructed attempts at relative dating. In particular, there was the problem of distinguishing Ninevite 5 material, of around 3000 B.C. or somewhat later, from material that belonged in the remainder of the 3rd millennium. We needed a pottery sequence to cover this span of time.

In 1966 there arrived, through Sir Max Mallowan, an anonymous donation aimed at encouraging 3rd millennium research, and it became much easier to make serious plans. Several sites, in reach of the School's existing base at Rimah, were considered for excavation. One which had produced a large amount of Ninevite 5 pottery was Karatepe, close to 'Afar itself, but this was a huge site unsuitable for the type of operation we had in mind; in any case it may not have had the vertical sequence required, and there were probably Hellenistic or Roman levels above. A much more attractive candidate was Tell Sha'ir, south of Rimah, whose contours suggested a small round fortified town; this was ruled out by logistic considerations, however, since it was impractically far from 'Afar, from which many of our workmen and all our supplies had to come. Several other sites were possible, but once we began thinking hard about Tell Taya, it became increasingly clear that this was the one to choose.

Lloyd had visited Taya in 1938, calling it Teir (the true form, Ṭāyah, was only established during the dig, at a conference on top of the mound, with local shepherds reciting the correct pronunciation to a group of distinguished Iraqi archaeologists). Lloyd's list gives Taya two stars, which indicates "less important sites attributed to the Moslem period", with the rider "probably Roman". It was an understandable reaction: even in 1967 another visiting scholar was to suggest that the site was mainly Sasanian. Such might have been my own

Fig. 56. Central mound seen from the north, across Wadi Taya, with half-eroded stone gate on left and enclosure wall on right.

conclusion when, in 1964, I first walked across part of the site, observing an abundance of stone wall footings and picking up thick sherds of incised pottery, had I not recently and repeatedly seen such pottery on sites that were plainly not Sasanian. It was associated, moreover, with some sherds of very fine ware, occasionally incised. This was material that we were beginning to think of as a late variety of Ninevite 5. "Extensive stone foundations," I noted then, "covering square kms all round and all seemingly third millennium."

The principal consideration in our 1966 choice of Taya, however, was not the wide extent of the site, since what we wanted first was a succession of levels, but the nature of the site's central mound, which did seem to have the requisite depth of deposit. It was about 9 m. high, and we were able to inspect a section in some detail, as one side had been eroded by the Wadi Taya stream, leaving a steep cliff. There was much 3rd millennium material that had fallen into the dry bed at the foot of the cliff, while a few sherds of early 2nd millennium painted Khabur Ware provided the end of the sequence we required. It seemed unlikely that there was much late deposit, as layers of 3rd millennium sherds were visible quite close to the summit; there were Islamic remains, but they were conveniently distant from the area we proposed to investigate. The date of the earliest occupation was uncertain: we did not positively identify any Ninevite 5 pottery, but there were incised and fine wares of the types already mentioned. We hoped therefore for a sequence covering most of the 3rd millennium, and reaching into the 2nd. The reality proved more complicated but no less rewarding.

It turned out, during our first season of excavation in 1967, that the central mound (fig. 56) owed its elevation primarily to a strong circular wall built in the mid-3rd millennium, Taya level 9. This wall had stone footings 3 m. high, with 2 m. of mud-brick surviving above; its thickness was originally about 1.6 m., but this was later (level 8) doubled by the addition of an outer skin constructed in the same way. Internally the wall was reinforced by projections, 2 m. long, that formed a series of compartments open on one side. The full diameter of the wall was just under 50 m., that of the area within the enclosure almost 40 m. The entrance was on the east, through an arched stone gateway half of which had disappeared over the cliff. Our excavations at the central mound, in various seasons, exposed parts of the gatehouse and of two monumental buildings that had presumably faced each other across an open space in the middle; one of the pair had a characteristic bent-axis temple plan, and contained fittings, and objects such as faience beads, that are often associated with temples. These solid structures were gradually surrounded and eventually in part superseded (levels 7–6) by rooms with narrower walls and a more domestic appearance. Then the enclosure was abandoned for a significant length of time, and was transformed by erosion into a round mound with a depression or crater on top.

The levels within the enclosure contained ample pottery, with evidence for successive temporary abandonments within the 3rd millennium sequence. Though it was difficult and sometimes impracticable, because of intervening walls and baulks, to establish detailed relationships between all the areas cleared, our 1967 season gave us much of the information we were after, and we could look with greater understanding at surface material from other sites. It was clear, first, that we had not got Ninevite 5; there is in fact a thin scatter of incised Ninevite 5 pottery on the ground south-west of Taya, and there is probably more at the mound of Mahmud Agha, further downstream on Wadi Taya, but a firm line of demarcation must be drawn between Ninevite 5 proper and the material of Taya 9–6 (col. pl. 5). This is the more important as there are superficial resemblances, between Ninevite 5 and Taya, which had misled both us and our predecessors. Obviously there is some degree of technical ceramic continuity, but there is also, at least in the 'Afar region, a break in continuity of settlement which the pottery reflects. For instance, there is a Ninevite 5 variety of fine grey or green pottery, in the shape of small straight-sided bowls with rounded bases, rimsherds from which are easily confused but not identical with those from larger ring-based bowls of Taya 8–7. Similarly, patterns of incised decoration on fine jars of Taya 9–7 immediately suggest a close relationship with Ninevite 5 methods of incision, and I have indeed seen one sherd of an unmistakable Taya type lurking among true Ninevite 5 sherds from Mallowan's deep sounding at Nineveh; but there are definite distinctions, and Taya lacks the Ninevite 5 technique of cutting clay to give a characteristic excised effect. In some ways the finest Ninevite 5 wares seem technically closer to those of Taya 8–7 than to those of Taya 9, as if the requisite ceramic skills were lost or less widely available in the intervening period. In chronological terms Ninevite 5 should be partly contemporary with Early Dynastic I in southern Mesopotamia, and Taya 9 with Early Dynastic III, while Taya 8–7 probably cover the Agade period; Taya 6 presumably overlaps the Ur III dynasty of the south.

Only half the height of the mound, however, proved to be occupied by these 3rd millennium deposits. On top there was a barren layer, level 5, when the eroded enclosure may have been used as an animal-pen, and above it no less than two major construction levels, Taya 4–3, of the early 2nd millennium, when Khabur Ware was in use. Taya 3, the later of these two occupations, was unusually rich in floral and faunal remains. It appears to be securely dated, in part, to the reign of Shamshi-Adad I of Assyria, since in one room we found a pair of cuneiform tablets bearing seal-impressions of Hasidanum, who is known to have acted as one of Shamshi-Adad's officials in this region. The tablets, which deal with a land transfer and a delivery of cattle, clearly belonged to individuals; official records of such transactions were found at Rimah. Taya 4–3 thus provided the first clear evidence that distinct stages in the development of Khabur Ware were to be found in the 'Afar region. The earlier phase, Taya 4, probably preceding Shamshi-Adad, produced some pots with both incised and painted decoration, and some shapes that did not recur later. It thus confirmed the suspicion, previously voiced by Mallowan, that his own finds of Khabur Ware at Chagar Bazar could hardly represent its earliest appearance. There is nonetheless a considerable divergence between the Taya 4 material and the "Old Assyrian" material from Ashur. It may be that Khabur Ware remained relatively scarce in places, like Ashur, which had probably been occupied continuously since the 3rd millennium and which also maintained closer links with southern Mesopotamia.

Above these early 2nd millennium levels was a Neo-Assyrian settlement of about the 8th and 7th centuries B.C. Much older sherds had been used as levelling fill in the foundations of this period, and these it was, visible in the section before digging commenced, which had formerly led us to assign most of the build-up of the mound to the 3rd millennium. The basic Neo-Assyrian structure was a substantial building with stone foundations that encircled the summit on much the same lines as the 3rd millennium wall. The rooms on this stone terrace had mostly been eroded away, but there were smaller structures within. Finally, in the topsoil above, we identified scraps of wall that were probably Parthian, interspersed with Sasanian or Early Islamic graves; it may be that the presence of this graveyard had protected the summit of the mound from incorporation into an Atabegi village which covered the southern slopes. The only other feature on top of the mound was the shell of a small house, resting on Neo-Assyrian foundations, which had been built and abandoned within living memory. The owner was said to have possessed a secret water supply, which never ran dry; we may have found this ourselves in 1972, a pool in a cavern beside Wadi Taya, a few minutes' walk from the mound.

The historical periods represented at Taya are the same as those during which the 'Afar plain in

Fig. 57. Stone wall footings in Outer Town.

general was thickly settled. We would expect comparable results at almost any site favoured in this way with permanent water, though the successive settlements would not necessarily have formed a single mound. The nearby site of Mahmud Agha was probably the equivalent centre of settlement in prehistory, but there are also scatters of a crude burnished ware (with the incised Ninevite 5), and of painted 'Ubaid pottery, on the fringes of the Taya town.

Our 1967 work left us little leisure for a close study of the remains away from the central mound. There were two small soundings: one was unproductive, but the other, across Wadi Taya on the opposite bank, produced large quantities of Taya 8–7 pottery and confirmed that, in this area, the date of the visible stone footings was much as it had appeared to be. Further confirmation, if any were needed, came during a visit in the spring of 1968, when the remains of what had surely been a stack of six grey stoneware beakers were found lying by a bulldozer track further to the south; this was a distinctive type of vessel, dated in the Khabur region to the Agade period. Our subsequent work, in 1968–9 and later, away from the central mound, has provided a broad picture of the town's development in the 3rd millennium; by then we had generous financial support from several institutions besides the School itself.

Stone wall footings, the plan of which was completed by George Farrant during the 1972–3 and 1980 seasons, spread all over the site, occupying some 155 hectares (383 acres) in all; there are 65 hectares of particularly dense stone remains (fig. 57). Correlations over an area this size raise obvious problems, but it seems probable that its occupation was largely contemporaneous with level 9 in the fortified central mound. The central mound was situated within an irregular area, the Inner Town, that was itself surrounded by another fortified wall. Against the base of this wall we found Taya 9 sherds, but they were in an exceptionally disturbed context, as if deriving from houses that had been demolished to provide stone for later structures.

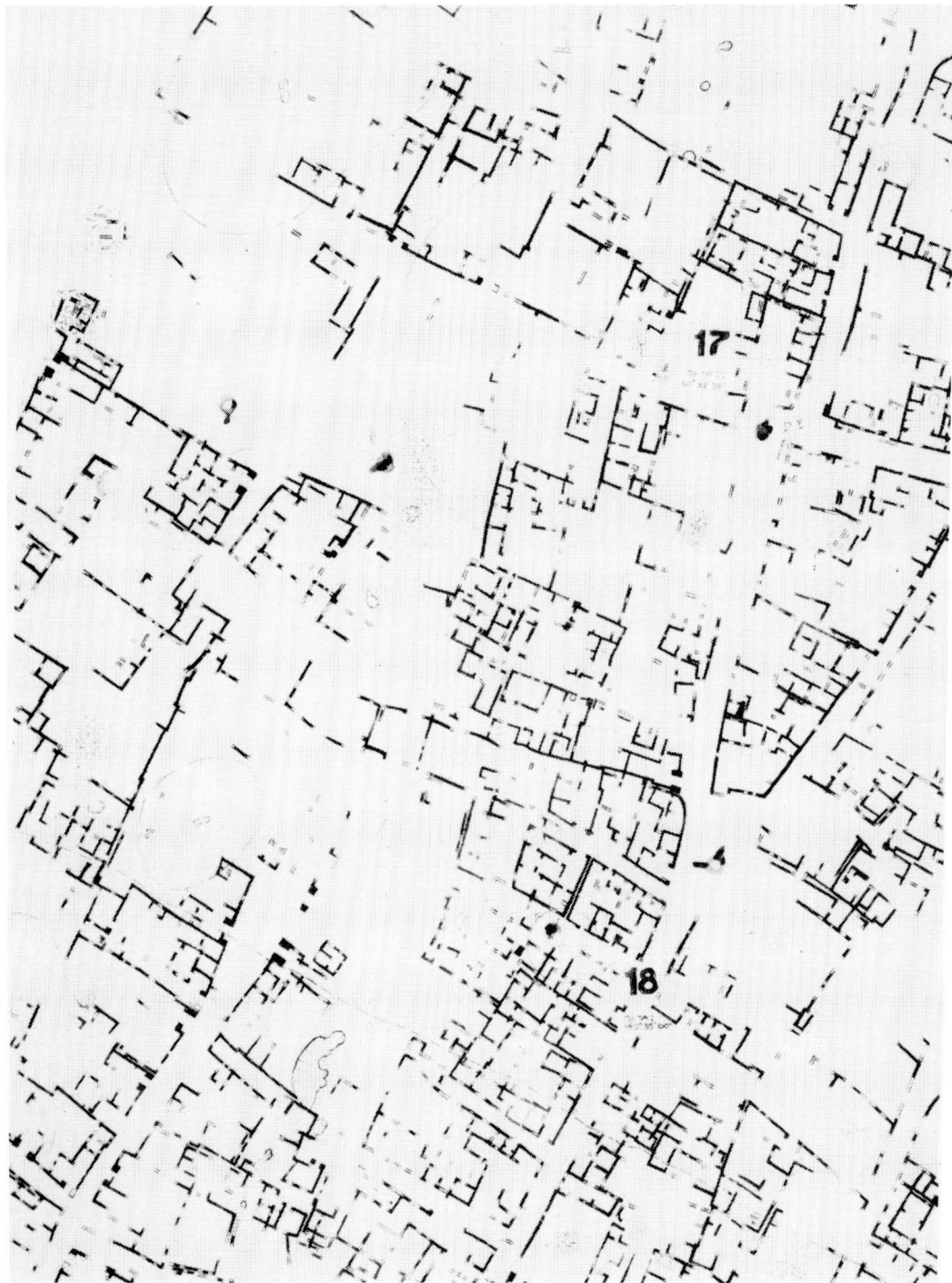

Fig. 58. Preliminary field drawing (1980) of stone wall footings in part of the Outer Town at Taya. Scale *c.* 1:1175.

There are Taya 9 sherds on the surface of the much larger area, outside the wall, which we call the Outer Town. This settlement seems to have grown rapidly, and to have come to a rapid end; the amount of pottery on occasional half-eroded floors in the Outer Town suggests a destruction or sudden abandonment.

This is clearly what happened in the one Outer Town building which we have excavated completely. It was roughly square, with a simple plan of rooms surrounding a courtyard; a well-made drain ran from the courtyard into the street. One room contained domestic equipment, and another seemed to have been a latrine. A third, below ground level, gave access to a funerary vault sealed by a stone. Inside were three skeletons, very poorly preserved but clearly adult, with pottery grave-goods; there would have been space for more bodies, and the small number implies that the house and vault were not in use for more than half a century or so, perhaps much less. In the fill by the entrance to the vault were fragments of a glazed faience beaker, the base of which was so thin that it consisted partly of glaze without any visible quartz-frit core; the translucent effect given by objects such as this probably provided the incentive for the invention of true glass, first extensively used in northern Mesopotamia some centuries later.

Occupation contemporary with levels 8–7 and probably 6 is attested in the Inner Town. In 1968–69 we cleared one substantial house and part of another in this area, but neither produced the amount of pottery or other material remains which our previous sounding had led us to expect. One inscribed amulet could be given an approximate date in the late 3rd millennium. There is probably also some occupation of levels 8–7 and later in the Outer Town, but little that has been firmly identified (apart from some Atabegi houses). Apparently the population of levels 8–6 was more concentrated than that of level 9 and was more concerned for its security; the series of abandonments or destructions attested in the central mound indicates that there was good reason to worry.

The plan of the Taya town provides a unique view of urban organization in the 3rd millennium, with major traffic arteries, open spaces, blind alleys, houses of various sizes, buildings that were probably small temples at some street junctions, industrial areas, notably potteries and a flint-knapping quarter, and so on (fig. 58). I hope that publication of our results, which ought to be supplemented by further investigations at the site, will follow in the near future. In the mean time there are three general points that deserve mention.

I have sometimes been asked what on earth a town the size of Taya was doing in northern Mesopotamia in the 3rd millennium'. Part of the answer must surely be that Taya is unique only in its exceptional state of visible preservation. This is owed to its stone wall footings, and to their position on gently sloping ground from which superincumbent mud-brick debris has been largely washed away. If Taya had been a conventional mud-brick site in a relatively flat plain, then the remains visible to a modern archaeologist would have consisted of the central mound – not particularly imposing by Mesopotamian standards – and the low rise of the walled Inner Town. The buildings in the Outer Town, the largest proportion of the site, would have been represented by little more than virtually invisible contours and a modest scatter of sherds. All Middle Eastern archaeologists are familiar, however, with the way in which sherds wander away from sites; sometimes they are even distributed by people taking soil from ancient mounds to fertilize their fields. We tend not to trust outlying surface scatters; but it may be that sites like Hadheil, a 3rd millennium town south of Sinjar whose main mound dwarfs the Inner Town at Taya, were also periodically ringed by extensive suburbs. The same could apply to many other sites whose size is liable to be judged primarily from the extent of their apparent build-up. Southern Mesopotamia, with its magnificent material culture, did not necessarily have the largest conglomerations of people in 3rd millennium Iraq.

A second point concerns the location of towns in general. Taya seems to have been important during only one period, the second half of the 3rd millennium. Its role in the region was presumably that filled previously by Karatepe, subsequently by Rimah, nowadays by 'Afar. Here, as in many parts of the Middle East and elsewhere, there is a range of possible sites for the major town, and its precise location at any moment will depend on chance or local political developments. The same applies on a wider scale to patterns of communication, which are seldom in practice controlled by considerations such as the location of one particular mountain pass or river crossing; there tend to be alternative patterns recurring at different times. In studying an area, one has to take account of the casual, unpredictable factors that may have affected the demography and the roads.

Thirdly, with the previous point in mind, it is surely time that Mesopotamian archaeologists concentrated a greater proportion of their energies on sites, like the Outer Town at Taya, that were widely occupied for not more than one or two periods of limited duration. It is only too easy to become bogged down, at vast expense of time, intellect, and money, in stratigraphical problems of small ultimate significance. Of course we do have to solve basic questions of sequence and chronology, and high sites do have their compensations: one may point topically to Mardikh/Ebla which produced, in a couple of rooms, after long years of excavation, a fantastic archive of a type that is still conspicuously lacking at Taya. But if we are really to understand more about how ancient societies functioned, we have to work horizontally rather than vertically. There is no intrinsic reason why sites with long continuity of occupation should regularly produce results of greater value than those available a few feet below the surface elsewhere.

Bibliography

J. E. Reade, *et al.*, Preliminary Reports on Tell Taya in *Iraq* XXX (1968), 234–64; XXXIII (1971), 87–100; XXXV (1973), 155–87.

S. Lloyd, 'Some ancient sites in the Sinjar district', *Iraq* V (1938), 123–42.

— 'Iraq Government soundings at Sinjar', *Iraq* VII (1940), 13–21.

S. Fukai et al., *Telul eth-Thalathat, vol. III: The Excavation of Tell V: the Fourth Season (1965)* (Tokyo 1974): for recent work on Ninevite 5 pottery.

Chagar Bazar

By John Curtis

Chagar Bazar occupies a central position in the Khabur basin in north Syria, with the Wadi Khanzir flowing just to the east of the site. Clearly visible from the top of the mound are distant mountains in most directions: Tur Abdin to the north, Jebel Abdul Aziz to the south-west, Kaukab to the south, and Jebel Sinjar to the south-east (col. pl. 6a). All the space in between, as far as the eye can see, is rich arable land, and it is probably this that accounts for the size of the town in antiquity. It was undoubtedly an important market centre. A contributory factor to its importance must have been its position at an intersection of routes. In the Roman period an east-west road linking Harran (Carrhae) and Ras al'Ain with the Tigris passed through Chagar Bazar, and we may presume that this was an important route in earlier times. Secondly the modern Hasseke-Amuda road, which runs from north to south and goes right past the mound, probably follows the line of an ancient track. In the chapter on Tell Brak David Oates has suggested that the route from the north Mesopotamian plain to the copper mines of southern Turkey, via Tell Brak, joined up with this road at Chagar Bazar.

The etymology of the name Chagar Bazar is uncertain, but according to one explanation proferred by a Kurd from the local village it is a combination of the Arabic *shagir* (vacant, unoccupied) and the Kurdish *bazaar* (market). This is an attractive suggestion, but lacks conviction from a linguistic point of view. There are a number of other possibilities, more plausible but less appealing, which we cannot go into here. The mound itself (fig. 59) is very heavily eroded and cut into by deep gullies, so much so that the highest part of the tell is almost completely separated from the main bulk of the mound. Nevertheless, Mallowan determined to dig here on the conclusion of his Khabur survey of November and December 1934. His choice of site was determined by the fact that great numbers of Halaf potsherds were found on the surface and he also thought that Chagar Bazar would provide a pottery sequence representative of the Khabur region from the prehistoric through to the historical periods. Further there was no substantial occupation after the middle of the 2nd millennium B.C., which meant that the early historical levels would be easily accessible. The excavation, on behalf of the British School of Archaeology in Iraq, took place in the spring of 1935 and 1936, and was continued for about a fortnight in 1937.

Information about the prehistoric occupation of Chagar Bazar was obtained from a sounding over 15 m. deep (Pit M) dug down from the ridge at the north-west corner of the mound (fig. 60). In this trench, which was 20 x 25 m. at the top, Mallowan

Fig. 59. View of Tell Chagar Bazar from the south-east.

Fig. 60. Contour plan of Tell Chagar Bazar (after Mallowan) showing excavated areas.

distinguished fifteen levels, ten of which belonged to the prehistoric period. In all of them potsherds of the Halaf period were found, and by analogy with material from other Halafian sites it can be deduced that the Halaf occupation at Chagar Bazar started slightly later than at Arpachiyah and continued down to the end of the Halaf period, covering the end of the 6th and at least the first half of the 5th millennium. A sample probably from level 11 or 12 has yielded a radiocarbon determination (P1487) of 4715±77 b.c.* Alongside the Halaf sherds in the three lowest levels were sherds of grey and black burnished ware, a type of neolithic pottery that is contemporary with and closely related to Amuq B ware, a class of pottery that is widespread in Western Syria and is named after the Amuq Plain where it has been studied in detail. Also found in these same three levels were sherds bearing Samarran motifs, testifying to contact with the Samarra culture of central Mesopotamia. A find of particular interest, from a relatively early Halaf level, is a copper bead. In the section of Arphachiyah we described how neutron activation analysis had been used to divide the Halaf pottery from there into groups and to demonstrate that some pottery found at Tepe Gawra derives from Arpachiyah. Using the same techniques, the Edinburgh team have also shown that the Halaf potters at Chagar Bazar obtained their clay from the local wadi. Further, in the late Halaf period pottery manufactured at Chagar Bazar was being used in at least five nearby villages to the north and northeast. Thus, Chagar Bazar must have been a production-centre of some significance, although the movement of pottery was not all in one direction — one sherd from Chagar Bazar was apparently brought from Tell Halaf.

The evidence from Pit M suggested that Chagar Bazar was abandoned at the end of the Halaf period and was not reoccupied until very late in the Uruk period or at the beginning of the Early Dynastic Period, *c.* 3000 B.C. However, potsherds that are unmistakably of 'Ubaid type were collected from the surface of the mound in 1981, testifying to at least some occupation in the intermediate period. It may have been on a limited scale, but only further excavation would confirm this. By contrast, sherds typical of the succeeding Uruk period were not observed, and their absence on a mound of this size is curious considering how widespread Uruk settlement was in the Khabur basin.

Details about the Early Dynastic to mid-2nd

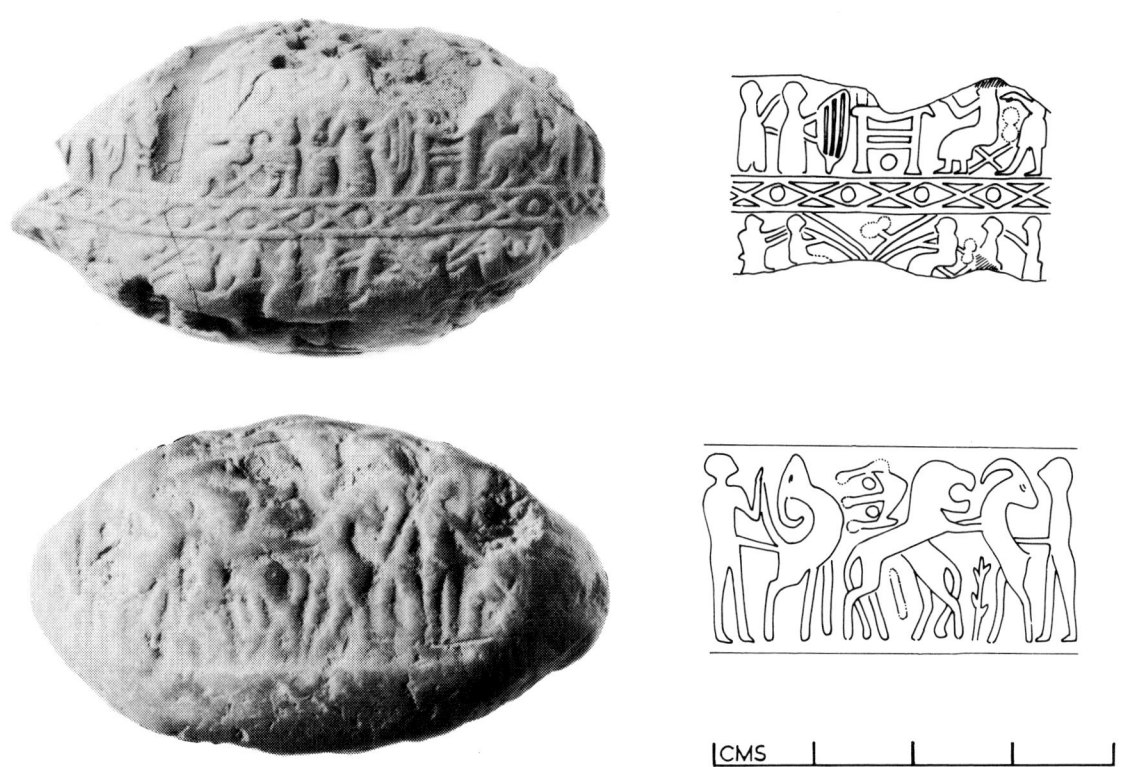

Fig. 61. Clay bullae from levels 3–2. Top: BM 131690; bottom: BM 129370.

*See p. 6

millennium levels at Chagar Bazar were mostly found in a series of interconnecting trenches describing a huge zig-zag, overall length nearly 200 m., along the crest of the northern part of the mound. Mallowan divided the occupation here into five levels, numbered from the top 1–5. None of them except the topmost was cleared on a scale sufficient to obtain meaningful architectural plans, but the thick walls and large rooms are probably indicative of a series of public buildings. Both levels 5 and 4 produced painted and incised pottery of Ninevite 5 type, suggesting that they should be dated to the beginning of the Early Dynastic Period, *c.* 2900 B.C. Of particular interest from a level 5 grave is a fragment of iron which analysis shows to contain no nickel and therefore to be of terrestrial rather than meteoric origin. Two more fragments of iron were recovered from level 3, but they have not been analysed. It is an interesting phenomenon that in most parts of the Middle East there are isolated examples of smelted ironwork from an early date, yet the widespread use of iron does not begin until the late 2nd or early 1st millennium B.C. The usual explanation for this curious state of affairs is that small quantities of iron were sometimes accidentally produced as a by-product of copper smelting. The iron derives either from the use of iron-rich copper ores or from iron oxide fluxes used to expedite the smelting of copper. The next two levels, 3 and 2, are also said to be closely linked together and homogeneous in character. Amongst the material from these levels, which are to be ascribed to the latter part of the Early Dynastic and the Akkadian periods, are "monochrome burnished black and grey ware(s) with rounded bases" and a couple of lozenge-shaped clay bullae. One of them (fig. 61, top) has a string-hole through the centre like the examples from Tell Brak (fig. 52). It is inscribed, and bears an interesting seal impression showing a banquet scene. The second example (fig. 61, bottom) is uninscribed but is again covered with seal impressions, this time showing a contest frieze. Both seal impressions are clearly late Early Dynastic in style, albeit with a rather provincial flavour, but the inscription is of Akkadian date. Here we have a clear indication that in outlying parts of Mesopotamia glyptic styles, or even the cylinders themselves, sometimes survive longer than the periods of which they are representative. The buildings of level 2 are said to have been largely destroyed by the foundations of level 1, and Mallowan believed there to have been an interval of several centuries between these two levels. The inference is that the site was abandoned during the Ur III period at least. However that may be, the earliest phase of level 1 is closely dated.

Some nine rooms were excavated of a large regular building which was probably a palace. In one of the rooms the greater part of a tablet archive was found, numbering altogether nearly 100 tablets or fragments thereof. Many of the tablets were resting on potsherds, some of which were identified as "coarse Khabur ware painted with red stripes." This is a fact of some significance to which we shall return later. The tablets were all written in the time of Shamshi-Adad I of Assyria (*c.* 1813–1781 B.C., according to the so-called 'middle chronology'), an Amorite who had not only seized the throne of Assyria but carved out for himself an empire embracing most of Upper Mesopotamia. To help in the administration of this large territory he installed his elder son Ishme-Dagan in Ekallatum, a city probably on the Tigris to the north of Ashur, and his younger son Yasmah-Addu in Mari. He seems to have given himself some sort of roving commission, but he was based at a place called Shubat-Enlil. To return to the Chagar Bazar tablets, they are mostly concerned with the issuing of cereals, principally barley, for the making of bread and beer, or for animal fodder. On one occasion Yasmah-Addu arrives with more than 3000 men, and both they and their teams of asses, horses and oxen all have to be fed. Although the texts are not at first sight particularly informative, they do give some interesting insights into the social conditions prevalent at the time. For instance, a study of the personal names in the tablets shows that the population of Chagar Bazar at that time was very mixed. People bearing Akkadian names were predominant, but there were sizeable minorities with Hurrian and Amorite or West Semitic names. Some texts make reference to a palace, presumably in Chagar Bazar, so it is clear the place must have been of some importance. Some scholars have sought to identify it with Shubat-Enlil, but this identification remains uncertain. There are a number of other candidates for the location of this site, including Tell Leilan, currently being excavated by a team from Yale University, and perhaps Tell Brak.

The building in which the tablets occurred was

Fig. 62. Grave 186.

destroyed by fire which accounts for the preservation of its contents. It is unfortunate that more of it could not have been excavated, as the pickings might have been rich indeed, but owing to its depth below the surface the cost would have been prohibitive. This destruction might have happened during the turbulent events of the twenty years following the death of Shamshi-Adad, in which time Zimri-Lim captured the throne of Mari and gained control over the Middle Euphrates area and the Khabur Valley, only to be dispossessed by Hammurabi of Babylon.

Above the burnt-out palace, if such it is, were a series of superimposed building levels which Mallowan divided into a number of phases of occupation. Nevertheless, he considered them sufficiently homogeneous to be bracketed together under the appellation of level 1. The plans recovered seem to be mostly of private houses, but owing to erosion on the sides of the ridge they are incomplete. A large number of graves were found in these levels (figs. 62-63). Although most of them were simple inhumations, the grave-goods were of considerable interest. Apart from the ever-present pottery vessels, the bodies were accompanied by a variety of objects including beads, amulets and bronze pins, daggers, spear-heads and axes. Some of the burials were in corbel-vaulted tombs made of mud-bricks, and one of these was particularly rich. In addition to the usual grave-goods, there was a head-band, earring and pendant, all in gold. It seems that most of these graves had been dug down from the floors of houses, a method of burial commonly practised in Mesopotamia, but we must not overlook the possibility that some may have been dug after the abandonment of a particular part of the site.

We have already seen how the tablets were associated with sherds of painted Khabur ware, and according to Mallowan this distinctive type of pottery was found all through level 1. This is an important point, which merits a short digression. Khabur ware is wheel-made pottery with monochrome painted decoration in red, brown or black (fig. 64). The designs are usually geometric, and include plain horizontal bands, hatched and cross-hatched triangles and other simple motifs in various combinations. The range of vessel shapes is, on the whole, as limited as the repertoire of designs. At Chagar Bazar, large jars with flat bases, high necks and wide mouths are the commonest form. There is also a whole series of unpainted vessels associated

Fig. 63. Grave 151.

with their painted counterparts, but this aspect of Khabur ware is not generally so well-known. The balance will doubtless be redressed by the publication of the pottery from Tell al Rimah, a site where all forms of Khabur ware are well-represented. This pottery was given its name by Mallowan after the great quantities of it encountered by him at Chagar Bazar, but its distribution is by no means confined to the Khabur triangle. Apart from north-east Syria it is spread across northern Iraq, and also occurs at a few sites in Turkey and Iran. Indeed, its occurrence at a site in the latter area—Dinkha Tepe—has promoted the most comprehensive study, by Carol Hamlin, of Khabur ware. What this wide distribution represents—if anything—in terms of ethnic movements, political homogeneity or economic contact is quite unclear. We are on firmer ground with the date at which Khabur ware was introduced; from the Chagar Bazar evidence and that from other sites excavated subsequently it is clear that it appears shortly before the reign of Shamshi-Adad. How long it lasted is more problematic. At Chagar Bazar there is limited evidence, in the form of at least one potsherd, of occupation in the Nuzi period. Level 1, then, might have lasted until $c.$ 1500 B.C. Whether the occupation was continuous is unclear, but the total accumulation of debris, in some places up to 6.5 m., indicates that it might have been. Did Khabur ware, then, continue in use until the middle of the 2nd millennium B.C.? The evidence from Tell al Rimah suggests that Khabur ware proper does not occur much after the reign of Hammurabi (1792–1750 B.C.). It is succeeded, probably after a break in occupation, by what David Oates terms "late Khabur/early Nuzi" pottery. This is superficially similar to Khabur ware, but can be distinguished from it. The vessels are thin-walled and generally finer, and the range of shapes is different. At Chagar Bazar this sort of

Fig. 64. Painted pottery from level 1. From left BM 125351, BM 125429, BM 125453. The vase on the right is probably later than the other two vessels.

pottery is also present, for example the button-based vases, and in all probability the pottery sequence here is similar to that observed at Tell al Rimah. Only more study of the pottery, however, would confirm this.

From this short account it should be evident that Sir Max Mallowan extracted an enormous amount of information from Chagar Bazar in just two full seasons of excavation. The project was a pioneering venture. As he himself modestly admitted at the time, though, some of his conclusions were necessarily temporary and a number of loose ends remained to be tied up. In his own words, "great argument, about it and about, will doubtless follow." In fact there has been practically none. The thirty-five years that have elapsed since Sir Max's last report on Chagar Bazar have seen little analysis of his findings, and only the tablets and the Halaf pottery have been accorded further study. It is to be hoped that now, with so much comparative material at our disposal, largely recently excavated, more scholars will turn their attention to this important and potentially rewarding site. Amongst the several problems to be resolved, perhaps the most important is the name of the site in antiquity.

We still do not know with certainty what it was called.

Bibliography

M. E. L. Mallowan, Reports on Tell Chagar Bazar in *Iraq* III (1936), 1–86; IV (1937), 91–154; IX (1947), 1–259.

— *Twenty-Five Years of Mesopotamian Discovery* (London, 1956), 12–23.

Carol Hamlin, 'The early second millennium ceramic assemblage of Dinkha Tepe', *Iran* XII (1974), 125–53.

T. E. Davidson and H. McKerrell, 'Pottery analysis and Halaf period trade in the Khabur headwaters region', *Iraq* XXXVIII (1976), 45–53.

T. E. Davidson and T. Watkins, 'Two seasons of excavation at Tell Aqab in the Jezirah, N.E. Syria', *Iraq* XLIII (1981), 1–18.

C. J. Gadd, 'Tablets from Chagar Bazar, 1936', *Iraq* IV (1937), 178–83.

— 'Tablets from Chagar Bazar and Tall Brak, 1937–38', *Iraq* VII (1940), 22–66.

O. Loretz, 'Texte aus Chagar Bazar', *Alte Orient und Altes Testament* I (Neukirchen-Vluyn 1969), 199–260.

— 'Texte aus Chagar Bazar und Tell Brak, Teil I', *AOAT* 3/1 (1969).

J. Renger, Review of Loretz, *AOAT* 3/1, in *JNES* 32 (1973), 261–5.

Tell al Rimah

By David Oates

While the excavations at Nimrud were drawing to a close the School was considering the choice of a site for its next major enterprise. A number of factors were taken into account. The School had been concerned since its inception with the history and prehistory of northern Mesopotamia, a field virtually neglected by other non-Iraqi expeditions whose interests at that time—with the exception of the Japanese at Telul eth-Thalathat—lay in Babylonia and Sumer. The obvious gap in Assyrian history was the 2nd millennium B.C., but it was abundantly clear from our work at Nimrud that the great Assyrian cities in the Tigris valley would not yield evidence for this period, because their favourable climatic situation had ensured continuous occupation in ancient times, and the massive remains of Late Assyrian monumental buildings deny extensive access to earlier occupation levels.

We therefore turned our attention to what appeared to have been the western frontier of metropolitan Assyria beyond the last outlying hill ranges that overlook the Jazira, the steppe between the Tigris and the Euphrates. Here we were near the edge of the rainfall zone, where modern rainfed crops are not consistently reliable and in this century control has passed from nomadic herdsmen to cultivators, reflecting the inter-related factors of climate and security. There is no evidence of any major climatic change in this region, and indeed the distribution of ancient sites from the prehistoric period onward conforms broadly with the limit of modern rainfall. The density of sites of all periods in the plain is impressive. Layard claims to have seen 150 mounds from the citadel of Tell 'Afar which overlooks the Jazira from the north-east, and in the course of travelling between Tell 'Afar and Tell al Rimah, 13 km. to the south, we found more than 120 sites in an area some 15 by 10 km. The first survey here was conducted by Seton Lloyd in 1938 and published in *Iraq* in 1939. He recorded a number of walled towns of medium size, all with evidence of 2nd millennium occupation, and when we followed in his footsteps twenty-five years later our choice for excavation fell on Tell al Rimah as an apparently typical site of its period with—an important consideration—relatively easy access to water and supplies.

The Site (figs. 65–66)

Tell al Rimah (The Mound of the Spears) owes its name, according to local tradition, to a tribal battle in the nineteenth century when Shammar warriors, then disputing the control of this area with the Jebour who were their predecessors as nomad herdsmen in the Jazira, planted their spears on top of the tell. The site consists of a central mound, measuring some 100 m. across at the base and rising to a height of 29 m. above plain level. It is surrounded by a roughly polygonal circum-

Fig. 65. Tell and walls seen from the south.

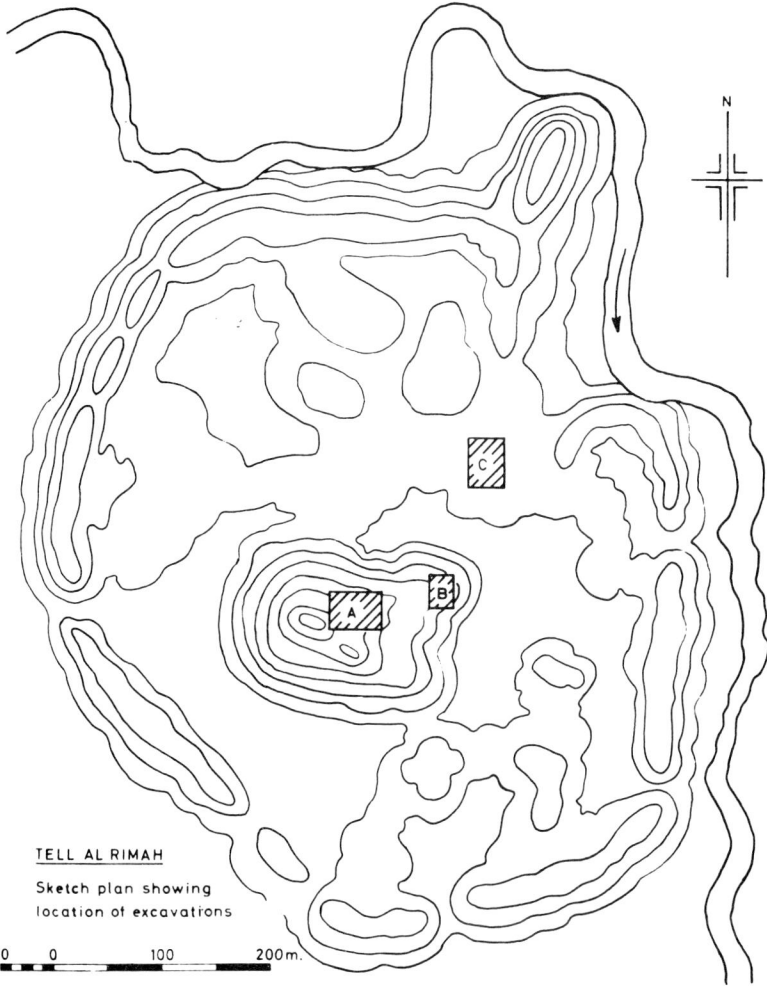

Fig. 66. Contour plan of Tell al Rimah (after Lloyd). A and C mark the sites of the temple and palace.

vallation about 600 m. in diameter with a re-entrant in the north-east corner where it is skirted by a modern — presumably also an ancient — watercourse that is now seasonal. Whether it was perennial at this distance into the plain in ancient times we do not know, but a change in the water regime might have occurred through denudation of the hillsides to the north and east. Between the outer defences and the central mound the superficial evidence for settlement is irregular, suggesting that it was concentrated for long periods in a few areas, virtually small tells in themselves, interspersed with considerable open spaces that were never occupied. This pattern is repeated on similar sites across the northern rim of the plain and in the Khabur basin of north-eastern Syria, and probably reflects their use as places of refuge in troubled times for the people of the countryside and their flocks.

We investigated the structure of the rampart only at one point on the north side, and here its remains consisted merely of a substantial earth bank with sloping sides, the material for which was probably extracted from an outer ditch that can be seen as a crop-mark in the fields beyond. The bank was partly overlaid by buildings of the mid-2nd millennium when the circuit of defences was clearly no longer maintained. In its original form it was almost certainly surmounted by a mud-brick wall, for at higher points around the perimeter the outlines of brickwork could be discerned as the winter vegetation dried out. We have no direct evidence for the date of the original construction, but it should logically be associated with the earliest occupation within the circuit, which is of the time of Shamshi-Adad I of Assyria c. 1800 B.C.

Excavations within the city

Within the walls work was concentrated in two areas, on one of the mounds in the lower town and on the high central tell. Our best sequence of occupation as well as the most precise dating evidence came from the lower mound, where we found over 6 m. of stratified material spanning the period from c. 1800 to c. 1200 B.C. with, at the top, the remains of a Late Assyrian settlement. In the middle levels the buildings were for the most part private houses with one or two small shrines, such as one might expect to find in a peaceful and moderately prosperous country town. They do not merit detailed description here, although they produced many interesting finds including, notably, the superb inlaid glass beaker (col. pl. 6b). In the lowest stratum, however, we came on the massive remains of an important public building shown by the documents within it to have been the palace of the rulers of the city in the Old Assyrian period.

The excavated area of the palace site, covering some 1000 sq.m., clearly revealed only a part of the whole complex but gives us a reliable outline of its history, in which there were three main structural phases. *Phase 1* is represented by a three-room suite with mud-brick walls on massive stone foundations

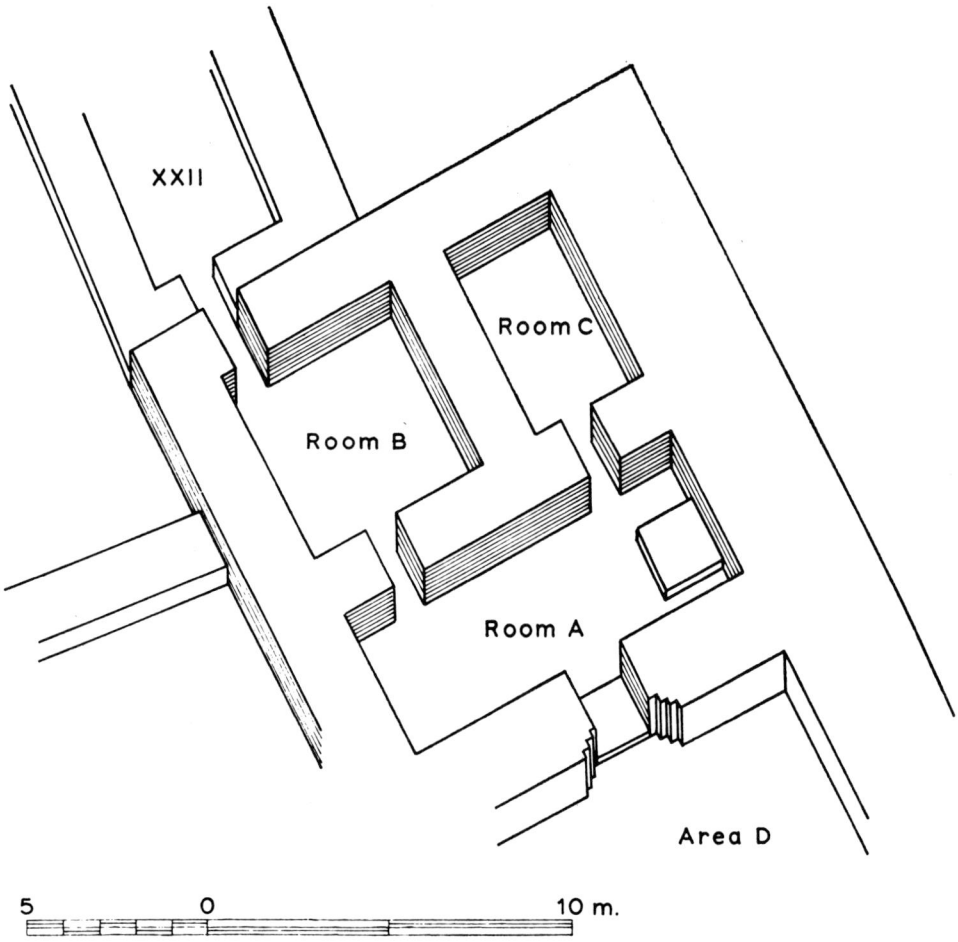

Fig. 67. Axonometric reconstruction of the Phase I reception suite in the palace.

trenched into virgin soil (fig. 67), and built against what appears to be an outer wall over 3 m. thick. The principal room of the suite (A) measured at least 10.20 m. long by 4.20 m. wide. It was entered by a doorway in the west wall ornamented with triple reveals, and with a raised, plastered sill. At the south end of the room was a low dais, identifying it as a formal reception chamber, and we presume that doorways in the east wall, now concealed under later brickwork, gave access to the two smaller rooms (B and C) that completed the suite on this side. The 'bent-axis' reception room, where the visitor enters through a door in one of the long walls and then turns to approach the place of honour, is a standard feature of north Mesopotamian villages to this day and has a very long history, but in antiquity it was common to both temples and palaces and does not in itself identify the suite as part of a religious or a secular building. In *Phase 2*, additions were made on the north and east sides of the suite on slightly different alignments and these walls remained to form part of the Palace in its final form.

Phase 3 (fig. 68) is marked by a much more ambitious development, the almost total rasing of the Phase I suite and its replacement by a grandiose throne-room and ante-chamber and two further courtyards, the larger of which formed the core of a new residential block. It is interesting to note in passing that the new throne-room suite was laid out on the plan that was later characteristically Babylonian, with an axial approach to the niche across the width of the ante-chamber. This is in marked contrast with the arrangement of the earlier and smaller reception chamber and may indicate the deliberate adoption of southern fashions, perhaps even a change in ceremonial. At some stage in its life this part of the palace was either damaged or briefly abandoned, then repaired with minor changes to the plan. When it was finally deserted and replaced by a building farther to the south we do not know, although on both archaeological and historical grounds a date about 1700 B.C. appears likely.

The debris associated with the construction, repair and final destruction of the various buildings produced a fascinating body of historical evidence in the form of seal impressions and tablets, vastly smaller in quantity than that from Mari but closely linked with it. It has also the interest of being the only such material so far found on a north Mesopotamian rather than a southern or Euphrates site. The texts and seal impressions have already been published and discussed in detail in *The Old Babylonian Texts from Tell al Rimah* and the arguments involved are much too complicated to be repeated here, but the main conclusions may be summarized. The seal impressions gave us the names of five rulers, derived either from their own seals or from those of their servants. They were Shamshi-Adad, certainly Shamshi-Adad I of Assyria, Samu-Addu, Hatnu-rapi, Ashkur-Addu and Aqba-hammu. The other four are attested in the Mari archives as rulers of a city, Karana, and there can be no doubt that this was the name of Tell al Rimah in the 2nd millennium. It seems probable that Samu-Addu was a client prince of Shamshi-Adad I who certainly had governors in this area. Hatnu-rapi and Ashkur-Addu—who may have been the son of Samu-Addu—were certainly independent kings who corresponded on equal terms with Zimri-Lim of Mari after Shamshi-Adad's death, while Aqba-hammu is described on the second version of his seal as 'servant of Hammurabi'. It is clear that the time range involved extends from some time in the reign of Shamshi-Adad—ill-defined because we have no detailed record of the extension of his control over Assyria—until late in the reign of Hammurabi whose suzerainty over the north can hardly be dated earlier than his 34th year when he finally subjugated Mari. The latest and most plausible chronological evidence we have from Babylonia accords with Assyrian records and would place Shamshi-Adad from about 1850 to 1817, and Hammurabi from 1828 to 1784 B.C. Returning to the buildings, it would seem likely that the smaller reception suite of Phase 1 was used by Samu-Addu as a client king and perhaps by other representatives of the Assyrian government in Shamshi-Adad's time, and that the more grandiose palace of Phase 3 was the result of Karana's emergence as a short-lived independent state after his death. There is some support for this suggestion in a letter from Mari that refers to 'the shining palace of Ashkur-Addu' and should apply to its most impressive phase.

The evidence of the tablets found in the palace confirms and elaborates this picture. They include a number of texts of Hatnu-rapi including letters from Zimri-Lim of Mari, the first king after the end of the Assyrian domination there. Zimri-Lim addresses Hatnu-rapi as an equal and an ally,

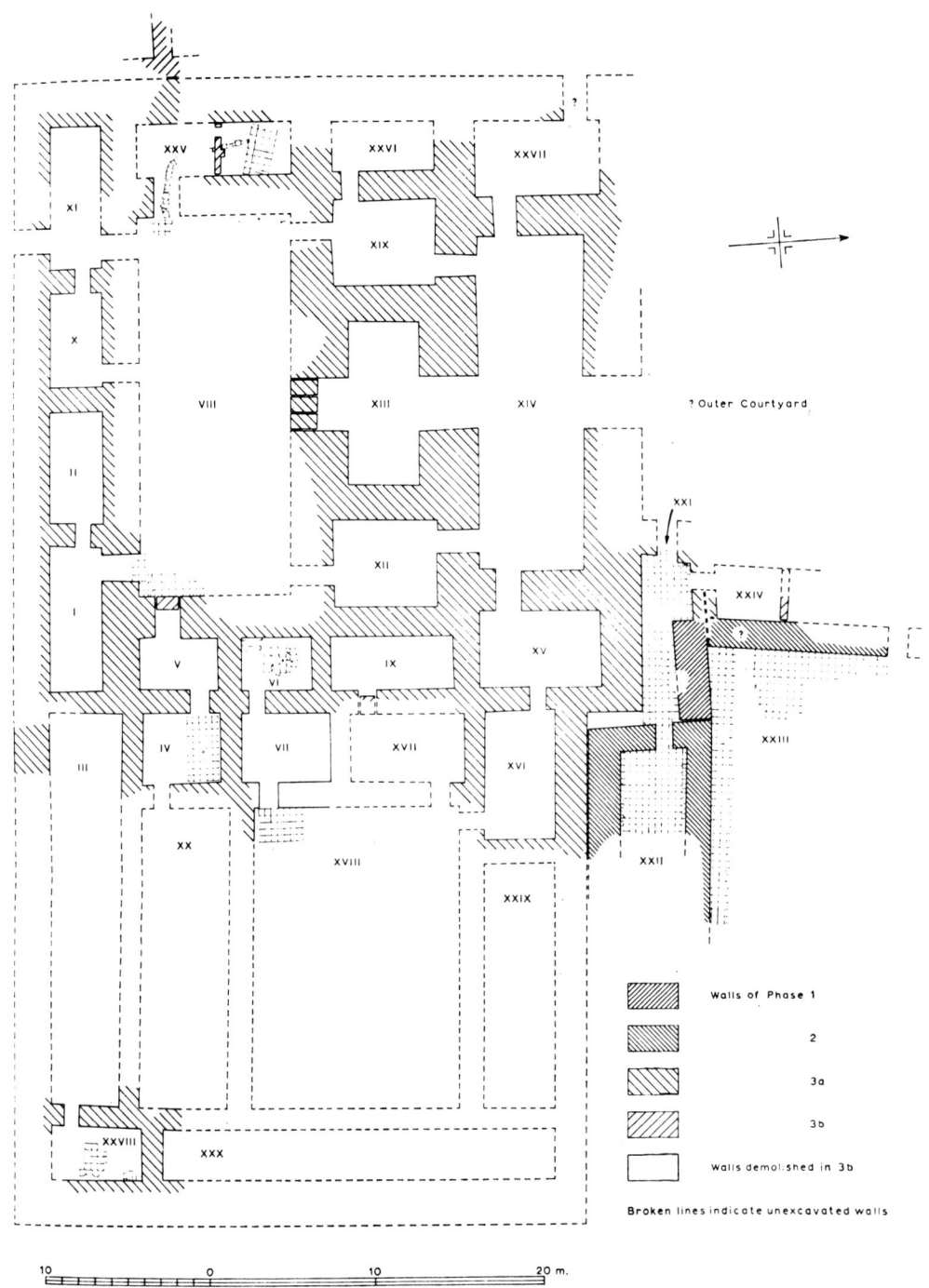

Fig. 68. Plan of the palace and adjoining buildings.

referring to a proposed meeting on the Khabur and requesting his assistance in repelling an attack by the king of Eshnunna, which lay in the Diyala basin east of modern Baghdad. Other royal correspondents include Zaziya of the Turukku whose territory lay east of the Tigris on the borders of Kurdistan and one of whose daughters was married in diplomatic alliance to Mut-asqur, grandson of Shamshi-Adad. But the most fascinating group of texts is undoubtedly the archive of the lady Iltani, daughter of Samu-Addu and wife of the last attested ruler of Karana, Aqba-hammu. She clearly acted as her husband's chatelaine and held considerable domestic if not political power, organizing the administration of his household and lands in his absence and keeping a wary eye on the social affairs of the city. She seems to have corresponded directly with a somewhat mysterious figure, Mutu-hadkim, who was evidently resident in the north and in a position to make firm suggestions, if not to give orders, to Aqba-hammu himself. Since a man of the same name is known from a letter in the Mari archives addressed to Ashkur-Addu as a Babylonian general in command of 10,000 troops, it is tempting to wonder whether he was not also Hammurabi's agent there after Aqba-hammu had declared himself formally 'servant of Hammurabi'.

With this historical framework in mind we turn to the excavations on the central mound, whose development reflects an astonishing change in the status of Tell al Rimah within the same period. Until then it had apparently been a large village or small town which had grown over the course of many centuries to a height of some 6 m. The earliest levels are not accessible to excavation, but surface pottery suggests that the original settlement, like many others in the area, goes back to the 6th millennium B.C. Early in the 2nd millennium the top of the mound was levelled to provide a foundation for the construction of a monumental religious complex. In its original conception this was apparently intended to incorporate a lower terrace surrounded by a temenos wall, a free-standing arcaded stair leading up from the main entrance on the east to a second terrace on which stood a large temple, and a third high terrace attached to the west end of the temple and approached from its roof. We have no means of knowing whether there was a second shrine on top of the third terrace, which is heavily eroded. This plan was never completed in full, and what was achieved shows evidence of two distinct stages of construction. In the first, the temple was completed and the high terrace behind it was carried up to a considerable height, but the second terrace on which the temple stood was not finished. In the second stage the high terrace was completed after an interval marked by the erosion of the existing brickwork, the main east stair was constructed from city level resting on three vaults of progressively increasing height, and the terrace at its head outside the main east gate was paved.

The plan of the temple (fig. 69) is of a classic Babylonian type that seems on present evidence to have originated with the architects of the Third Dynasty of Ur, and is only found in the north when contacts with the south were particularly close. The only distinctively Assyrian feature of the whole complex is the direct attachment of the high terrace to the back of the temple, for in the south ziggurrats were free-standing structures, each within its own temenos. The regularity of the temple plan at Tell al Rimah reflects the work of architects on an unencumbered site that had been cleared for the purpose, its sophistication suggests that they had been imported from some metropolitan centre, and the design of the building makes it clear that they had been brought in from Babylonia. Obviously Karana as a country town would not have been ambitious enough and could not have afforded such a lavish construction, and indeed could not maintain it when the community reverted in later years to its normal status. The temple, like the palace, has not yielded any legible foundation or monumental inscription that might have given us the name of its founder, but the temple could only have been built under external patronage and, since there was apparently no previous tradition of any such monumental religious building on the site, the patronage may be ascribed to political motives. Within the close chronological bracket for the early 2nd millennium history of the city that has been observed on the palace site, the most likely patron is Shamshi-Adad I, a usurper on the throne of Ashur who would have been especially concerned to exercise the traditional functions of royalty not only in the rebuilding of existing temples in the great cities, Ashur and Nineveh, but in affirming his control over outlying areas such as the territory of Karana through which ran the major route from Ashur to the Assyrian trading colonies in south-western Anatolia. To this inference we may add that the

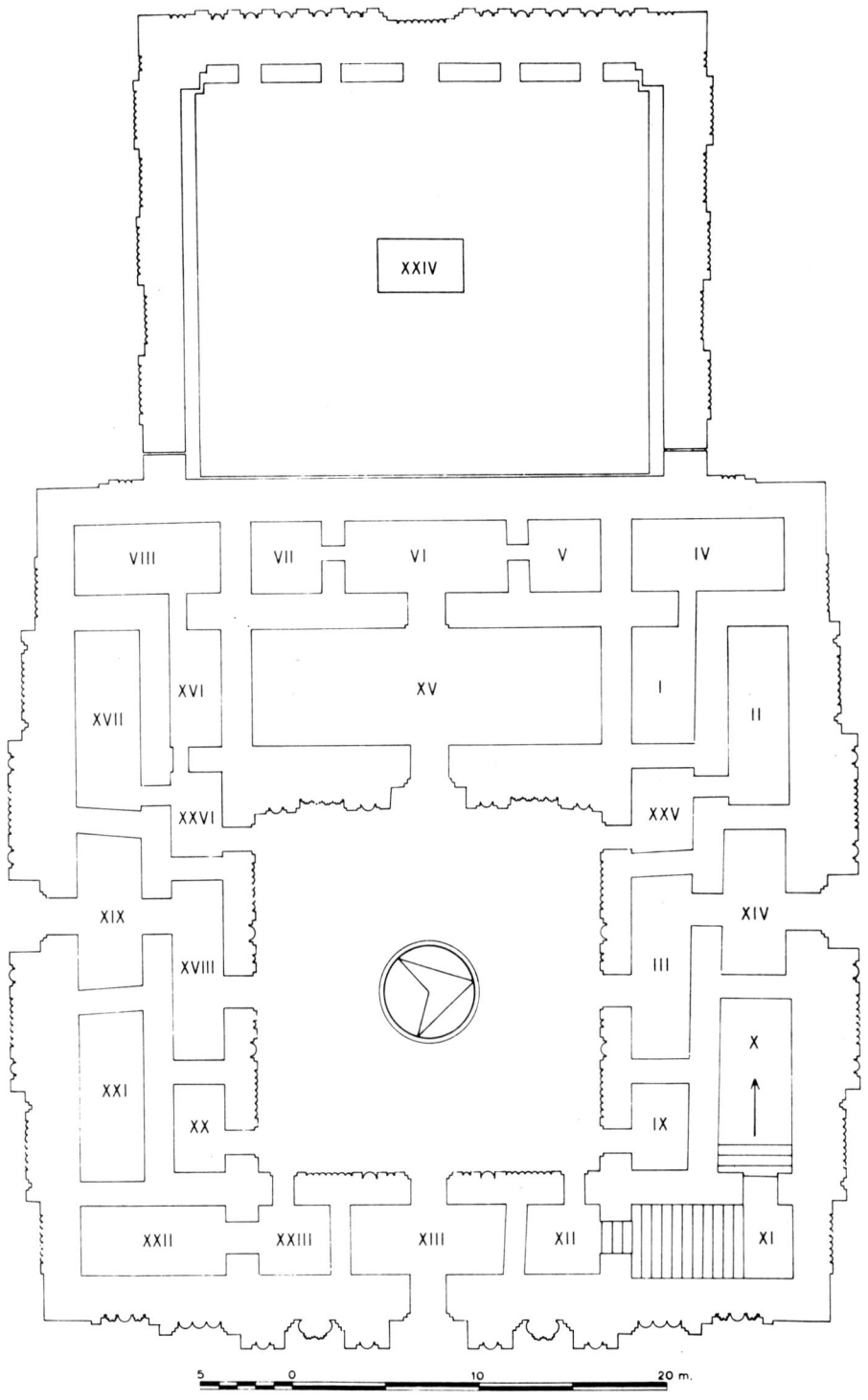

Fig. 69. Reconstructed plan of the temple.

temple of Ashur at Ashur itself was rebuilt by Shamshi-Adad on the Babylonian rather than the traditional Assyrian plan, and that before his conquest of Ashur he had, according to the Assyrian King List, spent some years in Babylonia where he would no doubt have become familiar with the latest fashions in architecture and developments in ceremonial. If we can then ascribe to him the original concept of the temple — and among the few tablets that are definitely associated with its first phase there is mention of a governor rather than a king — the second phase of the work was probably carried out by the independent rulers of Karana after Shamshi-Adad's death and the disintegration of his empire. It was certainly executed with much restricted resources. Although the main stair was built, the terrace that was originally intended to surround the temple and possibly also the high terrace on the west was never completed, and the north and south gates of the original plan were blocked from floor level. The city's rulers had been left with the temple as a white elephant, but were more concerned to establish their position in Mesopotamian politics, and therefore rebuilt the palace on a much grander scale.

At all events Karana reverted, after its brief period of patronage and then of independence, to the status of a country town prosperous enough but incapable of maintaining, much less replacing, the temple with which it had been endowed. There was a major attempt to reinforce the structure, probably about 1700 B.C., by the insertion of new supporting walls and arches, but thereafter the temple seems to have decayed slowly. The rooms around the courtyard were abandoned, perhaps because they were unsafe as they certainly were when we attempted to excavate them, and were gradually superseded by mid-2nd millennium and at the latest Middle Assyrian buildings of a much more flimsy nature. By about 1200 B.C. the only part of the original temple that remained in use was the focal point of the whole complex, the cella and ante-cella on the west side of the courtyard with some of their ancillary chambers. The result of this long period of neglect was an accumulation of occupation material within and over the walls of the Old Assyrian building which preserved them to a considerable height, in places over 6 m., and has thereby afforded us unique evidence not only of the elaborate decoration of the temple, but even of the methods of roofing employed in its first storey.

Within the temple the main approach through the east gate led across a courtyard some 19 m. square to the doorway of a broad ante-cella and, on the same axis, to the entrance of the cella. Another traditional feature of the Babylonian plan was an obviously ceremonial stairway reached from an angle of the courtyard. At Tell al Rimah it lay to the right of the main gate, leading up to a landing in the north-east corner of the building and thence turning left over the outer range of rooms along the north wall. Two important observations emerged from the excavation of this stair. The first flight was founded on solid mud-brick, but the second rested on eight transverse vaults of gradually increasing height, each supporting two steps. Secondly, the treads of the stair itself, which obviously emerged over the north gate-chamber, were entirely of unbaked brick and could not have been exposed to rain. We therefore inferred the existence of a second storey, of which vestiges were later found above a room north of the cella where the structure had been best protected from erosion by the mass of the high terrace behind it.

Vaults were also employed to roof most if not all of the ground floor rooms around the courtyard. They were constructed by a familiar method with the voussoirs laid radially, but their unusual feature to a modern eye is the high-pitched profile, of which a characteristic example is shown in fig. 70. The first few courses above the spring were slightly corbelled, and thereafter the voussoirs were turned at a gradual angle which permitted each to be supported by its predecessor and the adhesion of the mud mortar until the gap had narrowed to approximately half the original span, so that only the crown of the vault needed the support of scaffolding. This was obviously intended to economise in the use of timber, but the shortage of timber is a fact of Mesopotamian life that probably dictated the adoption of this method long before we find it at Tell al Rimah. In general, the builders of the temple display a familiarity with their techniques and material that can only derive from a long tradition. An example of this, particularly convincing because it occurs in an inconspicuous position, is the head of an internal doorway that still stands to its full height (fig. 70). Doorways of this size in ancient and modern buildings are usually spanned by timber lintels, often of poplar which is locally available. Here, however, the mason chose to build a flat arch, a feature which

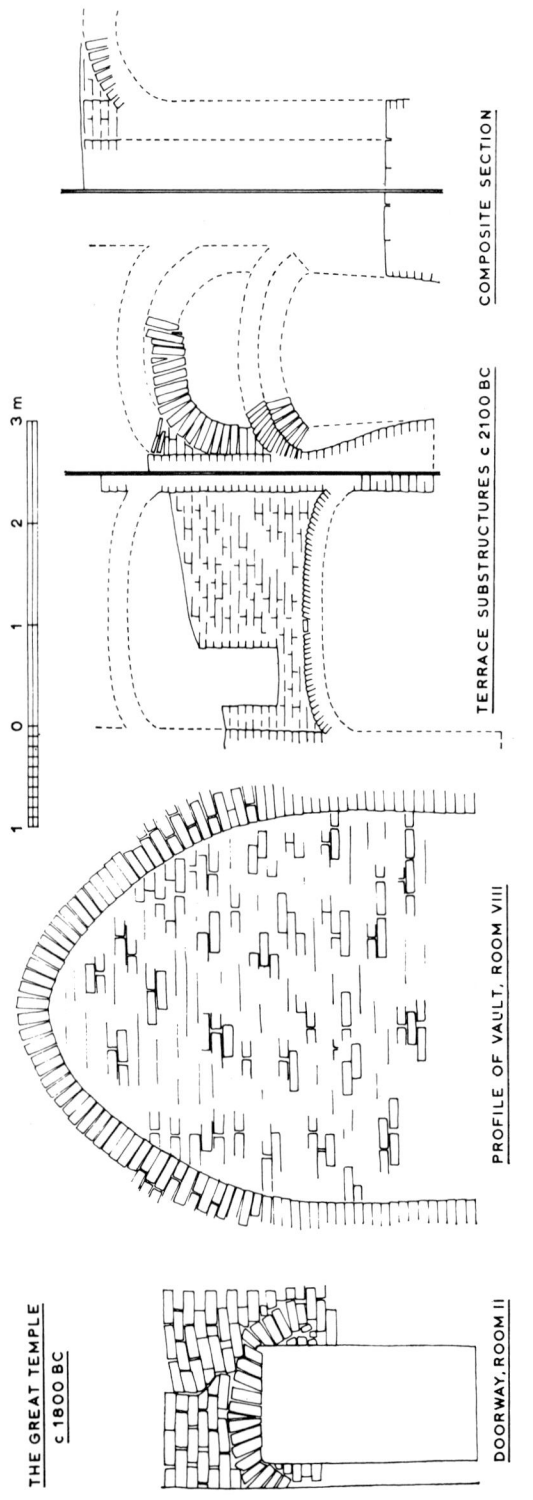

Fig. 70. Examples of mud-brick vault and arch construction.

one would have thought impossible to execute in unsupported mud-brick but which has survived for almost four thousand years.

Radial vaults were used in the only major reconstruction of the temple about a century later, and it is interesting that their profile was identical in significant details with those found in the only surviving rooms of the building that superseded the palace. Clearly the structural tradition that they represent continued at Tell al Rimah for a few generations after its brief moment of grandeur. There was, however, another technique of vault construction used in work that is more likely to have been carried out by local masons, in later repairs to the temple itself and much earlier in a terraced substructure far below the temple platform on the south slope of the mound, dated by pottery to the late 3rd millennium B.C. This method is commonly known as 'pitched-brick' vaulting, in which the need for timber centring is virtually eliminated by laying successive ring segments of bricks with their edges across the long axis of the vault. The laying starts from both ends simultaneously and each ring is inclined at a slight angle to rest on its predecessor, which supports it during construction. When the rings meet in the middle there remains a lozenge-shaped gap in the crown of the vault that is then filled with segments of diminishing size and finally plugged with brick fragments. Our earliest and most dramatic example of the use of this technique came from the late 3rd millennium building, which was clearly intended to support an upper terrace although nothing remained of the superstructure. It was a honeycomb of small vaulted chambers, accessible through low doorways opening off narrow passages, and at least three storeys high (fig. 70). The plan was irregular, since the builders obviously laid out the main lines of the supports required at the upper level and filled in the intervening spaces with a series of more or less flimsy structures erected by rule of thumb and taking advantage of earlier masonry where it existed. A very similar though much larger system of pitched-brick vaults was employed in the same way to terrace part of the Great Palace of the Byzantine Emperors in Constantinople in the 5th century A.D., and the technique was used in the famous Arch of Ctesiphon, south of Baghdad, in the 6th century Sassanian palace there. Although the evidence for continuity is lacking after the 2nd millennium at Tell al Rimah, where we have numerous examples, it seems reasonable to claim that this very distinctive method of roofing was a Mesopotamian invention. Moreover, our 3rd millennium vaults rested not directly against the end walls of the room as was the later practice but on pendentives, incurving triangles of brickwork in the four corners which are now the standard supports of a dome and were hitherto believed to have been invented some 2000 years later.

The second extraordinary feature of the temple that must be briefly described is the system of architectural decoration. The exterior of the building and the high terrace, together with the four internal facades of the courtyard, were elaborately ornamented with engaged columns, 277 in all. Of these 50 were of large size, about 60 cm. in width, standing either singly within rebated niches or in panels of four, and were all carved brick by brick to assume the form of spirals (fig. 71) or of two types of palm trunk that can still be seen today, one trimmed close to the trunk, the other with longer triangular frond scars. An exception to the standard pattern were two columns of quatrefoil plan in deep recesses in the towers that flanked the east gate, each with two palm trunks at the rear and two opposed spiral columns at the front. The other smaller columns were undecorated and normally arranged in panels of seven. This building is the only complete example we have of such an elaborate design, which might indeed have been submitted as a student's exercise for an architectural prize when baroque was the height of fashion, though there are individual examples of the use of engaged columns elsewhere. In the Bastion of Warad-Sin at Ur c. 1830 B.C. we find palm-trunk columns flanking the main entrance, and spiral columns have recently been reported on the facade of a building at Tell Leilan in north-eastern Syria which the excavator also associates with the time of Shamshi-Adad. We also, exceptionally in northern

Fig. 71. The western façade of the temple courtyard, showing a panel of four spiral columns and the entrance to the antecella.

Mesopotamia, found large blocks of stone originally used as impost blocks for the lintels of the east gate and the entrance to the ante-cella. Their outer ends were carved in high relief, the inner pair with the goddess Lama between two palm trees and a Humbaba mask, the outer with a second Humbaba and a bull-man, here unusually depicted in a long skirt. Only the Lama figure had ever been inscribed, and unfortunately the text was almost entirely eroded.

The import blocks from the ante-chamber doorway were actually found well below their original position at lintel height, reset on either side of the entrance at the mid-15th century ground level, some 2 m. above the original courtyard pavement. At this time there was a small room to the right of

Fig. 72. View of the Late Assyrian shrine.

the doorway in which we found a collection of glazed frit and glass objects including pendants and a large number of beads of various design. The presence of this material indicates a destruction level and, together with associated pottery, bears such a striking resemblance to the finds from Nuzi that they must be of approximately the same date, about 1450 B.C. It appears that the break in occupation, if any, was quite short since the level immediately above was of the Middle Assyrian period, perhaps reflecting the restoration of Assyrian power under Ashur-uballit c. 1380 B.C. When the end finally came we do not know, but we would guess about the end of the 13th century when Assyria was in disarray during the last years of Tukulti-Ninurta I and this part of the Jazira was probably experiencing the first impact of the nomadic Aramaean tribes. Since these events coincided with turmoil in the Levant and the depredations of the 'Peoples of the Sea', we may wonder whether a minor climatic change may have been a contributory factor, but of this there is as yet no evidence. The end of the Middle Assyrian occupation at Tell al Rimah produced another collection of glass and glazed frit objects, including the finest of a number of frit masks (col. pl. 6c). Our most poignant discovery, however, was a layer immediately overlying the Middle Assyrian marble dais in the cella, containing quantities of animal coprolites and covered in its turn by 4 m. of barren silt. Obviously the last purpose the temple served was a shelter for shepherds and their flocks.

By the 9th century B.C. when the Late Assyrian Empire was beginning to extend its power westward towards the Levant, the intervening territory in the northern Jazira was gradually brought back under control and may well have been resettled with some of the people transported from conquered territories who were first used as forced labour in the construction of the new imperial capital at Nimrud (Kalhu). We found evidence of settlement of this date on top of the low mound overlying the palace site and, in the form of large open villages, in many places in the surrounding countryside. But an entirely unexpected addition to our knowledge of this period was a small temple (fig. 72) of the standard Late Assyrian plan, which had been terraced into the side of the high terrace—by now obviously a grass-grown mound—and overlay its junction with the north-west corner of the temple. It consisted of an entrance flanked by two project-

Fig. 73. Stele of Adad-Nirari III.

ing towers, leading down the long axis of the antecella to a slightly raised cella, with a podium at the back surfaced with a slab of Mosul marble. Nothing was found on the podium but a series of depressions in the surface indicated that it had originally supported an enthroned statue. On either side of the entrance to the cella was a pair of orthostats, probably supports at floor level for engaged columns, and each carved with a lion mask with a dagger blade extending downward from its mouth. Another similar pair was found out of position and may have adorned the entrance of the temple. All had been inscribed but the inscriptions had been deliberately obliterated.

The most exciting find, however, was a royal stele of Adadnirari III, 810–783 B.C., which stood to the left of the podium with the king's hand raised in the standard gesture of salute to the deity and the symbols of the gods above his head (fig. 73). The stele, by contrast with some of its provincial neighbours of the same date, was obviously carved by craftsmen trained in the best tradition of palace sculpture. An inscription that covered the lower half of the slab had been partly and again intentionally defaced, but the missing portion could be reconstructed from the traces that remained. The surviving text included a dedication to Adad 'who dwells in Zamahu' and the king's name and titles with a brief account of events in his reign, sufficient to date the stele to 796 B.C. or just after. Unless the stele had been brought to Tell al Rimah from elsewhere, which seems unlikely, the temple was dedicated to Adad and the Late Assyrian name of the site was Zamahu, confirming that the existence of Karana had been forgotten for more than three centuries. Moreover, the presence of the temple and of a royal stele of this quality argues that Zamahu was an important local centre. The effaced lines of the inscription were of great interest, for they recorded the foundation of numerous settlements in the Jazira by Nergal-Eresh who is known as governor of Rasappa, the senior Assyrian provincial governor at this time who held the office for about thirty years and was effectively, in English terms, 'Lord of the Western Marches'. We do not know when or why the references to his achievements were deleted. Although he says that the new settlements were founded 'in the name of his lord', he gave his own name to one of them and may have transgressed his authority, especially in the eyes of later rulers concerned with increasing the control of the court bureaucracy over the provinces. The end of the Late Assyrian occupation of Tell al Rimah must have occurred some time in the late 7th century, and certainly before the final collapse of the Empire with the fall of Nineveh in 612 B.C. There are no signs of later settlement, and the site might well be described in the words that Ammianus Marcellinus used of Hatra, some fifty miles to the south 'vetus oppidum in media solitudine positum, olimque desertum'.

I should like to conclude this account with an acknowledgement of the help and support I received from all those who worked at Tell al Rimah over many seasons. None has been mentioned by name, but they will recognize their individual contributions as I most gratefully do.

Bibliography

D. Oates, Preliminary reports on Tell al Rimah in *Iraq* XXVII (1965), 62–80; XXVIII (1966), 122–39; XXIX (1967), 70–96; XXX (1968), 115–138; XXXII (1970), 1–26; XXXIV (1972), 77–86.

—*Studies in the Ancient History of Northern Iraq* (London 1968).

—'Early vaulting in Mesopotamia' in D. E. Strong (ed.), *Archaeological Theory and Practice* (London 1973), 183–91.

S. Dalley, C. B. F. Walker and J. D. Hawkins, *The Old Babylonian Tablets from Tell al Rimah* (London 1976).

S. Page (Dalley), 'A stela of Adad-Nirari III and Nergal-Ereš from Tell al Rimah', *Iraq* XXX (1968), 139–53.

H. W. F. Saggs, 'The Tell al Rimah Tablets, 1965', *Iraq* XXX (1968), 154–74.

D. J. Wiseman, 'The Tell al Rimah Tablets, 1966', *Iraq* XXX (1968), 175–205.

S. Lloyd, 'Some ancient sites in the Sinjar district', *Iraq* V (1938), 123–42.

Nimrud

By Julian Reade

In recent years there has been a great revival in studies of the Neo-Assyrian empire. This small kingdom, from its base in northern Iraq, maintained a position of hegemony over the Near East for two and a half centuries and eventually, in the 7th century B.C., imposed direct rule over an area extending from Iran to Egypt. A great wealth of material illuminating these developments was obtained from various Assyrian cities in the nineteenth and early twentieth centuries, but in many ways it remained poorly published and inadequately understood. Only now is its potential value for social and economic history being fully appreciated. This phenomenon is due in no small measure to the excavations of the British School, with support from other institutions, at Nimrud, the city which was once the administrative capital of Assyria (col. pl. 7a).

In 1852 Henry Rawlinson, one of the pioneers of Assyrian studies, had written off Nimrud as virtually exhausted. It was of course Professor Max Mallowan, Sir Max as he later became, who had the imagination to realize that a city like this might have more to offer than the sculptured palaces for which it was best known. The School's Nimrud excavations, the largest and longest-running project in which it has been involved, were initiated by Mallowan, with characteristic panache and determination, in 1949, hardly a time that can have seemed auspicious for the reopening of work at one of the biggest sites in Iraq. They were carried on annually, with two interruptions, up to 1963, with progress reports regularly appearing in the journal *Iraq*. Up to 1957, Mallowan was director in the field; he always retained a close interest in the work, and wrote the detailed account of all the excavations which appeared in 1966 as *Nimrud and its Remains*. I was myself frequently reminded, as a junior assistant in the last seasons, that Max was still present in spirit. In practice, however, from 1958 to 1962, the director was David Oates, while Jeffery Orchard took over for the last season in 1963. Thus it was Oates who was primarily responsible for the work at the arsenal or military camp, Fort Shalmaneser; the magnificent architecture of this building, with its seemingly limitless hoards of carved ivory, provided a fitting climax to the years of labour whose lighter side is characteristically described in *Mallowan's Memoirs*.

It is difficult, in 1981, when the main results of the School's Nimrud dig have long been familiar, to think back to the situation as it was before Mallowan arrived there. There is equally no point in attempting to summarize his own analyses of what was achieved. In this account, therefore, I shall concentrate in general terms on what are in my view some of the more significant aspects of the work. First of all, however, something should be said about the historical and geographical background.

Nimrud is situated on the north-east side of the Tigris, on a bluff overlooking the river, at a point where it is joined by a small tributary stream, about 35 km. downstream of the modern town of Mosul. A map made by the naval officer Felix Jones in 1852, at the time of earlier British excavations, shows the surroundings well (fig. 74). There is the wide flood-plain and, behind Nimrud, the rolling farmland of Assyria; in this district there is usually enough precipitation to ensure ample crops of grain. A bitumen source near the town provided a raw material widely used for waterproofing and other purposes in the past. The Tigris itself is fairly easy to cross in this vicinity.

The site of Nimrud was occupied in prehistory, but this is an age of which we know very little, since the early remains are deeply buried and have only been exposed in occasional nineteenth century tunnels on the mound. Mallowan identified painted Ninevite 5 pottery from these levels, which may be dated about 3000 B.C., while a stone cist grave of the mid-2nd millennium was still visible under the Burnt Palace in the 1960's. It is in the Middle Assyrian period, around 1200 B.C., that the town, by then known as Kalhu, emerges into the light of history as a provincial administrative centre. One building thought to have existed from an early date was the temple of Ishtar Kidmuri, and it was not far south of here, in a deep sounding, that Mallowan recovered archaeological evidence for the city's Middle Assyrian past: his material included glazed faience rosettes, probably from a temple, which were virtually identical with some later discovered by Oates in the ruins of Middle Assyrian Tell al Rimah. Again, however, at Nimrud, remains of this period were much too deeply buried for it to

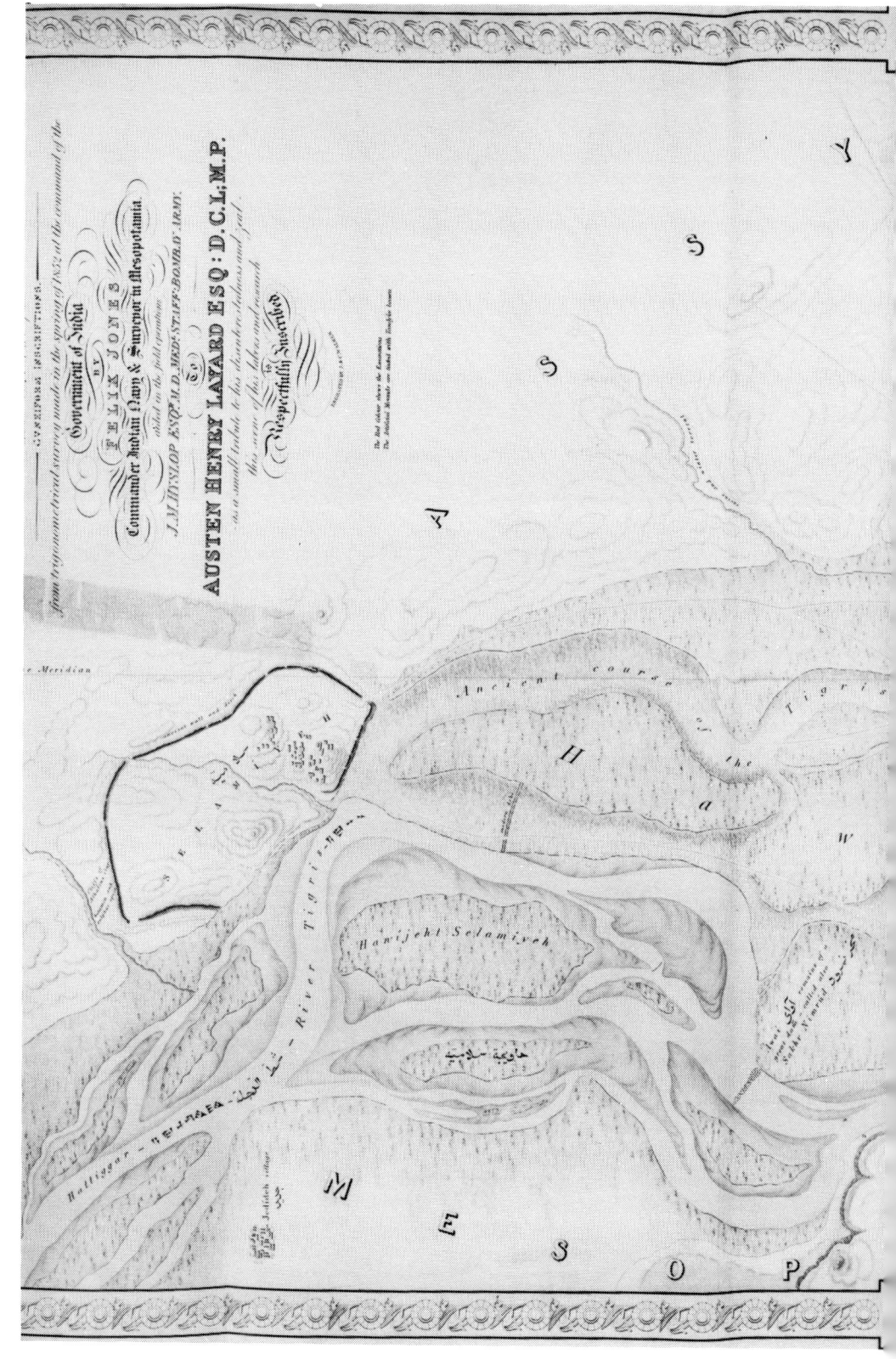

Fig. 74. Nimrud and its surroundings, surveyed by Felix Jones, 1852.

have been a suitable place to look for them on any extensive scale.

The man to whom Nimrud/Kalhu (Calah in the Bible) really owes its fame is Ashurnasirpal II, king of Assyria from 884 to 859 B.C. He continued the work of his royal predecessors by carrying Assyrian arms to the shores of the Mediterranean and re-establishing his kingdom as the dominant power in the Near East. It is not clear whether the king's main base at the start of his reign was the ancient Assyrian capital of Ashur, further down the Tigris, or the city of Nineveh in the other direction; but by 879 he had decided that he needed to construct a new capital between the two, a city that would both function as an imperial administrative centre and commemorate his reign in the time to come. He chose, then, the old town of Kalhu. The site is not where one would necessarily have expected a major city. On the other hand, there is yet another ancient walled town in the neighbourhood: this is Selamieh, marked on Felix Jones' map, possibly a Sasanian or early Islamic centre. The natural advantages of the area may then have been more apparent in antiquity than they are today, and they were enhanced by Ashurnasirpal's irrigation canal, which brought water to Nimrud from the Greater Zab river.

Among the most notable discoveries of Mallowan's early seasons at Nimrud was a stele of fine yellow stone, published by D. J. Wiseman. This was originally placed close to one of the main doors into the throneroom of Ashurnasirpal's palace; Layard's 19th century excavations had missed the stele by only a few feet. On it Ashurnasirpal recorded, below a small carving of himself, the celebrations at which he inaugurated his new palace on its completion. The text, written towards the end of his reign, besides recording in summary form his principal achievements, records how he repopulated Kalhu with people deported from at least eight lands which he had conquered; the lands included the Suleimaniye region in Iraqi Kurdistan, the region around Diyarbekir on the Upper Tigris in Turkey, various towns on the Syrian Euphrates, and the neighbourhood of Turkish Antakya, close to the Mediterranean. We are then given something not unlike a census figure for the population—specifically the number of guests who are said to have attended the inaugural feast. There were 69,574 in all; of these 47,074 were guests, male and female, from elsewhere in the empire; 5,000 were representatives of foreign states; 1,500 were government functionaries, presumably mostly resident at Kalhu; 16,000 were the people of the city of Kalhu. Clearly such figures are not precise, and need careful interpretation. Thus we might naturally understand the last 16,000 as comprising men, women, and children above a few years of age; and the city of Kalhu might naturally include in this context its extramural dependencies and peripheral villages. The details are arguable. On the other hand a thoughtful analysis of local resources by Oates, on the basis of observations made during the Nimrud dig, has shown that "without any external stimulus to its economy which might cause an artificial increase in the total population, the original city of Kalhu might have numbered at most 12,000 inhabitants." This figure might in optimum conditions be approximately doubled by systematic irrigation of the river valley. Oates' figures are based on the numbers of people who might have been supported by farming or ancillary activities carried on within a radius of some 7 km. of the city; if we include the inhabitants of more distant villages within the administrative sphere of Kalhu, then the maximum figure is higher still, say 25,000. Such calculations, admittedly very rough, do provide some kind of independent check on Ashurnasirpal's figures, and they suggest that his total of 16,000 or 17,500 for the permanent population of Kalhu and its hinterland about 860 B.C. is not merely possible but eminently reasonable, and does not deserve the suspicion sometimes attached to Assyrian statistics. There may in addition, during the construction of the city, have been many other conscript or temporary workers who may help account for the remarkable total of 47,074 Assyrians from other parts of the country.

At the same time we should not ourselves overestimate the numbers of men required for Ashurnasirpal's great project. Thus, one of the most important requirements was evidently the townwall. This was about 7.5 km. long, enclosing an area of some 360 hectares (fig. 75). This wall was built in part on stone foundations, terraced against the underlying conglomerate, and had buttresses or towers at intervals; at one point where fortifications encircle the citadel on the landward side Mallowan found traces of a double wall, with an extra defensive platform on the outside. But at one possibly typical point in the outer town, just west of the arsenal, the wall was found to be about 12 m.

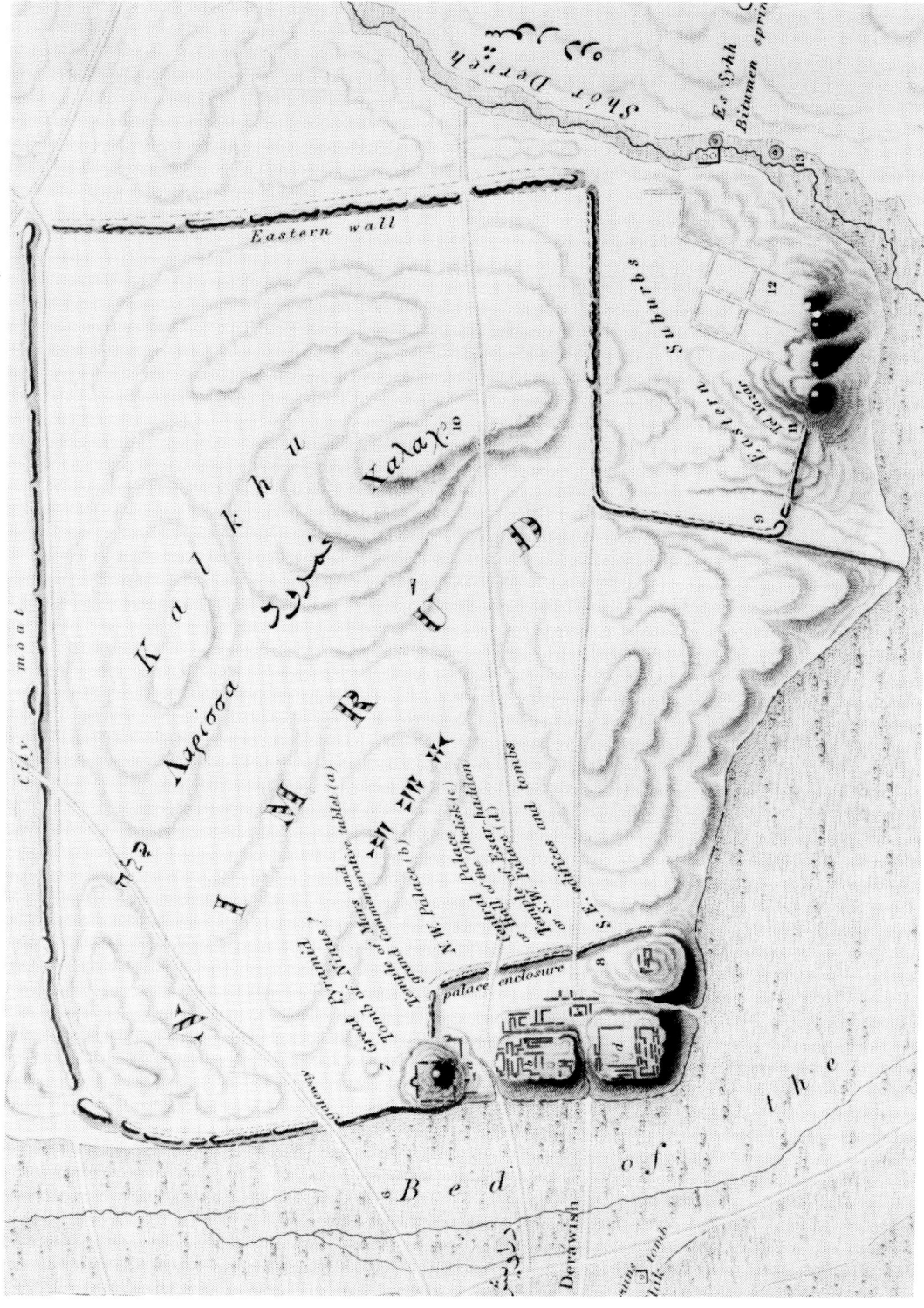

Fig. 75. The walls of Nimrud, as surveyed by Felix Jones in 1852, with the citadel at centre left and Fort Shalmaneser at lower right.

Fig. 77. Fort Shalmaneser: Esarhaddon's postern gate.

Fig. 76. West wall of Nimrud citadel, with ziggurrat in background.

wide, and this seems a fair minimum. Its average height may be taken as about 15 m., equivalent to the 120 brick-courses mentioned by Ashurnasirpal as the height of the citadel platform. If we then take the average Neo-Assyrian mud-brick with its surrounding mortar as being some 40 cm. square, we may estimate that the construction of the town-wall required some seventy million bricks. Such a figure gives at least some idea of the scale involved. Now, according to Mallowan, "those who have practical experience of building in the Near East will know that one man can comfortably lay 100 bricks in one day . . . this was the accepted rate of bricklaying in Assyrian times . . . it follows on this basis that 100 men can lay a million bricks in 100 days . . ." Or, 700 men could lay seventy million bricks in 1000 days. Whatever the deficiencies of these calculations Mallowan was surely right in concluding that it was "well within the capacity of the Assyrians to build the bare walls of Calah within five years."

On the citadel Mallowan exposed not only the mud-brick wall facing the inner town, at this point no less than 37 m. thick, but also the more elaborate frontage on to the Tigris flood plain. Here Ashurnasirpal's work seemed to be represented by a substructure of neatly cut blocks of limestone; these were largely concealed by an outer skin of much more massive blocks (fig. 76), dating perhaps from the reign of Tiglath-pileser III or Sargon in the late 8th century. Here, however, the kings responsible failed to leave inscribed records of their work at the points which came to be excavated. In one sector the stone wall was found to have been about 10 m. high; the upper courses were dressed, but the lower five, which would probably have been below the level of water from the Tigris, were left rough-hewn. This stonework provides an imposing contrast to the more vulnerable mud-brick structures most commonly associated with Assyria.

It was Esarhaddon, about 672, who was responsible for the finest surviving section of town-wall to be uncovered by the School. In the south-eastern corner of the town, below the great arsenal of Fort Shalmaneser, he refaced a particularly prominent section of the wall in stone, and at one point renovated a postern gate, giving it a corbelled archway of stone blocks (fig. 77). It is odd that the Assyrians, familiar as they were with various techniques of arching in brick, seem to have preferred corbelling when they came to work in stone, but the results have a monumental solidity. Esarhaddon ensured that his name would not be forgotten, as a text describing the work was inscribed in duplicate on each side of the entrance (fig. 78).

The School's work in the earlier seasons at

Fig. 78. Fort Shalmaneser: inscription on postern gate.

Nimrud was largely concentrated on the citadel, an area twenty hectares in size on a massive platform. Here the most famous building is unquestionably the North-West Palace of Ashurnasirpal, from which in the nineteenth century Layard extracted vast quantities of sculptured bas-reliefs, superbly preserved, which are now scattered across Europe and America. This was Layard's first discovery, and it was here appropriately that Mallowan commenced work in 1949. The plan of the palace, as left by Layard, showed the sculptured rooms enclosing a single courtyard, but we now know that this was only the heart of a much more elaborate building. On the north, outside the throneroom, was another much bigger courtyard, over 50 m. square, and it was on the far side of this that the School recovered in 1953 a cache of tablets forming part of the official correspondence of the Assyrian kings. These tablets, being published by H. W. F. Saggs, date from the last third of the 8th century, from the reigns of Tiglath-pileser III, possibly Shalmaneser V, and Sargon, and they confirm that the North-West Palace was still then being used as an administrative centre. They include a series of official reports from men stationed in newly conquered areas as far apart as Babylonia and Phoenicia, and illustrate the thoroughness with which the Assyrians approached the problems of imperial administration, and the degree to which central government concerned itself with the trivia of provincial administration. These letters, filed and abandoned when the court moved from Nimrud to Sargon's new capital of Khorsabad about 707, are in the same category as archives found in the last century at Nineveh, but refer to a slightly earlier period.

Elsewhere in the North-West Palace there were other remnants of the 150 years during which it had been a major royal establishment. Layard had found much: glass bearing Sargon's name; a magnificent collection of bronzes; and some elaborately carved ivories which probably derived largely from furniture sent as tribute, or collected as loot, from the merchant cities of Syria and Phoenicia. Indeed one of Mallowan's first finds was an ivory cow, lying on a small patch of floor which had escaped attention in the nineteenth century. As he remarked, it was a good omen for the excavations, and in due course ivories were to emerge in quantities that may seem incredible to those who never saw them. Some of the first groups, however, were notable for quality rather than quantity, for they came from deep wells in the North-West Palace where damp soil had ensured their preservation in exceptional condition. Mallowan tried three wells in all, but one of them proved too dangerous to clear. A second had been cleared to a depth of over 22 m. when work came to a hurried stop as the whole bottom of the well caved in with a thunderous roar. Among the finds already made there, however, was a group of oblong ivory and wooden boards with raised edges; the sunken framed areas had once been covered with a mixture of beeswax and yellow orpiment, and a few surviving fragments showed that this covering had been inscribed, with some two columns of 125 lines apiece on each board. The boards had originally been hinged together, and the outermost one in the ivory set gave the name of Sargon, the king for whom the book was made, and of the text: it was a traditional series of astrological omens, of a kind regularly consulted by Assyrian officials. Such board books are shown on Assyrian sculptures, and some had previously been found at Mediterranean sites, but these were the first examples from Mesopotamia itself.

A third well produced fragments of carved ivory furniture. One fine female head, nicknamed the Mona Lisa in contrast to another, the Ugly Sister, which came up shortly afterwards, was unusually large, 16 cm. high. The lady's hair, eye-brows, and pupils of the eyes were stained black, a colour which Mallowan suggested might originally have been the famous Tyrian purple. The exceptional nature of this group of ivories was confirmed by a pair of plaques each of which showed a lion killing an African under a floral canopy. Both had been embellished with gold leaf and with inlays of carnelian and lapis lazuli, while the curls of the African's black hair had been rendered by the insertion of gold-capped ivory pegs. The technique is a more sumptuous variety of one known from many other plaques, comparable in style, which were also overlaid with gold leaf but were inlaid with cheaper materials, red and blue glass or paste (fig. 79). Further fine ivories have since been recovered from this same well by the Iraq authorities, who have cleared it to a greater depth than Mallowan, with the limited equipment at his disposal, considered advisable.

The circumstances in which ivory furniture came to be thrown down wells are uncertain. Mallowan

Some of the North-West Palace rooms cleared by Mallowan were paved with stamped bricks not of Ashurnasirpal but of his son Shalmaneser III. Though it had long been known that this king continued his father's work at Nimrud, and that he was indeed responsible for the construction of the ziggurrat which is now the most prominent feature of the site, the School's excavations greatly illuminated the extent of his activities. For instance, the only main gateway to the citadel yet discovered was flanked by a stone lion of Shalmaneser III. Similarly, bricks of this king were found in two substantial administrative buildings on the citadel, one of which produced archives of governors of Kalhu in the 9th and 8th centuries, now published by J. N. Postgate. More traces of Shalmaneser's work were found by Mallowan in the south-eastern corner of the citadel. There was also a broken statue, apparently of the same king, from the vicinity of the Ninurta Temple at the northern end of the citadel, and another that was found in fragments at the base of the mound, presumably having been thrown from the walls. It was the city's arsenal or barracks, however, a massive complex to which the excavators gave the name of Fort Shalmaneser, that seems to have been his biggest single project. This was not on the citadel at all, but occupied a position in the far south-eastern corner of the town, a suitably remote place, perhaps, for the stationing of potentially riotous soldiery.

Fig. 79. Inlaid ivory plaque, in "Phoenician" style, from Fort Shalmaneser, SW 11/12.

The outer walls of the arsenal, to judge by surface indications, enclosed an area of about 750 by 500 m.; it is visible on Felix Jones' map, which even treats the enclosure wall of the arsenal as the town-wall itself. The main arsenal building, already observed by Jones whose map indicates the courtyards, measured some 350 by 250 m., and was itself fortified. Most of it was examined in the seasons when Oates was directing the School's excavations, and it is now one of the better understood Assyrian buildings.

It was dominated by a set of massive formal apartments in the principal one of which was a carved and inscribed throne dais, probably the finest piece of Assyrian sculpture to have emerged since the nineteenth century. On its sides were scenes of tribute, and on the front appeared a summit meeting between the kings of Assyria and Babylon. This monument, emphasizing Assyria's role as peacemaker rather than warmonger, had been presented to Shalmaneser by the governor of

first suggested that this might have happened during civil disturbances in Assyria about the end of Sargon's reign, but eventually preferred the Median sack of Nimrud about 614–612. Much depends on the status of the North-West Palace after it ceased to be a major royal residence. Thus, some of the sculptured wall-slabs in the state apartments seem to have been removed for re-use elsewhere before the sack of Nimrud, while those that remained in position were not subjected to the kind of conflagration that destroyed equivalent areas of other Assyrian palaces. This may imply that parts of the North-West Palace were already abandoned, in which case they would hardly have been suitable for the storage of objects decorated with gold. On the other hand some rooms, especially those around the outer courtyard, were still in use shortly before 614, since dated texts of this period have been found there. This is a problem which may yet be resolved by careful analysis of the building's internal stratigraphy.

Kalhu; the text was published by P. Hulin. It is now installed in the Iraq Museum, where it was transported with the aid of engineers and equipment generously lent by the Iraq Petroleum Company—a remarkable contrast with the days when Layard shifted much larger stones by manpower, wooden levers, carts, and rafts.

Only one of the main doors into this throneroom complex was fully excavated, but this produced another impressive monument now too in the Iraq Museum, a panel of brightly coloured glazed bricks which had originally been placed above the door. Fragments of such glazed panels had been known previously, from 19th century work, but this one could be reconstructed in its entirety. Other rooms of the main reception suites were lavishly painted, but it was not practicable to remove the fragile plaster, and it is now reburied (col. pls. 7b-c).

Outside the throneroom area were three oblong courtyards, with sides ranging between 50 and 100 m. in length, and a fourth area of comparable size which had been subdivided. One courtyard had, against one wall, a royal throne dais for outdoor reviews. The rooms lining the courtyards included residential units for officials and guards; workshops for craftsmen such as armourers and stonemasons; and many storage areas, including a wine-cellar. These busy parts were firmly separated, by intricacies of the architectural plan, from an extensive domestic area which included a female housekeeper's apartments. Various documents, especially wine-ration texts studied by J. Kinnier Wilson, S. Parpola and others, contain information about the many officials and different categories of government employee stationed in the arsenal; many of these texts are particularly valuable since they date from the first half of the 8th century, a period of imperial consolidation rather than expansion, and one which was previously very little known.

It was in Fort Shalmaneser that the School found the bulk of the carved ivories the recovery and conservation of which absorbed a large proportion of the expedition's resources during the final seasons at Nimrud. In some storerooms the fragments were to be found, not far below the surface, lying profuse as stones in a Cotswold garden. When freshly taken from the earth, they were pale yellow in colour, with a consistency not unlike that of processed cheese; later if allowed to dry untreated, they would become whiter and more brittle.

Various methods of treatment were tried, but the ones finally evolved were relatively simple and straightforward. The primary excavation of these objects, many of which were carved in exquisite detail, was largely entrusted to two supremely dexterous workmen, who extracted them on individual lumps of soil, which were then wedged securely on trays. Next there was the slow and perilous drive to the dig-house, where the ivories were placed on shelves, ready for further cleaning and consolidation with polyvinyl acetate. It was work often lasting far into the night, in which virtually all the staff, led by trained conservators from the London Institute of Archaeology, would participate. The problems were comparable with those presented by unbaked clay cuneiform tablets: for a few hours after exposure, the wet earth could

Fig. 80. Openwork ivory plaque in "Phoenician" style. From Fort Shalmaneser, SW 11/12. ND 12033, ht. 10.1 cm.

be easily detached from the soft ivory, and some of the most skilled practitioners preferred to do much of the cleaning then; alternatively one could wait until the ivory was harder, but then the earth was hard too, and had to be softened by repeated dabs of methylated spirit or acetone in order to separate it from the ivory surface to which it clung. Each case had to be judged on its merits, with some deserving priority treatment. Particular difficulties arose with those pieces that lay face-down, and which were liable to need their backs bandaged before they could be turned over. Perhaps the most difficult of all, and very numerous, were the larger segments of furniture, the surface and interior of which were frequently rotten; many of these were plain or decorated only with simple mouldings, but among them too were lions that required hours of devoted attention. The easiest were the fragments of plain veneer, which were also found in great quantities.

In one room a set of ivory chair-backs was uncovered, lying stacked as the Assyrians had left them, and in another there were the elements of what may have been a couch (col. pl. 8a). Mostly, however, the carved fragments were distributed pell-mell in the soil, mixed with mud-brick, and it was impossible to establish their original relationship to one another. The chaos was most vividly illustrated in one room, T 10, which had been burnt, so that the ivories were brown, black, blue, or, as the heat finally twisted them out of recognition, a greyish white. In a section through T 10 one could see veins of ash and ivory sandwiched between thicker layers of fallen brick, as if each successive collapse of a chunk of wall had thrown up a new shower of debris from the floor. These burnt ivories were much stronger, and easier to clean, than the others. Sometimes one only needed a soft brush, and had the satisfaction of being able to think about details as they emerged. There were the fragments with alphabetic inscriptions: a casual check in the small dig library revealed that one inscription was identical with that on an ivory from Arslan Tash in Syria, and gave the name of Hazael, probably the 9th century king of Damascus, as later published by A. R. Millard. There were the small fragments, shell rather than ivory, incised with marks that suddenly became recognizable as Hittite hieroglyphs, to be read by R. D. Barnett as the name of Urhilina, a 9th century king of Hama. And there was a continuous stream of minor observations, such as the way in which the different surface colours of stained polychrome ivories were echoed still by differential burning.

The question of the date and origin of the Nimrud ivories is one of great complexity. In broad terms one can distinguish three main groups: there are those which are closely related in style and subject matter to native Assyrian sculpture and painting of the 9th and 8th centuries, and which were presumably made in Assyria itself—most of these have been collected together in one volume by Mallowan and L. G. Davies; then there are those which show themes of unmistakably Egyptian origin, sometimes specifically associated with the XXIInd Dynasty (c. 945–718), and which mostly appear to have been made in areas such as the Phoenician coast and Palestine which had close commercial and other contacts with Egypt (fig. 80); and finally there are those which, while often influenced from Egypt, have their closest parallels in the art of central and northern Syria and southern Turkey, and which are therefore loosely grouped together under the label "Syrian" (figs. 81–82). It should eventually be possible, with careful analysis, to distinguish the products of particular towns or workshops. This can only be undertaken methodically when the primary publication of the ivories has been completed, but some interesting suggestions have already been made concerning the group of chairbacks from one room, SW 7, which were fully published by Mallowan and G. Herrmann. These were not only found stacked together, but were closely related stylistically, and I. Winter has shown that they are likely to have originated in the kingdom of Sam'al, north-west of Aleppo, about the middle of the 8th century. Presumably they originally belonged to a single batch of tribute or booty, and this raises the question of how far such shipments were in fact redistributed after arriving in Assyria. Perhaps some were simply left in store, with other goods of similar origin, so that their archaeological provenance may reflect the source of manufacture or, at any rate, the source from which the Assyrians collected them. Certainly ivories from particular rooms seemed sometimes to have distinctive features—there was a strong contrast, for instance, between the SW 12 and T 10 material, with the latter including much that was reminiscent of late 10th or early 9th century Tell Halaf ivories, but little or nothing plainly Phoenician. One explana-

Fig. 81. Ivory plaque in "Syrian" style. From Fort Shalmaneser, SW 11/12. ND 12154, ht. 12.7 cm.

more than once about 614–612, with intervening periods of abortive Assyrian salvage and tidying up, and we should not place too much reliance on the association of objects in any particular storeroom.

While the basic plan of this great arsenal building was probably determined under Shalmaneser III in the mid-9th century, the School's excavations showed that some of the residential apartments were only completed under his grandson, Adad-nirari III. There were naturally various changes and renovations during the two and a half centuries of the building's existence, not all easily dated, but the most important were those undertaken by Esarhaddon about 672. This king's work, like contemporaneous repairs to the city wall, seems to have been done with the intention of re-establishing Kalhu as administrative capital of the empire; any

Fig. 82. Ivory furniture element in "Syrian" style. From Fort Shalmaneser, SW 11/12. ND 12042, ht. 22.2 cm.

tion may be that T 10, a room in the state apartments, was furnished in the 9th century and remained in much the same condition for the next two centuries. The magazines, in contrast, SW 11–12, SW 37, and doubtless others, may have been repositories for interminable loads of ivory furniture and other precious but virtually unwanted goods that kept arriving from every Assyrian campaign to the west. Thus the brilliant red and yellow ochreous colours which stained the lower fill of SW 11 might have derived from a huge heap of textiles. On the other hand, all the rooms in Fort Shalmaneser, whatever their original function, are likely to have been ransacked by enemy soldiers such scheme lapsed on Esarhaddon's death, but some monumental architecture survived. Thus the new postern-gate at the south-western corner of Fort Shalmaneser led in to a ramp which ran, through a series of arched rooms, up to the internal floor level; at least one of the rooms was painted, probably with scenes of the king and courtiers returning from the hunt. At the head of the ramp stood what is still a massive mound encased in mudbrick. One of the most skilled Sherqati pickmen, in 1963, worked his way round this mound without finding any way in, and it is possible that there were rooms at a high level, approached by an internal staircase through R 10 or by an external staircase on the west. A sounding on top of the mound exposed part of a structure, Assyrian or later, with its floor not far below the surface.

On the citadel mound, too, work continued after Ashurnasirpal and Shalmaneser. The most significant building of a later phase cleared by the School was in the south-eastern corner. This entire area of the mound had been something of a puzzle to the nineteenth century excavators, whose operations were hampered by a large amount of Hellenistic debris; the underlying Assyrian remains were vaguely known as the South-East Palace, but incorporated at least three distinct buildings. One of these, the Nabu Temple, was investigated by Mallowan and Oates, who were able to establish its original plan and trace its history from its foundation under Adad-nirari III to the end of the Assyrian empire. This building, with its two sets of twin shrines, had probably developed by the late 7th century into the principal religious building of Kalhu, and part of it may even have been rebuilt after the fall of the empire.

Appropriately, this temple of the god of writing produced useful written documents. Some belonged to the scholarly library, with classic works such as the Epic of Gilgamesh and much more technical literature, to be published by D. J. Wiseman. One tablet apparently listed different areas of the temple, making possible an unusual correlation between textual and architectural evidence. Other tablets published by Barbara Parker, later Lady Mallowan, illuminated one of the functions of the temple as an agricultural bank, advancing grain to farmers for repayment after the harvest. Yet more dealt with the elaborate arrangements whereby Esarhaddon hoped to fix the succession to the Assyrian throne after his own death.

Known as the Vassal Treaties, these last documents are in the form of agreements between Esarhaddon and various Median chieftains from the eastern fringes of the empire: the chieftains swear to support Ashurbanipal as next king of Assyria, and fearful curses are invoked for disloyalty. This was one attempt to cope with an odd failing in the structure of the 7th century Assyrian state, the lack of a clear method of royal succession, and it is ironical that internal rivalries arising from this settlement were eventually to play a significant part in putting Assyria at the mercy of the Medes. The room in which the treaty documents were found also contained burnt wooden furniture overlaid with bronze, and much ivory veneer carved in the Assyrian style of the 9th century. In this case Mallowan suggested that objects had been brought from different parts of the temple, heaped together, and set alight.

While the abandonment and destruction levels of 614–612 naturally contributed some of the most informative items found by the School at Nimrud, there were also areas where stratigraphic sequences could be observed. This was most clearly illustrated by the work of D. and J. Oates in the vicinity of the Nabu Temple. For instance, in the lane between the Nabu Temple and the so-called Burnt Palace to its west, nine distinct phases could be distinguished, ranging in date from before Ashurnasirpal to the Achaemenid period. Unfortunately the evidence preserved was insufficient for the establishment of a pottery sequence covering this length of time; such a sequence would be invaluable for studying the evolution of settlements in metropolitan Assyria under successive dispensations. For the imperial period we have to be satisfied with the great quantity of 7th century pottery recovered from several areas of the site and partly published by Joan Oates. On the other hand there was an unexpected bonus in the Oates' work on post-Assyrian Hellenistic layers above the Nabu Temple: here there was a succession of small buildings, with superimposed floors, which could be closely dated by coins, pottery, and other small finds. As a result, we know almost more about the ordinary material culture of Assyria in the 3rd century B.C., a time of political obscurity, than we do about comparable things in the times of imperial expansion. The work in the Hellenistic levels was naturally a more conventional archaeological operation than the normal Nimrud task of clearing masses of fallen mud-brick from inside enormous one-period rooms.

There can be few spots, at or near Nimrud, that escaped assessment by Mallowan's practised eye. Many of them seemed suitable for a sounding, which might grow into an extended operation, and the excavators were rewarded with more information than can possibly be discussed here. There was the complex of private houses along the eastern side of the citadel; there was the painted palace of Adad-nirari III in the north-western corner of town; there were the excursions to Abu Sheetha and elsewhere. Especially significant, for future excavators, were the soundings, relocating walls originally cleared in the nineteenth century, whereby Mallowan encouraged and facilitated subsequent restoration work by the Iraq authorities. It was probably Mallowan too who cleared a pair of ruined colossi in the centre of the citadel, and so guided Meuszyński's Polish expedition on its way to the rediscovery of Tiglath-pileser III's lost sculptures. It was not inappropriate that this continuation of the School's work should have been undertaken by a team from Poland, a country for which Mallowan had a very high regard; sadly, the murder of Meuszyński, elsewhere in the Middle East in 1976, brought the work to a premature close. The Iraq authorities, however, have gone on, successfully transforming Nimrud into a major tourist attraction, something far removed from the empty mound where the School began work in 1949.

Today, if one was starting a fresh series of excavations at Nimrud, one would have other aims and expectations than those which took Mallowan to the site. There may be regret for some of the things that were not done then, but for the positive results there can only be admiration: for the vast amount of work finished and published, for the multifarious discoveries which we owe to Mallowan, Oates, and their many collaborators. It was an achievement on a nineteenth century scale, something there is no prospect of emulating.

Bibliography

M. E. L. Mallowan, *Nimrud and its Remains*, 2 vols. (London 1966).
—*Mallowan's Memoirs* (London 1977).
A. H. Layard, *Nineveh and its Remains*, 2 vols. (London 1849).
A. A. Agha and M. S. al-Iraqi, *Nimrud* (Baghdad 1976).
J. N. Postgate and J. E. Reade, 'Kalhu' in *Reallexikon der Assyriologie* V (1977–80), 303–23.
D. Oates, *Studies in the Ancient History of Northern Iraq* (London 1968).

Numerous articles by various authors in the journal *Iraq*, especially volumes XII–XXV (1950–63), and final publications in the continuing series *Ivories from Nimrud* and *Cuneiform Texts from Nimrud*.

Balawat

By John Curtis

The background to the British School's excavations at Balawat makes curious reading. The first excavations here were by Hormuzd Rassam in the spring of 1878. He had been drawn to the site, 15 km. north-east of Nimrud, by reports that some fragments of embossed bronze bands which had reached Mosul in the previous year and then been distributed had in fact been found at Tell Balawat by chance during the digging of a grave. According to his own accounts Rassam soon found the main part of the monument, which is now known to have been a pair of gates set up by Shalmaneser III (858–824 B.C.). To the wooden door-leaves were nailed sixteen bronze bands decorated in *repoussé* with scenes showing the Assyrian army on various campaigns. As the wood had long since rotted away, the find resembled to Rassam "a gigantic hat-rack with the top rising to within four feet of the surface of the ground, and the lower portion gradually descending to about fifteen feet deep". Another, smaller pair of gates, of Ashurnasirpal II (883–859 B.C.), was found about sixty feet to the north-west of the first pair. There is again a total of sixteen bands, but they are in poorer condition. As well as scenes of the Assyrian king on campaign, there are illustrations of hunting expeditions and of events taking place in Assyria. In addition to these two sets of gates, Rassam also found in a building on the north side of the mound an inscribed stone coffer which contained two stone tablets, all bearing an inscription of Ashurnasirpal II. This gives the ancient name of the site — Imgur-Enlil — and records the building of a temple dedicated to the god Mamu.

Doubts about the reliability of Rassam's account were first voiced by Wallis Budge who visited Balawat in 1889 and concluded that no large-scale excavations had ever taken place there, and that the mound was too small to contain monumental buildings such as the gates must have belonged to. L. W. King, whose publication of the Shalmaneser III gates remains the definitive work on the subject, was of the same opinion as Budge and even went so far as to describe Rassam's account as "an absurdity". Thus matters stood until 1942 when Professor Seton Lloyd visited the site in connection with his work as Technical Adviser to the Iraq Department of Antiquities. He saw no reason to disbelieve the truth of Rassam's statements, and indeed found that the topography of the mound and the nature of the surviving monuments matched his description in every way. But actual excavation was needed to dispel altogether the lingering doubts sown by Budge's malicious accusations. In 1956, therefore, Sir Max Mallowan decided, as a corollary to the work at Nimrud, to make an investigation of Balawat. The work was supervised mainly by Miss Marjorie Howard assisted by Dr. Joan Oates. In his book, Rassam gives an amusing account of the difficulties he encountered at Balawat on account of the large numbers of graves on the mound. These belonged to the inhabitants of the two neighbouring villages of Balawat and Kabarli, and many were the quarrels about who the graves belonged to, whether the digging should be allowed to continue, and so on. The upshot was that for the most part Rassam was obliged to dig in tunnels nearly 2 m. below the level of the graves, which needless to say severely restricted his operations. By 1956 the situation had changed little, with the result that the British School expedition was able to dig in only two confined areas. Although the work (carried out in 1956 and 1957) was on a very limited scale, it was nevertheless sufficient fully to vindicate Rassam's integrity as well as greatly further our knowledge of the site.

In the north-east corner of the mound (fig. 83) much of the plan of a small temple was uncovered, with a central courtyard giving access to the north-west to an ante-cella and a cella, or shrine, and to the south-west to a secondary courtyard off which opened a room of unknown function and a second, smaller shrine (fig. 84). A range of rooms which had once existed on the north-east side of the temple, probably administrative in function, had largely been eroded away, but in one of them was found a collection of forty tablets of an economic and legal nature. It was in the principal shrine of this temple (col. pl. 8*b*) that Rassam had found the stone coffer and tablets of Ashurnasirpal II, as a result of which the temple could be identified as the Temple of Mamu. Fortunately for posterity, and for the vindication of his good name, Rassam dug only in this one room; it was therefore left to the British School expedition to find in the adjacent room, under 5 m. from the limit of his excavation, the remains of a third pair of wooden gates overlaid

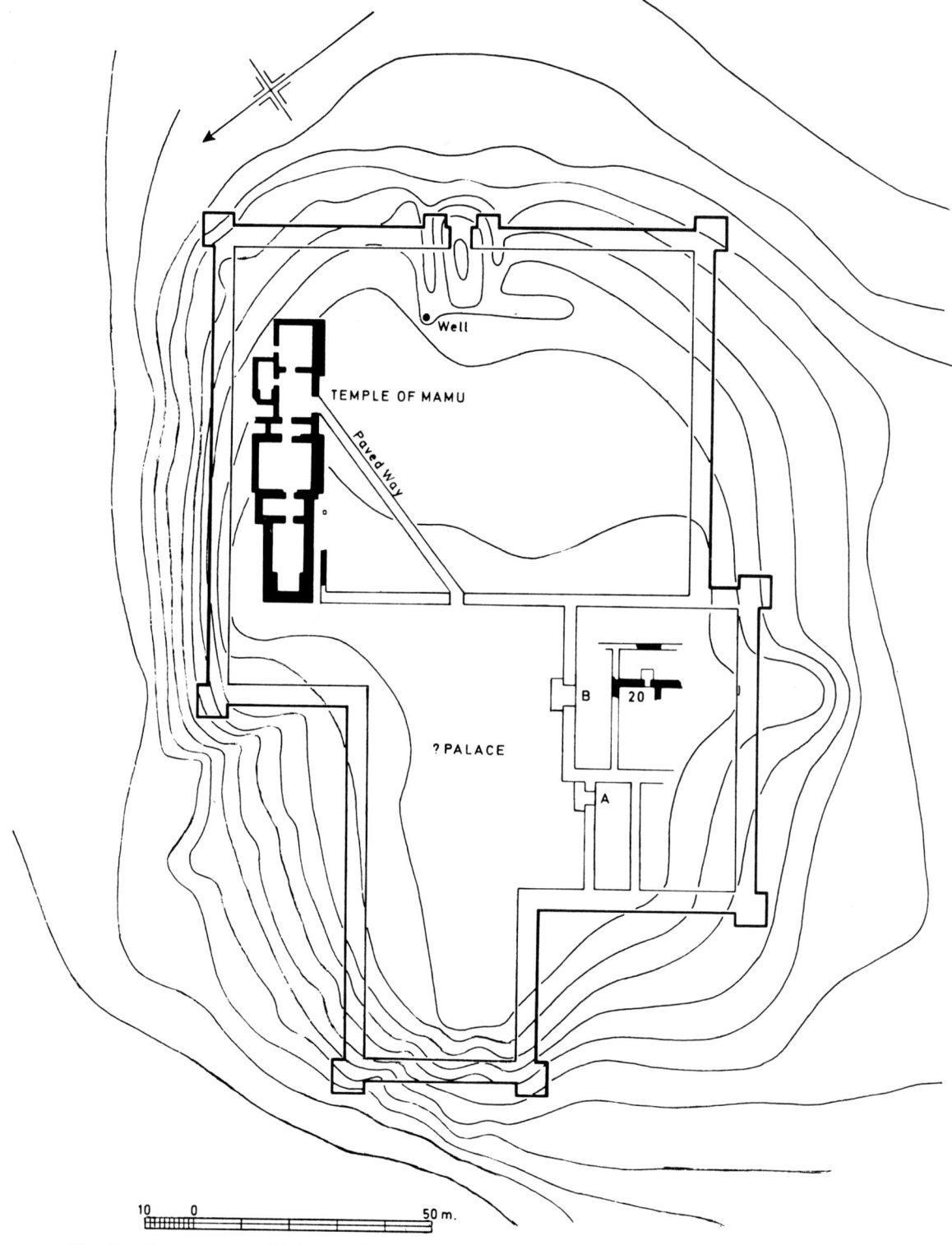

Fig. 83. Contour map of Balawat, showing buildings excavated in 1956-57 and David Oates' suggested reconstruction of the citadel plan.

Fig. 84. Excavations in progress in Temple of Mamu, viewed from shrine at N.W. end.

with strips of embossed bronze. They stood at the entrance to the central courtyard, and opened into the ante-cella. It was especially gratifying to the excavators that these gates are in fact mentioned in the stone tablets of Ashurnasirpal referred to above. He says that in the Mamu Temple he "constructed cedar doors" and "fastened them with bronze bands (and) hung (them) in its doorways". (Translation by A. K. Grayson).

The second area in which the 1956–57 expedition was able to dig at Balawat was c. 75 m. to the west of the Temple of Mamu. Here they cleared a room lined with stone slabs of which one was still in position. Very probably this is the small room excavated by Rassam "paved and walled with small marble slabs" most of which were given to local villagers. The significance of this discovery is that Rassam describes his room as being "about twenty-five feet to the south-west of the large monument" (i.e. the Shalmaneser III gates). It was therefore possible to suggest that two appropriately situated hollows must have been the sites of the two pairs of gates found by Rassam, and to mark them on a modern contour plan of the mound (A and B on fig. 83). David Oates has suggested that the two pairs of gates were incorporated in a palace, and might have flanked the entrances from a courtyard to two reception rooms built by Ashurnasirpal II and Shalmaneser III respectively. The stone-lined room would then be another smaller reception room behind, corresponding with an arrangement known from the North-West Palace at Nimrud.

As with the two sets of Rassam gates, the third pair has a total of sixteen bronze bands nailed to wooden leaves. The wood had been heavily burnt in antiquity (fig. 85). When found one door was ajar while the other was in a closed position. The door-leaves had been securely fastened to huge circular door-posts and turned with them. The flat part of each band is nearly a metre in length, and as with the other gates the bands are extended to encircle the door-posts. Bronze sheathing covered the bottom and the edges of the door-leaves; it was inscribed on the inside edges of the leaves, where the doors meet. In contrast to the other gates, there were no bronze pivot-casings fixed to the bottom of the door-posts; rather, the wood turned directly in a hollow stone. On the bands are various narrative compositions depicted by the techniques of embossing and chasing. These will be published in full by Dr. R. D. Barnett, together with the Ashurnasirpal gates found by Rassam. Included in this book will be Miss Howard's masterly drawings of the gates, plus some notes by her on their excavation. Barnett's preliminary description of the bands is that they show "scenes of the surrender of Kudurru of Suhi, of Bīt-Adini, of Carchemish, of Urartians, Phoenicians and others whose names are lost". Only one of the bands has been published so far (here fig. 86, top), but this is amongst the most interesting. It shows the city of Imgur-Enlil (Balawat), identifiable by a cuneiform epigraph above, as a fortress with towers and castellations. To the right, having just issued forth from a gateway which David Oates believes to be that of the citadel, is Ashurnasirpal II, escorted by three attendants. He receives tribute from Kudurru of Suhi. Another of the bands, published here for the first time (fig. 86, bottom), again shows Ashurnasirpal standing outside the gateway of a city,

Fig. 85. The charred remains of the gates of Ashurnasirpal II in the Temple of Mamu.

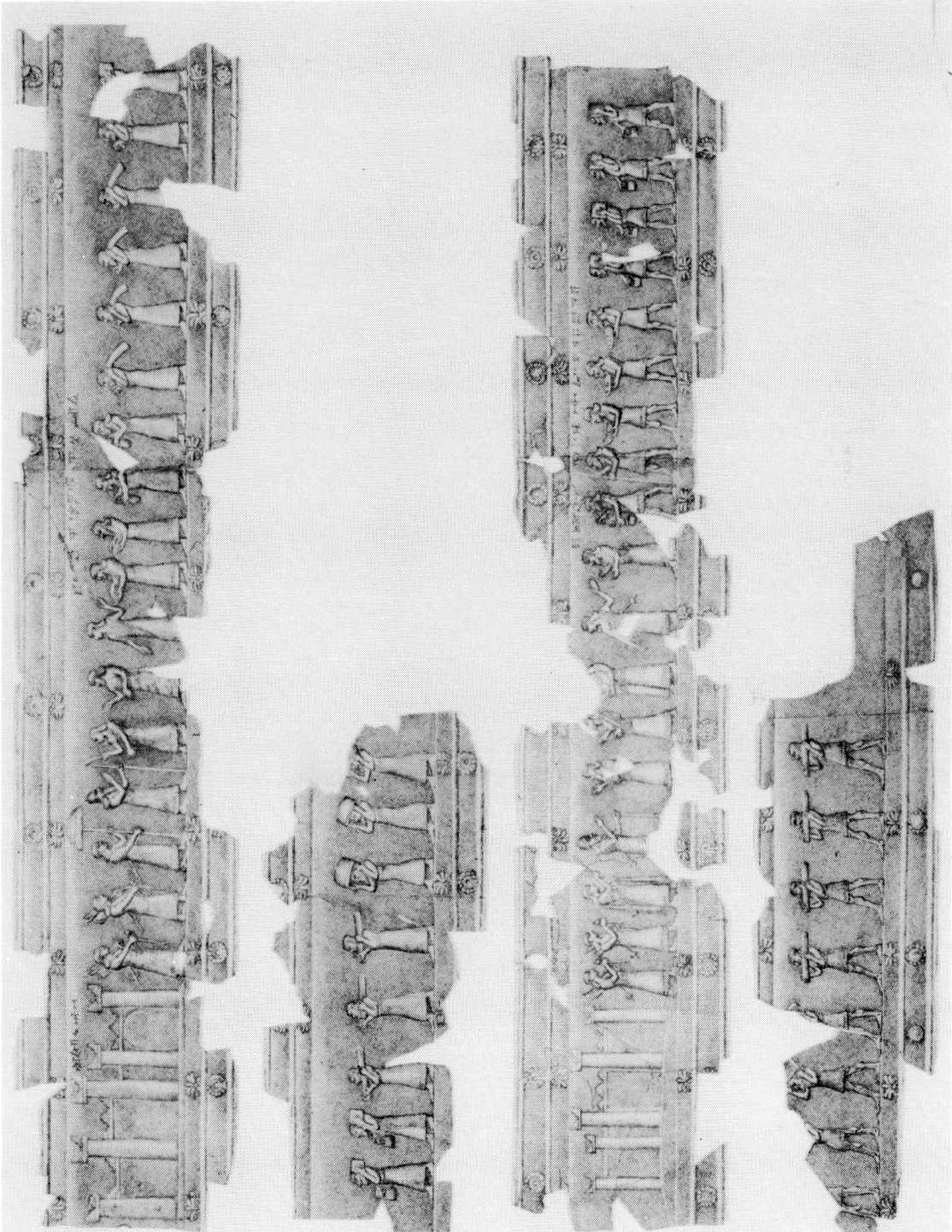

Fig. 86. Two bands from the newly-excavated gates of Ashurnasirpal II. Drawings by Miss Marjorie Howard.

probably Balawat but not labelled as such. This time he receives tribute from Ualtu(?) the Azamaean. These newly-discovered gates are now one of the prize exhibits in the Iraq Museum, Baghdad.

The bands from all three pairs of gates were probably made in the same sort of way, but only those of Shalmaneser III have been subjected to a careful examination. It seems that the first step was to trace the outlines of the design on the surface of the bronze with a graver. The metal was then turned over and placed face down on a bed of bitumen. Because of the thinness of the bronze strips the traced outlines would have shown through to the back, and the design could have been embossed by hammering out the figures and motifs from behind. While the bronze strips from the recently discovered gates were being restored in the British Museum the opportunity was taken to analyse some of them by x-ray fluorescence. This revealed a bronze with a tin content of around 10%. In two cases (out of four) at least 1% of zinc had been added to the alloy.

Apart from Balawat, pieces of bronze gate overlay have been found at all the major Assyrian sites except Nineveh. At Nimrud, Layard found three large fragments of bronze strips in Chamber I of the North-West Palace. There are scenes showing chariots and the king receiving officials and tributaries. At Khorsabad both Place and Loud found fragments of gate overlay, in the Adad and Nabu temples respectively. Motifs include ploughs, horses, bulls, a lion, a chariot, and mythical and human figures. Small bits of embossed bronze found in the throneroom of Sargon's Palace are also presumed to be from ornamental gates. At Ashur fragments of bronze overlay from a door were found in the Anu-Adad Temple reconstructed by Shalmaneser III. The strip is decorated with a frieze of figures flanked at top and bottom by a design of eight-spoked wheels or rosettes. Some pieces of bronze overlay and some bronze nails, which Andrae thought must have come from decorated gates, were also found in the Tabira Gate. Further, news has recently reached London that bronze gate-coverings have been found by an Iraqi expedition at Tell Hadad (Sirara) in the Hamrin. These were apparently set up in a temple of Nergal built by Ashurbanipal.

We have, then, archaeological evidence for wooden gates decorated with embossed bronze strips at five Late Assyrian sites—Balawat, Khorsabad, Ashur, Nimrud and Tell Hadad—and during the reigns of four rulers—Ashurnasirpal II, Shalmaneser III, Sargon and Ashurbanipal. Such gates were set up in palaces—at Balawat, Nimrud and perhaps Khorsabad; in temples—at Balawat, Ashur, Khorsabad and Tell Hadad; and perhaps in gateways if we accept the evidence from Ashur. Clearly it was a fairly standard practice in Late Assyrian times to set up decorated gates of this sort, and this impression is confirmed by the Assyrian royal inscriptions. We first find reference to such gates in the reign of Adad-Nirari I (1305–1274), and sporadic references down to the reign of Ashurnasirpal II. Thereafter they are more common, with most of Ashurnasirpal's successors refering to metal bands on gates, usually of bronze or copper but sometimes of more precious metal. For example, Esarhaddon says that he decorated the gates of the restored Temple of Esagila at Babylon with bands of gold and silver.

It is of interest to note that a parallel tradition of decorating wooden gates with metal overlay also existed in Phoenicia. This is known to us from the Biblical accounts of the building of Solomon's Temple, in which we are told that the doors were overlaid with brass and gold, presumably by Hiram of Tyre. In view of the antiquity of the practice in Assyria, however, there is no reason to suppose that it was derived from Phoenicia; if anything, the Phoenician tradition may be derivative from the Assyrian. Similarly there are no grounds for believing, as some scholars seem to have done, that the gates were executed by non-Assyrian craftsmen. From the large body of Late Assyrian bronzework which has survived and the wide range of forms it is clear that Assyrian smiths were every bit as competent as their contemporaries in producing cast and hammered bronzework of a high quality. Stylistically and iconographically the scenes on the bands are typically Assyrian, and there is a tradition of narrative art in Assyria going back at least to the Middle Assyrian period.

At this point we must return to Budge's claim that the mound of Balawat was too small to have boasted such important monuments as the gates. In fact, Budge was quite mistaken about the size of the site. A survey carried out in 1956–57 showed that the town walls enclose an area of about 64 hectares, which although small by comparison with Nineveh and Nimrud (750 hectares and 360 hectares respectively) is nevertheless quite sizeable by provincial standards. Further, David Oates has convincingly demonstrated that Imgur-Enlil was a town of some strategic importance: it must have been a stopping-place on the Assyrian road from Nineveh which crossed the Greater Zab at Tell Abu Sheetha and went ultimately to Kirkuk (Arrapha). Why there should have been a royal palace here is not quite clear, but one possibility is that it was a country residence not too far from Nimrud. Alternatively, it may be that the town was of such religious importance, perhaps because it housed the shrine of Mamu, god of dreams, that the monarch felt it necessary to have a seat there. One difficulty that remains to be answered is why the gates here should have survived in such good condition whereas at the other Assyrian sites only traces of such gates were found. It cannot be that Balawat was abandoned before the end of the Assyrian period and thus escaped the attentions of the marauding Medes and Babylonians, for one of the tablets found here dates to the reign of Sin-shar-ishkun, testifying to occupation in the late 7th century. Also, traces of a destruction were found here consistent with that noted at the more important Assyrian sites. The only explanation seems to be that the destruction of Balawat was a half-hearted affair, with the participants not bothering to rip the bronze bands from the gates as they did elsewhere. Perhaps the invaders had already vented most of their anger and hatred on the Assyrian capitals, symbols of many years of oppression and domination. After the sack Balawat seems to have been abandoned, and was apparently not reoccupied until the Hellenistic period.

Bibliography

H. Rassam, *Asshur and the Land of Nimrod* (New York and Cincinnati 1897).

David Oates, 'Balawat (Imgur Enlil): the site and its buildings', *Iraq* XXXVI (1974), 173-78.

Barbara Parker, 'Economic tablets from the Temple of Mamu at Balawat', *Iraq* XXV (1963), 86-103.

R. D. Barnett, 'More Balawat Gates: a Preliminary Report', in *Symbolae Biblicae et Mesopotamicae Francisco Mario Theodoro de Liagre Böhl Dedicatae* (Leiden 1973), 19-22.

A. K. Grayson, *Assyrian Royal Inscriptions. Part 2: From Tiglath-pileser I to Ashur-nasir-apli II* (Wiesbaden 1976).

E. A. Wallis Budge, *By Nile and Tigris*, 2 vols. (London 1920).

Seton Lloyd, *Foundations in the Dust* (revised ed. London 1980).

Ain Sinu—Zagurae

By David Oates

In the autumn of 1957 the School made a brief sounding at the Roman site of Ain Sinu, some 90 km. west of Mosul and 30 km. east of Beled Sinjar, Roman Singara (fig. 87). It lies on the upper southern slopes of an outlying ridge of the Jebel Sinjar—Jebel Ishkaft hill chain and has a commanding view of the plain to the south and east. The pass of Gaulat between Jebel Sinjar and Jebel Ishkaft, the easiest of only three widely separated ways through the hills to the upper Khabur basin and Nisibin, is some 5 km. away to the north-west. The caravan track to the pass from the main crossing of the Tigris at Mosul runs behind the ridge just north of the site, and the traditional road from Mosul to Beled Sinjar passes directly through it. It has a good water supply from perennial springs, which were channelled in the Roman period to their present outlets through underground tunnels or *qanāt*. Previous survey coupled with the evidence of the *Tabula Peutingeriana*, a compilation of Roman route books which seems to have drawn considerably on 3rd century evidence, pointed decisively to the identification of the site as Zagurae.

The ruin-field extends for over a kilometre along

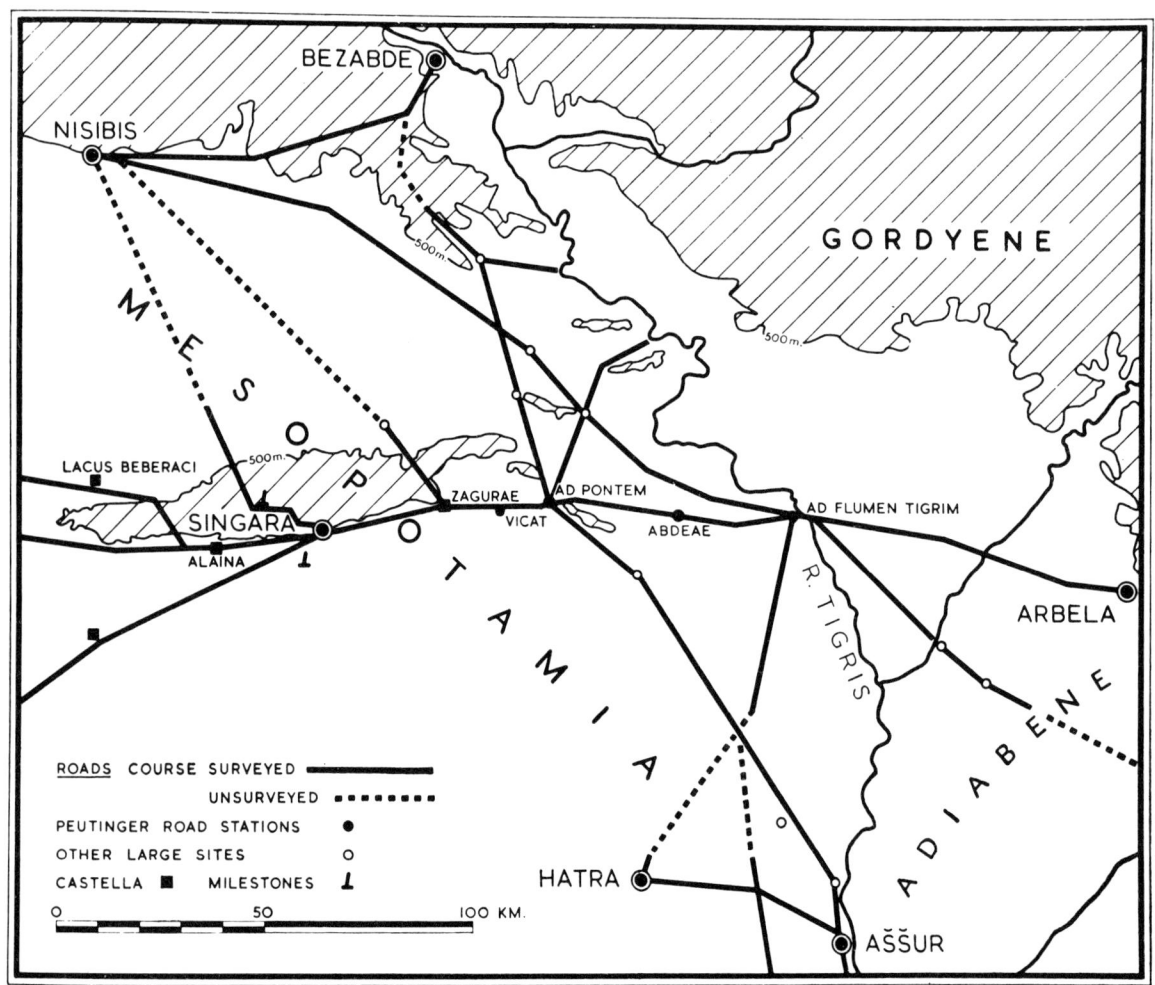

Fig. 87. Map of northern Iraq at the beginning of the 3rd century A.D.

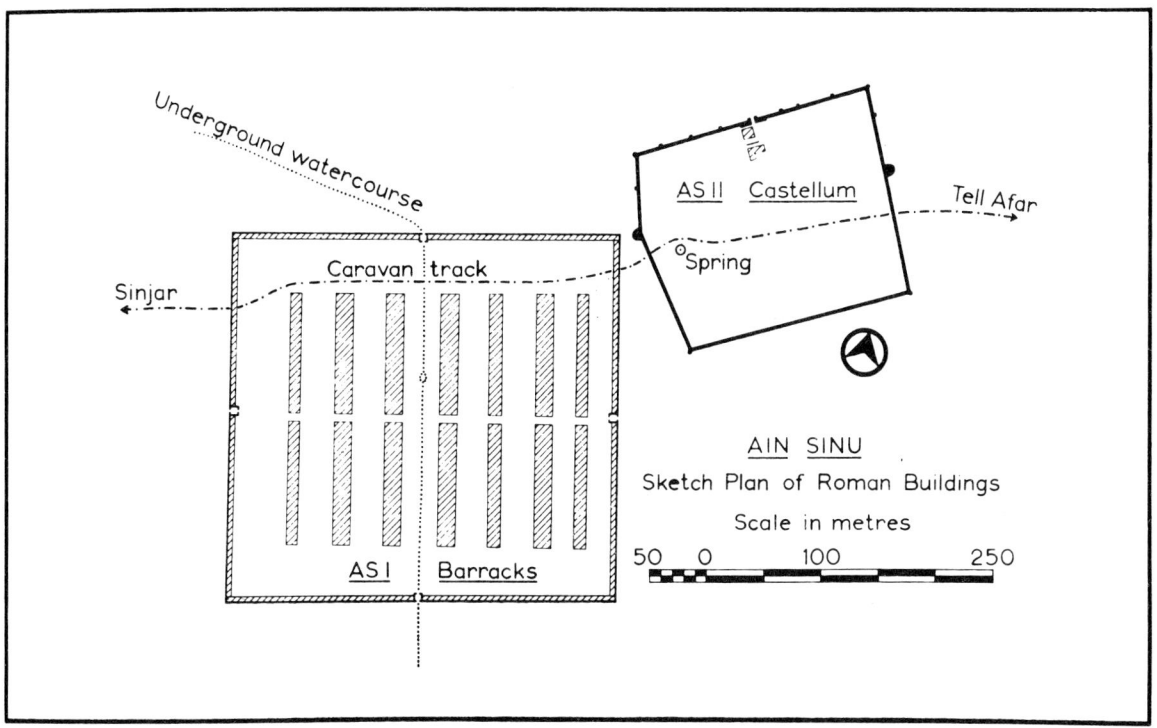

Fig. 88. Sketch plan of Roman buildings at Ain Sinu.

the Mosul-Sinjar track, and on superficial evidence many of the buildings appear to be medieval though there may well be earlier occupation beneath. We investigated two obviously important structures at the western end, AS I and AS II on the accompanying plan (fig. 88). AS I was a barracks some 330 m. square, enclosed by a casemate wall with four axial entrances and seven pairs of barrack blocks, each with eleven interconnecting pairs of large rooms — presumably living quarters — faced across a wide open space by smaller chambers that looked like store-rooms. By the standard conventionally accepted in the western Roman Empire, at eight men to a room of similar size, the barracks could have housed upwards of 2000 men. Whether they were cavalry or infantry we do not know, though the wide spaces between the barrack blocks might have been intended for tethering animals. This was not, however, a legionary camp of the standard type since there is no sign of a *praetorium* or headquarters building. Two other similar, though smaller, examples with barracks but no headquarters are known from Poidebard's air reconnaissance in the upper Khabur basin, one close to Tell Brak on the Wadi Jaghjagh, the other some 28 km. to the west at Tell Bati. The late Sir Ian Richmond suggested to us that they might have been training camps for recruits, either *auxilia* or legionaries of the three legions, I–III *Parthicae*, which were raised largely to man Septimius Severus' extension of the Roman frontier in Mesopotamia to the Tigris. However that may be, AS I was hastily built and perhaps at an inconvenient season — there was little straw in the bricks — and to judge by the paucity of occupation material, was used for a short time and then simply abandoned. There was no sign of violent destruction and we found only four coins, one inside and the others in debris outside the north wall. They were dated between A.D. 216 and 235, and all came from Mesopotamian mints, Resaina, Edessa and Nisibis, the activity of which reflected the need for small coinage among the newly established garrisons. Those from Resaina bore the vexillum and, under Caracalla, the number of the Third Parthian Legion which had its base there.

AS II was a *castellum* of a more familiar type, approximately rectangular and measuring some 200 by 180 m. The outer wall was of rubble and mortar faced with roughly dressed limestone blocks and there were probably four gates, again axially placed. We dug the north gate with one of its two guard chambers and found large fragments of a baked-brick vault which had spanned the entrance, and appeared to have been constructed by the pitched-brick technique. Inside the gate was a mud-brick building of four rooms, and to the south of it a larger structure of which only five rooms could be cleared because of an overlying medieval ruin. The headquarters building probably lies beneath the same debris, roughly in the middle of the fort. In the excavated area, c. 40 by 15 m., the contrast with AS I was very marked, for we found a mass of pottery, a broken glass vessel and some bronze and iron objects including spear or javelin points, arrowheads, a sling bullet and armour scales as well as a number of coins. The pottery comprised glazed and painted wares, a particular type of thin ribbed cooking ware and jars with diamond-impressed decoration. The whole inventory could well have come from Hatra, the capital of an Arab kingdom in the Jazira to the south, which had long served as an outlying fortress of the Parthian Empire but briefly admitted a Roman contingent after the Arsacid dynasty had been overthrown by the Sasanians. The three Latin inscriptions from Hatra, two of them recording the presence of the *Cohors IX Maurorum,* can be dated between A.D. 235 and 242.

Hatra fell to the Sasanians at the latest in the mid-3rd century, at or before the time when Shapur I captured the Roman frontier city of Dura Europos on the middle Euphrates where the destruction level has produced much comparable pottery. The question that remains is the date of the destruction of the *castellum* at Ain Sinu, and it is significant that among the 25 3rd century coins we found in both buildings there was none of Gordian III (A.D. 238-244) who mounted the last major campaign in the Severan tradition, marked once more by prolific issues from the provincial mints. It seems most likely that the site was overrun during the northern campaign of Ardashir I in the summer of A.D. 237.

Ain Sinu remains the easternmost Roman site that has been excavated, however briefly, and gave us a vignette of history from the end of the 2nd through the first 40 years of the 3rd century, when Septimius Severus first extended, and his less competent successors tried to maintain, Roman control over northern Mesopotamia as far as the Tigris. This policy unsheathed a dagger aimed at the heart of Parthia and undoubtedly contributed to the downfall of the Arsacid dynasty with whom Rome had long maintained uneasy but essentially stable relations.

Bibliography

D. and J. Oates, 'Ain Sinu: a Roman frontier post in Northern Iraq', *Iraq* XXI (1959), 207-42.

D. Oates, *Studies in the Ancient History of Northern Iraq* (London 1968).

A. Poidebard, *La Trace de Rome dans le Désert de Syrie* (Paris 1934).

Acknowledgements

Trustees of the British Museum: figs. 18–24, 61 (photographs), 62–64, 74–75, 86.
British School of Archaeology in Iraq: figs. 49, 54, 79–82.
John Curtis: figs. 1, 59–60, 61 (drawings), col. pls. 6a, 7a, cover.
Diana Kirkbride: figs. 2–9, col. pl. 1a.
David and Joan Oates: figs. 10–17, 48, 50–53, 55, 65–73, 76, 83–85, 87–88, col. pls. 1b, 2a, 4a–4c, 6b–c, 7b–c, 8b.
Nicholas Postgate: figs. 35–47, col. pls. 3b–c.
Julian Reade: figs. 56–58, 77–78, col. pl. 5.
Michael Roaf: figs. 27–34, col. pls. 2c, 3a.
David Stronach: figs. 25–26, col. pls. 2b, 8a.